The Apple® Macintosh™ Book

Cary
Lu

Drawings by
Rick van Genderen

PUBLISHED BY
Microsoft Press
A Division of Microsoft Corporation
10700 Northup Way, Bellevue, Washington 98004

Library of Congress Cataloging in Publication Data
Lu, Cary, 1945-
The Apple Macintosh Book
Includes Index.
1. Macintosh (Computer)   I. Title.
QA76.8.M3L8   1984   001.64   84-3839
ISBN 0-914845-00-4

Printed and bound in the United States of America

3 4 5 6 7 8 9   HLHL   8 9 0 9 8 7 6 5 4

Distributed to the book trade in the United States and Canada
by Simon and Schuster, Inc.

Disclaimer

The opinions in this book are strictly those of the
author and do not necessarily represent the views
of Microsoft Corporation, Apple Computer, Inc.,
or any other company.

Introduction

Section One

Section Two

Section Four

Acknowledgments

This book comes out of a conversation between Bill Gates of Microsoft and Steve Jobs of Apple. Jobs's development team was hard at work on the then-secret Macintosh, which was many months away from introduction. Microsoft was busy writing application programs and helping Apple with the Mac interface and many other design issues. Bill suggested that Microsoft's new publishing division prepare a book as well.

Nahum Stiskin, general manager of Microsoft Press, asked me to write the book shortly afterwards. I replied that I had never heard of any microcomputer that was sufficiently interesting to write a whole book about. Nahum insisted that I go to the west coast and see the Macintosh in action.

Here is the book.

Many people helped in its preparation. Among the staff of Apple Computer, I especially thank Chris Espinosa, Martin Haeberli, Mike Murray, Mike Boich, and Guy Kawasaki. Almost everyone at Microsoft seems to have helped at one time or another. Jeff Harbers, leader of the Macintosh software development group at Microsoft, played a key role, along with others in the group. Despite the extraordinary pressures of completing extremely complex products under an absolute deadline, everyone patiently answered questions and offered suggestions. These people really understand how the Macintosh and its software work; any errors are mine alone.

At Microsoft Press, Joyce Cox and Salley Oberlin contributed outstanding editing; Elaine Foster, Bonnie Mackay, and Marianne Moon put in long hours turning the manuscript into finished form. Art director Karen-Lynne de Robinson, along with Nick Gregoric, Sue Cook and Chris Stern, turned out the visual portion of this book. I also thank Barry Preppernau and Larry Levitsky.

Fellow author Steve Lambert shared the pleasures and frustrations of working with hardware and software under development and provided much valuable advice and insight.

At a critical time, Ellen Chu came in and read several chapters. She didn't say much; she just threw them out and rewrote them. She was right.

Cary Lu

February 1984
Boston, Massachusetts

A note to software developers: Because of Microsoft's early start, this first edition of *The Apple Macintosh Book* is weighted toward Microsoft programs. Future editions will describe software and hardware from all companies.

Introd

Computers Should
Work Like People

Computers are supposed to help us get work done quickly, easily, and effectively. So why have they become cloaked in mystique? Because most computers are difficult to use. So difficult, in fact, that we hear about "computer literacy" as if everybody must learn a new language. Computer enthusiasts haven't helped by talking computer jargon that obscures rather than clarifies. And so the mystique has grown: To work with a computer, we must think like a computer.

Nonsense. Computers should work the way we do.

That's what the Macintosh™ is all about. Mac works the way we think; unlike most computers, it doesn't force us to change our language and work habits for its sake. We do need to learn how to use the Macintosh, but since most steps are analogous to the way we already work, learning is quick and easy. With this book to guide you, learning will be even quicker and easier.

If you already own a Macintosh, this book will soon have you working productively on your machine. If you are trying to decide whether to buy a Mac, this book gives information that should help with comparison shopping. If you don't plan to buy a Mac and are just interested in this innovative computer, this book offers a complete reference, covering present and future Macintosh products as well as how the Macintosh can work alongside other computers.

The Macintosh is a visual computer, one operated as much with symbols and pictures as with words. This book is also visual. With or without a Macintosh in front of you, you will *see* how easy it is to use and what its screen looks like in action.

Before the Macintosh, even people who liked computers accepted an initial period of suffering before they became productive or had any fun. Not so with Mac. Whether you're new to computers or an old hand, Mac's visual technology means that those periods of frustration are now over.

HOW TO USE THIS BOOK

The Apple® Macintosh™ Book has four main sections. The brief opening section, Chapters 1 and 2, introduces you to Mac and explains how to set it up. The two chapters contain only the bare essentials; each topic is taken up in greater detail later. If you've had little experience with microcomputers or if you haven't yet set up your Mac, you will want to read this first section, or at least leaf through it. Otherwise, you can skip to Section Two.

The second section, Chapters 3 through 11, guides you through some Macintosh uses. Everyone should read Chapter 3, which gets you up and going on Mac in minutes. Chapters 4 through 10 show how to make Macintosh software work for you. No need to read these chapters in order—just read about the programs that interest you.

The third section, beginning with Chapter 12, takes up each part of the Macintosh in detail, discussing each component and explaining how it works and interacts with other parts. Although you don't have to read these chapters to get Mac going, you will find them useful as you gain experience with the machine. This section also describes how Mac software works. Other topics include maintenance, the Macintosh versus the IBM® PC, and future developments.

Section Four is for those interested in further details about the Macintosh. Specialized applications, such as drawing, photography, and advanced communications techniques have been gathered together in Chapters 26 through 30 for those who want or need to know about them.

A glossary and an index complete the book.

HOW MUCH DO YOU NEED TO LEARN?

Depending on your situation, you may only need to learn a single program—a word processor, perhaps. And you may not even need to learn everything about that program. As you become more comfortable with Mac, you'll want to learn more, but set your own pace. Learn as much as you need to when you need to.

One key to successful computer use is clearly understanding your needs; fill those needs instead of trying to learn everything about computers. Don't be lured into pursuing some ill-defined notion of "computer literacy." Remember, Mac is a tool for making your life easier, not more complex.

Section

In the Beginning

Welcome to the Macintosh revolution: What is the Macintosh? Is it right for you? This section introduces you to Macintosh and tells you where and how to set it up; it reviews Mac's major components and their functions.

Chapter *Getting* 1 *Acquainted*

Must a computer work like a computer? Must we all think like computers to benefit from them? Most of us want a computer that works the way we do, with familiar concepts and images.

Computers process information. How you work with a computer depends on how you present information to it and how it presents processed information back to you. This interaction is known, in computer jargon, as the interface between human and computer. The Macintosh's key innovation is its visual interface.

OLD AND NEW INTERFACES

When you turn on most conventional microcomputers, you are greeted with a cryptic A>. If you don't already know what to do next, you usually won't find out without wading through a thick manual.

Thousands of people have struggled to master this cryptic interface. It's not impossible to learn, but it takes time and concentrated effort—not only the first time, but each time you need the computer for a new task. If you want to write a letter, for example, you might have to type, without error, *WORDPROC B:LETTER.TXT,* followed by several more commands before you can even begin.

Suppose you want the letter double-spaced; you have to know in advance to type something like ^OS 2 or \SP2.

But when you turn on the Macintosh, you get something quite different—a visual interface that resembles a desktop.

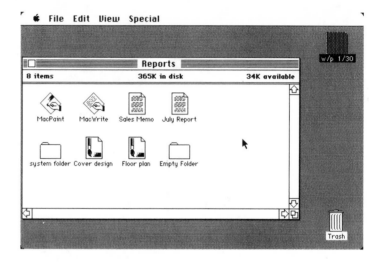

If you wanted to write a letter on a real desk, you might first pick up a pen and pull out a sheet of paper from a file folder containing stationery. With Mac, you do nearly the same thing; you pick up "pen and paper" by selecting a symbol, called an icon. For the MacWrite™ word-processing program, the appropriate icon shows a hand holding a pen.

Next, you use the mouse to choose File from the words at the top of the screen and Open from the list of things you can do with files.

Now you're ready to write your letter. If you want to change the spacing, you choose one of the three small symbols representing pages that appear in the center of the screen. The first page symbol shows single-spacing, the second a space and a half, and the third double-spacing. For a double-spaced letter, you select the double-spacing symbol, and your letter appears on screen, double-spaced. It's that simple.

Which do you prefer? The old-fashioned, cryptic interface or Mac's visual interface?

MACINTOSH RIDES THE CREST

The Macintosh rides the crest of a new wave: computers that work with familiar ideas and symbols and mimic objects we already use.

The ideas behind Macintosh were originally developed at XEROX's Palo Alto Research Center and, in 1981, led to the landmark XEROX Star®, the first commercial computer with a visual interface. Apple's Lisa™, launched in 1983, brought the price of such machines below $10,000—much less than Star, but still too high for most individuals and many businesses. Now the Macintosh offers a visual interface for considerably less, enabling many more people to enjoy its benefits.

WHAT YOU NEED

When you buy a Macintosh, you need:

- The Macintosh hardware package.

- Some applications software; for many people, the MacPaint™ and MacWrite combination will be the best starting package.

- A box of blank disks.

A computer's physical parts—keyboard, screen, printer, wires, and so on—constitute the hardware package. You can touch hardware.

Software, or programs, are the instructions you need to turn a collection of hardware into a word processor, a number cruncher, or a game machine. You can't touch software, although you can touch the hardware it is stored on. Hardware is useless without software and vice versa.

In the coming months and years, you will be able to choose from hundreds of programs, each turning your Macintosh into something different. Some of the Macintosh programs vying for your attention may be exactly what you need.

WRITING YOUR OWN PROGRAMS

If you find programming interesting and want to learn to program the Macintosh, by all means do so. But don't feel that you have to. Most people who use computers will never write a program. After all, excellent programs have already been written, so why duplicate the effort? Good word-processing software can take one skilled person several years to prepare; you may prefer to do other things with that time.

As microcomputers become more common, chances are that a program meeting your specific needs will appear. But if you have a special requirement for which no program exists, you can write the program or have someone else write it. Either way, computer languages available for Mac will take advantage of its special features, and programming will be easier than on earlier microcomputers.

KEEPING UP WITH NEW PRODUCTS

You may find yourself caught up in the craze to get the latest and greatest of each software or hardware accessory. If you enjoy doing this, fine; but remember, familiar products that work well may be enough. Many new products will boast glamorous features that may be irrelevant to your needs.

Remember, too, that every time you change programs, your work will inevitably be disrupted until you learn the new one. Although the Macintosh design makes this period short compared with other computers, you should weigh the potential benefits against the liabilities. In a business, be especially careful before changing programs and procedures.

IS MACINTOSH RIGHT FOR YOU?

No computer can be all things to all people, and the Macintosh will not suit everyone. You may not find it suitable if you must have:

- Complete compatibility with another microcomputer model.

- Specific software that runs on another micro-computer but not on Mac.

- Several programs running simultaneously— a specialized, high-performance task for computers.

- Very high-capacity disk drives, capable of storing a company's accounting information, for example.

- A color display screen.

Some of these restrictions will be eliminated as Apple and other companies introduce Macintosh accessories.

At this point, most computer books start telling you how a computer works and explaining the difference between a bit and a byte, RAM and ROM. But you don't need to know any of this to use Mac successfully. If you're curious, Section Three deals with Mac's insides.

The next chapter shows you how to set up the Macintosh computer. If you have one already set up and are familiar with basic terms like keyboard, disk drive, and mouse, go to Chapter 3.

Chapter 2 *First Steps*

Let's suppose you have just purchased a Macintosh. Before you open the box and spread its contents out on the floor, find a comfortable, properly lit place to set your Macintosh up. You will probably want the keyboard at typing height, a little lower than your desk or dining table. Adjust your chair so you're seated comfortably; the fatigue some people feel when working for long periods at a computer usually comes from poor lighting or an uncomfortable chair or desk setup. If two people of different heights share the computer, keep a chair cushion handy.

Although the Macintosh takes less space than most other microcomputers, it still needs an area at least two feet wide and two feet deep. The mouse needs part of that space: about a square foot to either the left or right, depending on your preference. The mouse will work on any flat surface; just keep the area reasonably clean—no liquids or food debris. The printer will take another square foot or so.

Avoid placing your Macintosh next to a heating vent or radiator. Exposure to high temperatures might damage it or, more likely, its magnetic information-storage disks. Generally, if you can stand the temperature, Mac can, too.

Don't put the computer in direct sunlight, and make sure the area behind it is neither brilliantly lit nor very

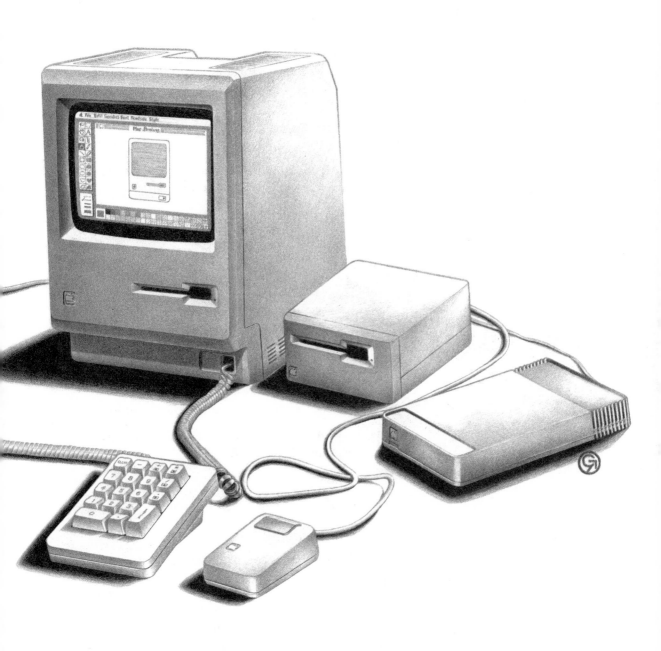

dark; otherwise your eyes will have to readjust constantly for the difference. No lights should shine directly on the screen; position them to avoid glare. If you have bright overhead office lights, a shade or hood over the screen may help.

Once you have settled on the most convenient location, you are ready to unpack and assemble your Macintosh.

UNPACKING AND ASSEMBLY

When you open the Macintosh box, you will find in addition to the manuals and warranty cards:

- The main computer unit, including a display screen and a disk drive.

- A keyboard.

- A coiled keyboard cable.

- A mouse with a cable.

- A power cord.

- A small plastic part labeled INTERRUPT RESET, which you can install on the left side.

- Several disks containing Macintosh software.

- A battery for a clock/calendar. This may be installed already.

Follow these steps to set up your Macintosh:

Position the main computer unit and keyboard.

Plug in the keyboard.

The keyboard cable has plugs like those on a telephone. One end plugs into the back of the keyboard, the other into the front bottom right of the main computer unit.

Never plug this cable into a telephone line and never plug a telephone cable into any Macintosh component; the telephone line's electrical characteristics are completely different, and damage might result.

Plug the mouse cable into the back of the main unit (leftmost plug as you face the rear).

When right side up, the plug fits easily. If you have trouble pushing it in, you have the wrong jack or the wrong orientation. Never force a plug! A small, knurled knob secures the plug to the computer.

Plug the power cord into the main unit and an AC power outlet (120 volts AC in North America).

If the power supply is irregular in your area or if you've had problems with other equipment, see Chapter 21 for suggestions.

If you are outside of North America, make sure that the electrical supply is the correct voltage. The power line frequency (50 or 60 Hz) doesn't matter, but the voltage must be correct. If you use a transformer, it should have a capacity of 60 watts or 60 VA.

Save the little plastic piece labeled INTERRUPT RESET.

You won't need to install this piece for now.

Once you have plugged everything together, you're ready to start. If you ever need to move your Macintosh, the safest way is to disconnect all the cables and move each unit separately.

TAKING CARE OF THE MACINTOSH

Although you should give your computer the same care and respect that you'd give any other valuable object, it is no more fragile than a television set and fairly hard to damage.

You cannot harm Macintosh hardware by any combination of typing on the keyboard or handling the mouse. Generally, you can only alter or erase software or lose data by deliberate choice. We'll go over simple safekeeping steps as they come up.

TAKING CARE OF YOU

Don't work steadily at any computer for hours on end; plan to stretch your legs at least every hour or so.

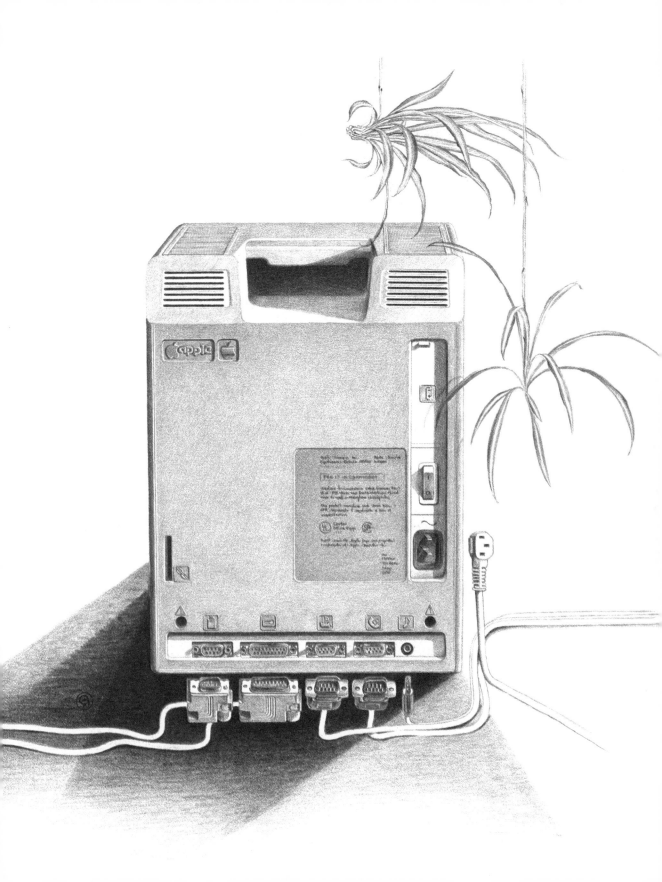

Don't forget to eat, and remember to talk occasionally with your fellow workers or your family and friends.

USING NEW PRODUCTS

Whenever you work with hardware or software for the first time, take a little extra care. Don't invest a lot of time entering data at the beginning; make sure that the program does what you need first. Enter a little data and check the results; print from the program to make sure everything works. Only after you are confident of both the program and your ability to use it should you invest the time in intensive work.

A FEW WORDS ABOUT EACH COMPONENT

Here's a quick rundown on each component. You won't need more information to operate a Macintosh successfully, but you may want to learn more after you have some experience; you will find more detail in Section Three.

The Main Computer Unit

For now, you need to know only two things about the main unit: how to turn it on, and how to adjust the brightness. You can leave the machine on constantly if you wish; just turn the screen brightness down whenever you're not going to use it for several hours.

Disks and the Disk Drive

The disks store information magnetically. They fit, one at a time, into the disk-drive slot just below the display screen. They can only go in right side up; the plastic disk jacket has a small arrow showing the correct orientation.

When you are finished working, you should use the Finder to eject all disks. I'll explain this shortly; for now, just note you should eject all disks before turning off the power.

Disks store several kinds of information in units called files. Functionally, a computer's files resemble the paper file folders in your filing cabinet. Stored information includes:

System and Finder information. When you first turn on the Macintosh, you must insert a start-up disk in the disk drive. The computer transfers System and Finder information from the disk into its memory and onto the screen. (We'll see what these terms mean in the next chapter.)

Application programs. In most cases, programs that turn your Macintosh into a graphics tool or word processor must be on the same disk as the System and Finder information. Once the Finder is in memory, you'll need to indicate the program you want, and it, too, will be transferred into memory.

Data. Information you enter when using a program, or information needed by a program, is stored in data files. Data files don't always have to be on the same disk with the program, although some programs will be easier to use if the data files are handy.

You can keep these different kinds of information on the same disk, but if they must share space with an application program as well as the System and Finder, you won't have room to do much work. In Chapter 11, we'll look at how to set up disks to solve this problem.

Don't be concerned if you don't follow all the subtleties of this discussion just yet. We'll take up these topics again, and you'll soon be fluent with disks and files.

The Keyboard

You'll use the keyboard (and mouse) to enter information and to tell the Macintosh what to do with the information. The Macintosh keyboard has all the familiar typewriter keys and a few extra ones. The typewriter-like keys produce all the familiar letters and symbols. If you hold a key down, it will automatically repeat.

The Shift key works just like a typewriter's; when you hold it down, you get capital letters and punctuation marks instead of lowercase letters and numbers. But the Caps

Lock key works a little differently than a typewriter's shift lock: It stays engaged when you press it, and releases on a second press. When the Caps Lock key is engaged, you get capital letters as you would expect, but you still get numbers, not the punctuation marks above them. For punctuation marks, you must press the Shift key and the number key at the same time, even if Caps Lock is engaged.

Two keys you won't find on a typewriter, the Option and Command ⌘ keys, work like two more shift keys. You press them at the same time as another key. The Option key serves several purposes, including generating special symbols for foreign languages or scientific equations. The Command key shouldn't concern you if you are just starting out; it is a shortcut to instruct the computer to do something, such as eject the disk or delete a word. We'll cover its functions when we start using software.

The last non-typewriter key is the Enter key. You'll use it most often to tell your Macintosh you've finished with some typing.

A last word of warning: If you are in the habit of typing the letter "l" for the number 1, or a letter "O" for zero, you'll have to change your ways. Sorry. The difference is very important to computers.

The Mouse

Along with the keyboard, the mouse lets you work with the Macintosh. We'll cover it in Chapters 3 and 15.

ADDING ON: HARDWARE ACCESSORIES

There are four add-on accessories you should consider buying. They are all simple plug-in units.

Two accessories are probably essential:

A second disk drive makes computing much easier by providing more storage for programs and data. Although you can limp along with a single disk drive, a second one makes many tasks so much easier that you should regard it as a necessity rather than an option. For example, with two disk drives you can copy disks or move information from

disk to disk without constantly swapping disks during
the operation.

The Macintosh will accept only one additional microfloppy disk drive. You can add more storage with different
accessories.

A *printer* produces text and graphics on paper, and
nearly every Macintosh owner will need one. At least
initially, only the Apple ImageWriter™ printer works with
the Macintosh for every application, but accessory
hardware and software should eventually let you use other
printers. For now, if you have an ImageWriter printer, plug
it in with the supplied cable. The larger plug goes into the
printer, the smaller one into the computer.

Two other accessories are useful but may not be
essential to your work:

A *numeric keypad* provides an adding machine-like
set of keys, handy if you often work with numbers. The
keypad also improves some Macintosh operations by
giving you more keyboard options, but it isn't necessary
for most software.

A modem lets you communicate with other computers by telephone. It converts information from your computer into sounds that can travel by an ordinary telephone line; it also does the reverse, changing sounds generated by a distant computer and its modem back into information your computer can understand.

You're now ready to start using your Macintosh computer.

A Macintosh Sampler

Working with Macintosh: This section describes how to perform basic operations with the Macintosh interface and introduces you to software available for the Macintosh. You can see how programs work before you buy them, with a step-by-step example for most programs.

Chapter 3 Fundamental Operations

*T*his chapter covers the basic information you need to start using your Macintosh, but it does not replace Apple's excellent manuals. If you have a Macintosh, I suggest you read the manuals and use this chapter as a supplement; if you do not have a Macintosh, this chapter will introduce you to its operation. We'll discuss starting the system, learning to use the mouse, handling icons and windows, and working on the Macintosh Desktop. These operations are fundamental ones that you will perform many times with a Macintosh; they will soon be second nature.

STARTING UP THE MACINTOSH

After you have plugged all the Macintosh components together:

Turn on your Macintosh.

Mac produces a single acknowledgment tone from the speaker and an image showing a disk with a question mark appears on the screen.

Any disk that will start up a Macintosh has all the features you need to perform the operations described in this chapter. A disk that can start up a Macintosh is called a system, or start-up, disk. Such disks can also have other names if they contain application programs. A system disk containing MacWrite and MacPaint, for example, might be called a Write/Paint disk.

Insert a system disk into the disk-drive slot.

The disk drive whirs as it loads start-up information from the disk into the computer's electronic memory. A little wristwatch appears on the screen, meaning you must wait until Mac finishes its task.

LOOKING AT THE DESKTOP

After the disk drive stops, you see the Desktop on the screen; this is part of the Macintosh's visual interface. The icons, or pictures, on the Desktop represent places for finding, storing, and discarding information. The first icons you see are:

- The disk you've just inserted.

- A trash can.

A window may open as well. If so, try to ignore it for the next five minutes. If the window gets in the way, scan ahead to "Closing a Window."

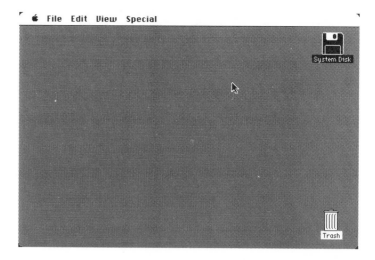

USING THE MOUSE

Because you use the mouse for so many operations, you need to get accustomed to moving it. Among other things, it is your primary tool for pointing at and selecting items on your Desktop so you can work with them.

Mouse operations are illustrated in this chapter with specific examples, but the actions are applicable to many situations.

Move the mouse around your desk.

The pointer on the screen follows the mouse movements. You cannot move the pointer off the screen, no matter how far you move the mouse itself.

The pointer you see now is shaped like an arrow; however, the pointer can take on other shapes, as we'll see later.

Pointing

Move the pointer over an icon.

Whenever you move the pointer to an icon or other object, you are pointing at the object. The exact spot you are pointing at depends on the pointer's shape. With the arrow, position the arrow tip over the object.

Clicking

Point at the Trash icon.

Press and release the mouse button once.

This action is called clicking. You click objects that are on the Macintosh Desktop.

When you click the white Trash icon, it turns black. The black color indicates that you have selected that icon. Selecting an icon means that your next action will apply to that icon.

Move the mouse to the disk icon and click it.

The Trash icon turns white again, and the disk icon turns black; you have changed your selection from one icon to the other.

Click anywhere on the Desktop outside the icons.

This cancels your previous selection. Now none of the icons on the Desktop is selected.

Dragging

Move the pointer over the Trash icon.

Press and hold down the mouse button.

Move the mouse while holding the button down.

You use this essential operation, called dragging, in many ways. As you move the mouse, the icon's outline moves with it.

Release the mouse button.

When you release the button, the icon pops over to the location of its outline.

Dragging allows you to move icons from place to place on the screen; it is analogous to shuffling paper around on a desk.

Move the two icons around on your Desktop.

Practice dragging to get a feel for it.

Pressing

Pressing means that you position the pointer and then press the mouse button, holding it until an action is complete. Pressing differs from dragging because you don't move the mouse while pressing the button. We will get to an operation that requires pressing shortly.

OPENING AN ICON

To find out what information an icon represents, you must open the icon; you can think of this as opening a drawer in a filing cabinet.

Click the disk icon (the system disk).

First you have to select the icon you want to open. (Remember, point at the disk icon and click the mouse button once.) The icon's color reverses from white to black, to show that it is selected.

Move the pointer to the words at the top of the screen.

This line of words is the menu bar. The words are categories of commands you can have the Macintosh perform.

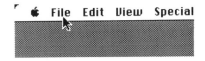

Point at File .

Press and hold down the mouse button without moving the mouse.

A list called a menu appears; you've "pulled-down" the File menu. The menu entries are things you can do with the icon you've selected—in this case, the system disk. You choose from a Macintosh menu as you would choose a dish from a restaurant's menu.

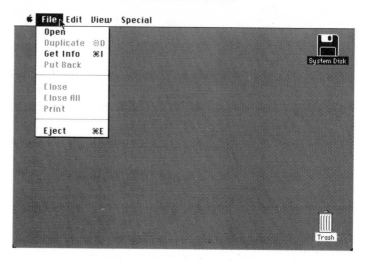

The complete File menu appears when you pull it down, but all choices on the menu may not be available; you can't close anything, for example, because you haven't yet opened anything. Available menu choices appear in black letters; unavailable ones, such as Close, appear in dimmed or gray letters.

Still holding down the mouse button, move the mouse so that the pointer moves down the menu.

As you move down the menu, the available choices are highlighted in turn; the words reverse from black on white to white on black.

Position the pointer over **Open** .

The word Open is highlighted.

Release the mouse button.

You select a menu item by releasing the mouse button when the item is highlighted. In Macintosh terms, you have chosen Open from the File menu.

The disk window now opens up.

Double-Clicking

To open an icon faster, point at it and click the mouse button quickly twice; this action is called double-clicking.

LOOKING AT THE DISK WINDOW

What you see now are the contents of the system disk; you have in effect opened a window displaying the disk contents. Each icon in the window represents a file on the disk. Some files may be application programs; others may be documents or drawings; still others may represent information needed by the Macintosh or used by a program.

Windows are an important part of Mac's special interface; they are used by many Macintosh programs. The operations described here apply to most Macintosh windows, not just the disk window.

Moving a Window

You may need to reorganize your Desktop by moving windows around.

Point at the black-banded bar at the top of the window and drag it with the mouse.

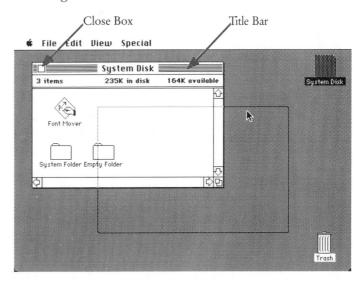

The area with the black bands is the window's title bar. Dragging the title bar moves the entire window. As with icons, the window's outline follows your movement.

Release the mouse button.

The window moves to the location of its outline.

Changing a Window's Size

To reduce clutter on your Desktop, you can make a window smaller; to see more of a disk's contents, you can make its window larger.

Point at the size box at the lower right corner of the window and drag it with the mouse.

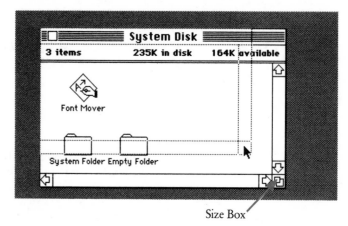

Size Box

The top left corner of the window remains in place and the window's size is adjusted following your mouse movement. Practice changing the window location and size, finishing up with a fairly small window. Notice that some of the icons drop out of sight as the window gets smaller.

Scrolling

Sometimes a disk may contain more files, represented by icons, than you can see in the window at one time; to move invisible icons into view you need to scroll the disk contents past the window.

Click a scroll arrow.

Clicking the arrows moves the disk's contents past the window by a small increment (a line if you're looking at text).

Click in the gray area of a scroll bar.

Clicking in the gray area instead of the arrow moves a larger increment (a pageful if you're looking at text).

Position the pointer over a scroll arrow and press the mouse button without moving the mouse.

Remember, this action is called pressing; it's a fundamental mouse operation.

The disk contents scroll by the window until you release the button.

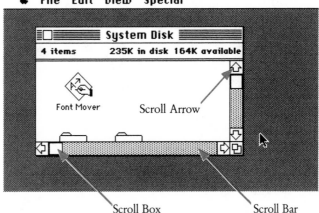

Drag the scroll box.

This action brings hidden icons directly into view. The scroll box indicates the relative location of a window with respect to the contents.

Some windows do not permit resizing or scrolling and therefore lack a size box or one or both scroll bars. If a disk window is big enough to display all the contents of a disk, the scroll bars turn solid white, and you can't scroll the window.

OPENING MORE THAN ONE WINDOW

You can have several windows open on the screen at the same time.

Double-click the Trash icon.

Double-clicking is a fast way to open an icon. (Remember, point at the icon and quickly click twice on the mouse button.)

This opens another window. It's empty because there is nothing in the trash.

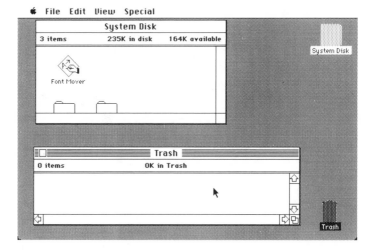

The window with black bands across its title bar is the active window. The black bands have disappeared from the disk window's title bar, showing that it is no longer active. (You might have to hunt around for the disk window if the Trash window has covered it up. Move or resize the Trash window if necessary.)

Click anywhere in the disk window.

The black bands are back in the disk window's title bar, showing that the disk window is again active.

Drag the disk window's size box so that the window overlaps but does not obscure the Trash window.

Click anywhere in the Trash window.

The Trash window moves on top of the disk window and the black bands switch into its title bar. If you have several overlapping windows on your Desktop, the active window will always be in front.

Closing a Window

You may close your windows in either of two ways:

Choose Close from the File menu; *or*

Click the close box in a window's upper left corner.

Close Box

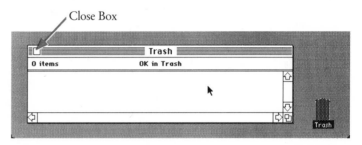

Close the Trash window; leave the disk window open.

WHAT THE DISK WINDOW TELLS YOU

Now that you can manipulate windows, let's take a closer look at the system disk window.

Click the disk window to make it active.

Drag its size box to make a large window.

The words and icons you see tell you which items you have stored on the system disk and how much space they take up.

A disk can hold only a finite amount of information. The top line in a disk window tells you how many items are on the disk, the total storage taken up by the files on that disk, and how much space is still available for additional items. The units are thousands of characters, or kilobytes (KB).

The icons represent individual files of information on the disk. Some of these files are application programs; others contain software the Macintosh itself needs to operate; still others contain resources you will find useful once you start working with the application programs.

You can use the menus to find out more information about disk files.

Choose `by Name` from the `View` menu.

(Point at View on the menu bar, drag the mouse to highlight by Name, and release the button.) The icons disappear, and a list of files appears in alphabetical order. Along with each file's name, you have its size and kind, and the date the file was last modified.

	System Disk		
Size	**Name**	Kind	Last Modified
0K	**Empty Folder**	folder	Tue, Jan 24, 1984
13K	**Font Mover**	application	Tue, Jan 24, 1984
146K	**System Folder**	folder	Wed, Jan 18, 1984

Pull down the `View` menu again, holding down the mouse button.

These choices represent ways you can organize the list of files. If you choose by Date, for example, the files are listed starting with the one most recently changed.

Drag to `by Icon` and release the mouse button.

Click any file icon.

Choose `Get Info` from the `File` menu.

A new window opens, showing information about the file.

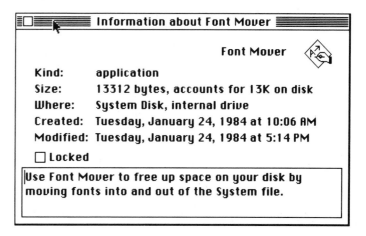

To close the Get Info window, you can either:

Click the close box in the Get Info window; *or*

Choose `Close` from the `File` menu.

TAKING A BREAK

Choose `Close All` from the `File` menu.

Choose `Eject` from the `File` menu.

After a few seconds, the Macintosh pushes the disk out of the disk drive. Turn off the power if you wish.

To restart, simply turn on the power and insert the disk again.

DESK ACCESSORIES

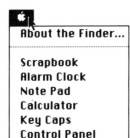

The Apple menu in the menu bar opens the way to the Macintosh desk accessories. You can use the desk accessories at any time, regardless of other activity — whether you are using a program or not, whether any windows are open or not.

Point at the Apple symbol at the far left of the menu bar.

Press and hold the mouse button.

Drag the mouse down to highlight `About the Finder...`.

Release the button.

Some information about an important program called the Finder appears on the screen. The Finder creates your Desktop, shows you which files are on the disk, copies files from disk to disk, and much more. You've been using the Finder throughout this chapter.

Click anywhere to get rid of the Finder information.

Go back to the Apple symbol and pull down its menu again.

The rest of the items in the menu are desk accessories. (Your menu may not be in the order shown.)

Choose each accessory in turn.

Click the accessory's close box to put it away.

What Do the Accessories Do?

Scrapbook saves material from one program and lets you move the information to another program or within the same program.

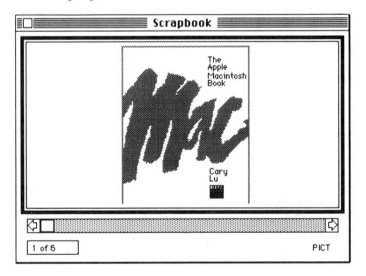

Alarm Clock displays a small box with the current time. Click the small symbol on the right to add a calendar. Now click the small alarm-clock icon. You can set the alarm by moving the cross-hair pointer over either the hours or minutes and clicking; then click the up or down

arrow to set the time. Turn the alarm on by clicking the bell icon on the left.

Note Pad gives you a place to type text notes. You can tear off sheets (the Note Pad gives you eight) by clicking the upturned corner. Clicking the lower left corner below the diagonal line flips the Note Pad back a page. Mac beeps if you try to put too much text on a sheet. We'll use the Note Pad in the next section.

Calculator is a general-purpose four-function calculator. Like the hand-held calculator you probably have on your desk already, it works algebraically. Use the mouse to click the numbers or functions you want; the results appear in the calculator's display panel. You can also enter numbers and functions from Mac's keyboard. The ✻ symbol denotes multiplication.

Key Caps displays a miniature Macintosh keyboard that tells you which characters your real keyboard generates. Press a few keys on the real keyboard or click them on the Key Caps display with the mouse and watch what happens; the keys are highlighted on the Key Caps display and appear in the blank bar above it.

Hold down Shift, Option, Caps Lock, or a combination of these keys on the real keyboard and watch what happens; the display keyboard is transformed into a variety of symbols and graphics characters.

Puzzle will look familiar; you can play with it when the boss isn't looking.

Control Panel lets you adjust the speaker volume (drag the sliding control up or down), set the repeat rate of the keys (turtle for slow, hare for fast), adjust the rate the pointer flashes, set the clock/calendar, and other features; see your manual for details.

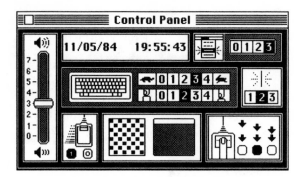

Again, you may want to close everything to take a break before we move on to practice a major operation: editing text.

EDITING TEXT

For most Macintosh application programs, you will use the same general methods for entering and editing text. We'll practice these operations using the Note Pad, since all system disks have one.

Choose Note Pad from the Apple menu.

If the first page has writing on it, turn to the next clean sheet by clicking the upturned left corner.

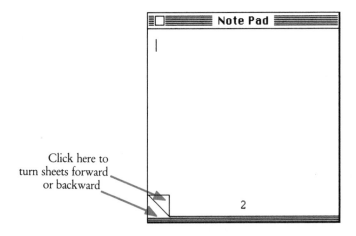

Click here to
turn sheets forward
or backward

You should now see a blinking vertical bar at the top left of the Note Pad page; this bar marks the text insertion point. Anything you type appears at this point. This insertion point is used by all application programs for text entry.

Type two or three lines.

If you make a mistake, hit Backspace and retype.

Your text appears on the Note Pad, pushing the insertion point ahead of it. Notice how the words wrap around to the next line when you get to the edge of the page. You don't have to hit Return at the end of each line as you do on a typewriter; Macintosh software does it for you.

Inserting Text

Suppose you have left out a phrase in the second line of the text you just typed. You want to go back and insert the phrase where it belongs.

Move the mouse so the pointer lies somewhere within the text.

Notice how the pointer changes shape as it moves onto the Note Pad, becoming an I-beam. You can use the I-beam pointer to mark where in the text you wish to insert the phrase you left out.

Move the I-beam pointer to anywhere on your second line of text and click.

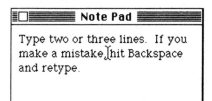

The blinking insertion point, which was at the end of your text, moves to the location of the I-beam pointer. If you now type in the missing phrase, it will be inserted in that location, pushing the insertion point and the existing text ahead of it.

Practice moving the insertion point around your text.

Move the I-beam pointer to a blank area at the end of a line and click.

The insertion point appears at the end of the text in that line.

Move the I-beam pointer to the blank area following all the text you have typed and click.

The insertion point appears at the end of the last line of the existing text.

Deleting Text

Click so the insertion point appears somewhere within the text.

Press the Backspace key.

Using the Backspace key is the simplest way to delete something; backspacing removes the character to the left of the insertion point.

You can also use Backspace to delete more than one character at a time. But first, you have to use the I-beam pointer to select what you want to delete.

Move the I-beam pointer to the beginning of the text you wish to delete.

Drag the I-beam pointer to the end of the text you want to delete and release the button.

Note that the text is now highlighted.

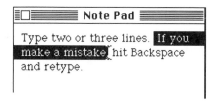

Hit Backspace.

Gone!

```
Type two or three lines.  hit
Backspace and retype.
```

Once you've selected text with the I-beam pointer, you also have three other ways of deleting it:

Choose Cut from the Edit menu; *or*

Choose Clear from the Edit menu; *or*

Hold down the Command key (⌘) while typing x.

Using the Command key is a shortcut to an operation; you simply hold down the Command key and type a letter instead of using the mouse to pull down and choose from a menu. The Command key equivalents for menu items are shown next to each item. From now on, this kind of instruction will be given as: Type Command-x.

Changing Your Mind

If you delete the wrong thing, Macintosh gives you two ways to repair your mistake:

Choose Undo from the Edit menu; *or*

Type Command-z.

Either operation restores your last deletion.

Choose Undo again.

The selection is deleted again. Undo reverses whatever your last move was; if your last move was to restore a deletion, then Undo deletes the restoration. You cannot undo more than one previous step.

In some programs, the Undo menu item changes to reflect your last action. It might say Restore Row if you've just deleted a row, but the item will always be in the same menu location.

Erasing the Note Pad

Select the entire text by dragging the mouse down over all the lines.

Choose **Cut** or **Clear** from the **Edit** menu.

These actions erase the entire practice sheet.

Closing the Note Pad

Click the Note Pad's close box.

If you don't erase what you've written, your text is stored in a file on the disk named Note Pad when the window closes. The next time you use the Note Pad, you'll find your notes right on the page where you typed them. Try it. To end this practice session:

Close the Note Pad window.

Close any other windows you might have opened.

Close the system disk window.

You can close windows one at a time by clicking each close box or all together by choosing Close All from the File menu.

Choose **Eject** from the **File** menu.

The disk drive ejects the disk.

TURNING OFF THE MACINTOSH

Do not turn Mac off before using the File menu to eject your disk. If you turn off the computer before ejecting the disk, you may lose some information that Mac has not yet stored on the disk (see Chapter 16).

A NOTE ABOUT PHILOSOPHY

As you learn more about the Macintosh, you will find that the best programs use a consistent philosophy. Such programs will have no unpleasant surprises.

For most Macintosh operations, you always select something first, then choose what you want the computer to do with it. Thus you select a file, then choose Get Info; you select a portion of text, then choose Cut or Copy.

A few programs, by their nature, don't work quite in this fashion. In the MacPaint program (the next chapter), you select a tool first, and *then* you do something with it. Yet selections of an area within MacPaint follow the normal rule: Select first, then choose what to do with it.

Most application programs will also use the same two ways of finding out more specifically what you want them to do: conversational dialog boxes and more urgent alert boxes.

Dialog Boxes

As you work with Macintosh, application programs will at times put dialog boxes on the screen in response to your actions. For example, a dialog box might ask you the size of paper in your printer. Some dialog boxes merely ask a yes/no question.

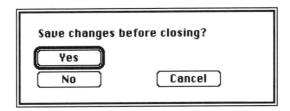

In most dialog boxes, you make choices by clicking buttons or items on a list. The next step depends on the dialog box. Often, you click a button labeled Yes or OK when you are satisfied with your choices, or you click a button labeled Cancel to close the box and return to the previous step. You cannot proceed past a dialog box unless you click an appropriate button.

One special form of dialog box is a mini-finder—
a listing of the files on the disk that were created by the
application program you are using. A related form is a
mini-list, which might, for example, contain the font
choices available for a particular program.

Alert Boxes

An alert box is similar to a dialog box, but is used to
warn you of a potentially serious problem. An alert box
might tell you that your word-processing document is getting too long to store on the disk, for example. In most
cases, you must acknowledge the alert box by clicking an
OK button.

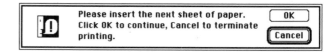

WHAT TO READ NEXT

The next seven chapters describe some major software types. Most Macintosh users will want to read the
next chapter on MacPaint and the first part of Chapter 5,
MacWrite. Read the other chapters if you are interested
in the software.

Since this chapter has covered only the essential
operations to get started, you may want to skip to Chapter
11, which covers disk organization. The information in
Chapter 11 is important for any productive work on
a Macintosh.

Chapter MacPaint
4

Once you have your Macintosh up and running, it's time to try an application. Let's begin with MacPaint.

The superb MacPaint program by Bill Atkinson is the essence of Macintosh. At its simplest, MacPaint is a fabulous drawing program. But it offers much more. You can use it to create designs—your company logo, for example—that you can incorporate into documents created by other programs. You can print your logo along with the text you write with your word-processing program or create an illustration to dress up your graphics program. Conversely, with suitable techniques or accessories, you can turn a graphics image from virtually any source into a MacPaint drawing.

What's more, MacPaint is fun. Even people with no tolerance for computer games find MacPaint absorbing and rewarding. No matter what your reasons for buying a Macintosh, make sure you have MacPaint.

STARTING THE PROGRAM

Like many other application program disks, the MacPaint disk is a system disk; it contains the information necessary to start up the machine. Assuming you have turned Mac on:

Insert the MacPaint disk.

Double-click the disk icon to open the disk window (if necessary).

MacPaint

Double-click the MacPaint icon; *or*

Click the MacPaint icon and choose `Open` from the `File` menu.

MacPaint fills the screen and, after a few seconds, gives you a blank drawing window labeled Untitled. You'll give it a title when you are ready to save your drawing on your disk.

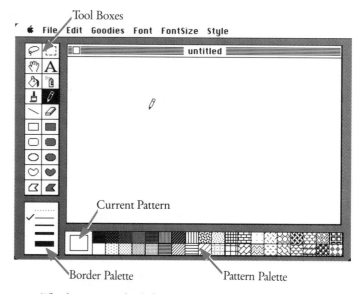

Tool Boxes

Current Pattern

Border Palette   Pattern Palette

The boxes on the left contain several drawing tools— a pencil, a paintbrush, an eraser, a can of paint, and so on, plus several ready-made open and filled shapes.

The border palette at the lower left shows lines of different thicknesses; you select these to control the border width of the open and filled shapes.

The boxes along the bottom make up the pattern palette. The current pattern selected from the palette is shown in the large leftmost box. We'll see how these patterns are used in a moment.

LEARNING TO DRAW

The best way to learn what each tool does is to experiment. Some tools are self-explanatory: The pencil lets you draw free-form; the paintbrush paints with lines and patterns; and the eraser erases.

 Click the pencil to select it from the tools.

You can select any tool by clicking it.

Move the pointer to the drawing window.

The pointer changes shape in the drawing window depending on which tool you're using. Now it's a pencil.

 Drag the pencil to draw something—anything.

When you've finished drawing, release the button. Drag the pencil again to draw another line.

 Click the straight line in the boxes to the left of the drawing window.

Move the pointer into the window.

The pointer changes shape to a crosshair.

 Drag anywhere in the window and release the mouse button.

The line tool permits you to draw only straight lines (at some angles the line is a little bumpy because each line is made up of discrete points).

Press Shift and drag another line.

The Shift key is a "constrain" key; when it is depressed, you can only draw vertical, horizontal, and diagonal (45-degree angle) lines. Any line you draw will be automatically adjusted to one of these orientations.

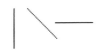

Drawing Predefined Shapes

 Click the open rectangle in the center left tool box.

Point anywhere in the drawing window and drag to another point.

51

Release the mouse button.

The starting and finishing points of the dragging action mark the diagonal corners of the rectangle.

Similarly, you can select other open shapes and indicate what size they should be by dragging.

If you press the Shift key while you drag the rectangle, it will be drawn as a square; pressing Shift while dragging the ellipse will draw a circle.

Moving Part of the Drawing

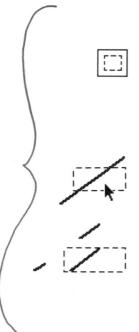

You can move any part of your drawing if you select it first.

Click the dotted-line rectangle in the top tool box.

The dotted-line rectangle is called the selection rectangle.

Move the pointer into the drawing window.

Drag the selection rectangle so that it surrounds the part of your drawing you want to move.

Position the pointer inside the selection rectangle.

Drag the rectangle and its contents to the new location.

Release the mouse button.

This action deposits the rectangle's contents in the new location.

Click in a blank area or choose another tool to get rid of the selection rectangle.

Erasing Part of the Drawing

There are four ways to erase part of a drawing.

Click the eraser icon, and drag it over what you want to erase; *or*

Select an area using the lasso (in the top left tool box) or the selection rectangle and hit Backspace; *or*

Select an area with the lasso or selection rectangle and choose **Clear** from the **Edit** menu; *or*

Choose the white pattern and use the paint brush to paint over what you wish to erase.

Erasing the Whole Drawing

Getting rid of your doodles is easy; simply:

Double-click the eraser.

Undoing the Changes

You can always undo your last step—but only the last step.

Choose **Undo** from the **Edit** menu;

Type the ` (top left) key.

Adding Text to the Drawing

You can add titles, labels, and captions to your drawings simply and quickly with MacPaint.

Click the letter A to select it from the tools.

Choose **New York** from the **Font** menu.

Choose **18 point** from the **FontSize** menu.

Points are a measure of type size; ordinary printed text is generally 10 to 12 point (see Chapter 26 for more information).

Choose **Bold** from the **Style** menu.

Click an open area in the drawing window.

Type a title or a label.

You can change the font and size by making a different choice from the menus.

Style	
✓Plain	⌘P
Bold	⌘B
Italic	⌘I
<u>Underline</u>	⌘U
Outline	⌘O
Shadow	⌘S
✓Align Left	⌘L
Align Middle	⌘M
Align Right	⌘R

**New York
18 point
bold**

Moving to Another Portion of the Page

The drawing window shows you only part of the whole drawing page, which is 8½ by 10 inches. If you fill the drawing window and want to move to another portion of the page:

 Click the hand icon.

Drag the hand in the drawing window.

If you drag the hand upward, the drawing moves upward, exposing a fresh portion of the page below it; if you drag the hand downward, the window moves down, exposing a fresh portion above it; and so on.

To work on large drawings, move the drawing half a window at a time.

Because it takes a little time to bring a fresh portion of the page into view, the wristwatch icon appears to tell you to be patient while Mac finishes its task.

LEARNING TO PAINT

Macintosh's tool boxes contain three tools for painting: a paintbrush, a regular can of paint, and a spray can of paint. We'll experiment with them here.

 Click the paintbrush.

Move the pointer to the drawing window and drag the paintbrush.

To select a brush of a particular size and shape:

Double-click the paintbrush; *or*

Choose `Brush Shape` from the `Goodies` menu.

A window appears with the size and shape of the current brush outlined by a box.

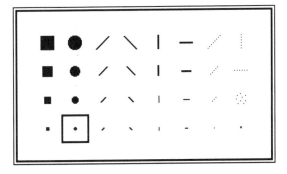

Click any brush size and shape.

You cannot continue painting until you make a choice; if you don't want to change the brush, you must click the already-selected size and shape in the box.

When you click a size and shape, the window disappears.

Drag the paintbrush in the drawing window.

The brush paints with the current pattern.

Using the MacPaint Palettes

Choose another pattern from the palette along the bottom of the screen.

Choose the filled rectangle from the tools to the left.

Move the pointer to the drawing window.

Drag the pointer diagonally across the window and admire the results.

Choose a different border width from the border palette.

Drag across the drawing window again.

Choose a different shape (for example, the filled oval) and again, drag the pointer.

Experiment with different tools and patterns; try the paintbrush and spray can, using different patterns.

Filling an Area with a Pattern

Choose the open rectangle from the tools.

Draw a rectangle.

Choose the paint can.

Move the paint can into the rectangle and click.

If the blank white pattern is selected, nothing will happen; click another pattern and try again.

Creating a New Pattern

Double-click a pattern that is close to the one you'd like to create.

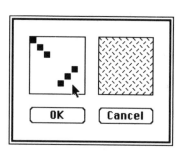

A dialog box comes up with the pattern detail greatly magnified on the left and the overall pattern on the right.

Click individual squares of the pattern in the left box.

Each individual square represents a dot on the screen. Clicking individual squares changes their color; black squares become white, white ones become black. The box on the right shows what the overall pattern looks like when you change individual dots. When you are satisfied with the new pattern:

Click the OK button.

When you click OK, the modified pattern replaces the pattern you originally double-clicked. The pattern change is saved with the drawing on disk.

If you change your mind, click Cancel.

A MACINTOSH SELF-PORTRAIT

Let's put some of these techniques together and have the Macintosh draw a self-portrait. (Whether you, the hardware, or the software is actually doing the drawing is a semantic question I will ignore.)

Choose the rounded-corner open rectangle from the tools and the second border from the border palette.

Move the pointer to the drawing window and drag from top left to bottom right to form the body of the Macintosh.

Draw the screen the same way, using a smaller square-corner open rectangle.

Choose the straight-line icon from the tools.

Hold down the Shift key while dragging a horizontal line to indicate Mac's recessed lower front face.

Choose the filled rectangle.

Choose a uniform gray dot pattern.

Drag to form the keyboard connector.

Choose the open rectangle.

Drag and build the disk-drive slot from two rectangles.

57

Using the selection rectangle (upper right tool box), select the area where the two disk-drive rectangles overlap.

Choose Fat Bits from the Goodies menu.

Fat Bits shows you a magnified portion of the drawing, surrounded by the flickering selection rectangle. Each black square represents a dot on the screen. You need to remove some dots to create the shape you want.

Choose the pencil from the tool boxes.

Move the pencil into the drawing window and click on each dot you wish to remove; drag the pencil to remove several dots at a time.

Clicking the pencil changes a square from black to white or white to black; if you click in a white area, you create dots. If you take out too many dots, use the pencil to put them back in.

The results appear in proper scale in the inset at the upper left corner of the drawing window.

Click the inset to restore the original drawing window.

Choose a suitable pattern for Mac's screen—horizontal lines, perhaps.

Choose the paint can, move it to the rectangle that represents the screen, and click to fill in the screen.

For some finishing touches:

Choose the filled rectangle and drag a small rectangle for Mac's Apple logo.

To touch up the Apple logo:

With the selection rectangle, surround the Apple logo and choose Fat Bits from the Goodies menu.

Use the pencil to remove dots so you end up with something that looks like an apple.

Label the drawing; try the Venice font at 14 point:

Choose Venice from the Fonts menu.

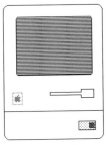

Macintosh

Choose 14 point from the FontSize menu.

Choose Plain from the Style menu.

Select a location and type in the label.

One last touch. If something isn't positioned exactly to your taste:

Choose the selection rectangle from the tool boxes.

Surround the misplaced part of your drawing.

Use the pointer to drag the surrounded part of your drawing to precisely where you want it.

Click in a blank area to clear the selection rectangle.

Choose Show Page from the Goodies menu to see where your drawing will appear on the 8½ - by 11-inch page.

The dotted rectangle represents your drawing window.

Press the mouse button and drag to move the drawing window anywhere you want it on the page.

The printed version will match your final choice.

Choose Save As ... from the File menu to name and save your handiwork.

Type in an appropriate name and press Enter.

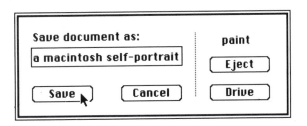

Your Macintosh self-portrait will be saved as a file and will be given a special icon that will appear in your disk window.

Choose `Print` from the `File` menu to print your picture.

What you see in the MacPaint drawing window is only about a third of a single 8½- by 11-inch page. What you get when you print is the whole page. If you've been experimenting, you may have miscellaneous doodling on parts of the page outside the drawing window.

If you are interested in using the Macintosh and MacPaint to create quality graphics, see Chapter 26 for some specific techniques.

Chapter 5 Word Processing

Almost everyone who buys or uses a computer eventually does some form of word processing on it. In fact, many people use their machines for nothing but word processing. With a computer, writing and editing anything from a letter to a book becomes easier, faster, and far less messy.

Instead of scrawling out drafts by hand or banging out innumerable versions on a typewriter, you type your text into the computer one time only, changing words and phrases on the screen as you type. The computer allows you to move paragraphs, delete sections, and add new sections—all without having to retype pages over and over. When you like what you've written, you can print a precisely formatted copy immediately.

At least that's the way it should be. A major challenge for word-processing program developers has been to give you on paper exactly what you see on the screen—not an easy task. With traditional word processing, you could rarely be sure exactly where new pages of text began, much less see italics or headlines on the screen.

Macintosh has changed all that. At last, what you see *really is* what you get.

Several word processors with different features will be available for the Macintosh. Which one is right for you depends entirely on your own writing needs and style. This chapter highlights two of the first word-processing programs available for the Macintosh: Apple's MacWrite, designed for short, simple writing jobs; and Microsoft® Word, designed to compete with dedicated word processors.

The guides to MacWrite and Microsoft Word in this chapter give you just the flavor of each program; they are not exhaustive and some functions are explained using the simplest operations rather than the fastest ones. For a more complete description, refer to their respective manuals.

The chapter concludes with a brief look at Think Tank, a specialized word processor designed to create and manipulate outlines.

MACWRITE

MacWrite is a simple, handy word processor. It works well for people who have never used a computer or word processor before, as well as for users with straightforward needs; anyone can get some productive work out of Mac-Write in an hour. MacWrite does not have the elaborate functions necessary for major word-processing jobs.

Starting MacWrite

For this practice session, you'll need the Write/Paint disk, or any start-up or system disk containing the MacWrite program.

Insert the disk.

The menu bar and the Desktop icons appear. If the disk window is not open:

Double-click the Write/Paint disk icon; *or*

Click the Write/Paint disk icon and choose `Open` from the `File` menu.

The disk window opens, showing icons that represent what's stored on the disk. You'll select the MacWrite icon to begin word processing.

MacWrite

Double-click the MacWrite icon to open it.

The Desktop clears and the wristwatch appears, telling you to wait for the MacWrite document window to open.

The window, labeled Untitled, opens.

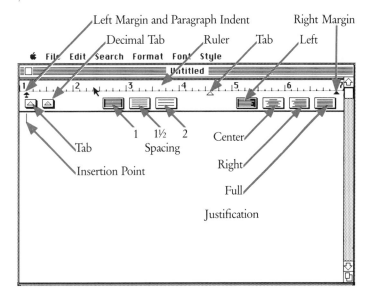

Notice the blinking vertical bar at the top left margin; this marks the insertion point (equivalent to the cursor in other word processors) where the text you type will appear.

Type a few sentences—anything.

Backspace and retype to correct minor typing errors.

To MacWrite, any text typed into the window is called a document. Imagine that you are typing on a long paper scroll that advances past your window as you add text.

Notice what happens when you get to the end of a line: MacWrite automatically bumps words to the next line without your having to press Return; this is called word wrap. The only time you have to press Return is at the end of a paragraph.

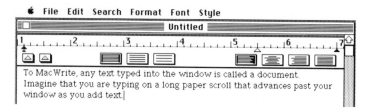

Inserting and Adding Text

With the mouse, you can move the pointer anywhere within the text. You use it to position the insertion point so you can add text. You can only add text at the insertion point.

The insertion point will only appear within or at the end of your text; you cannot put it in the white space following the text or in the margins.

Move the pointer into the text area.

The pointer changes shape when it's in the text, becoming an I-beam pointer. Whenever you're working with text on a Macintosh, you will see the I-beam pointer and can use the same basic operations described here.

typing on a long⌐paper scroll

Position the I-beam pointer between two words and click.

The blinking bar marking the insertion point appears wherever you click within the text.

typing on a long papyrus or paper

Type a few words.

The extra text is inserted at the insertion point, between the two words.

Move the pointer to the last line or below the last line and click.

Type another sentence.

The sentence is added to the end of your text.

Hit the Return key several times.

You use the Return key if you want some blank lines.

Type in more text.

What if you change your mind? You didn't really want to add any text after all. As with other programs, you can undo your last step.

Choose `Undo Typing` from the `Edit` menu.

Undo reverses your last action, back to the last click of the mouse.

If you change your mind again, you can get your typing back by undoing the Undo Typing command.

Choose `Redo Typing` from the `Edit` menu; *or*

Type Command-z.

For the next sections, you will need a few lines of text on the screen. You can type more text in now, or you can use some text that is already on the disk. If you want to use an existing disk file, you need to clear the text you've just written from the screen. In most cases you will want to save your work. These operations are described briefly here and in more detail later.

Saving a Document

Choose `Save` from the `File` menu.

A dialog box comes on screen, asking you to name the file.

Type a file name.

Click the Save button.

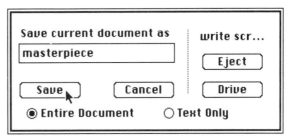

The disk drive turns on, and your document is saved on the disk.

After the file is stored, you can resume working on your document; or if you want to leave the MacWrite program completely:

Choose Quit from the File menu.

If you have made any changes since the last Save, a dialog box asks if you want to save your current work. If you are just experimenting, click No, and nothing will be saved. If you want to save the latest version:

Click Save.

If the file has no name ("untitled"), a new dialog box asks for a file name.

Type in a file name and click Save.

After you save the document, the Desktop with the disk window reappears.

Reading in an Existing Document

In the disk window, locate a file you want to work with. Make sure that the file you select is a MacWrite document.

If you open a file icon, the system will automatically start the program that generated the file and read in the file information.

Double-click the file icon.

The contents of the file you have chosen appear in the document window.

Formatting with MacWrite

With conventional word processors, setting the format of your document—the margins, tabs, line spacing, and alignment—often takes more effort than typing the text. MacWrite uses visible rulers with special markers to make setting formats easy and elegant.

When you start a document, MacWrite supplies a ruler with a preset format that you can keep or change. The ruler corresponds to the text area on a standard 8½- by 11-inch sheet of paper; the full margins do not appear in Mac's document window.

Notice the format of the text on your screen. Changing this format simply requires moving the margin or indentation markers and selecting the spacing and justification, or alignment, icons.

Margins and paragraphs

The two markers on the ruler to the left are for the left margin and the paragraph indent. The triangle marks the left margin and affects any word-wrapped text; the arrow marks the paragraph indent and affects only the first line of each paragraph (any line immediately following a Return). These two markers move independently. The triangle on the right marks the right margin.

To drag a margin marker, position the pointer carefully on the triangle and drag.

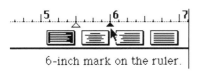

6-inch mark on the ruler.

Drag the right-margin marker to the 6-inch mark on the ruler.

Drag the left-margin marker to the 1½-inch mark on the ruler.

Drag the right margin marker to
Then drag the left-margin

Notice what happens to your text.

Drag the paragraph-indent arrow so that it is on top of the left-margin marker.

If you drag both the left-margin and indentation markers to the same position, all your text lines up on the left margin with no paragraph indents.

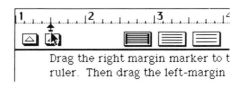

Drag the right margin marker to t
ruler. Then drag the left-margin

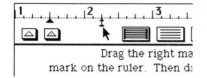

Drag the right ma
mark on the ruler. Then d

Drag the indent arrow first to the left and then to the right of the left-margin marker.

Dragging and placing the indentation marker to the right of the left margin marker gives you normal paragraph indents; dragging it to the left gives you hanging indents—the first line of each paragraph extends farther left than the rest of the text.

Tabs

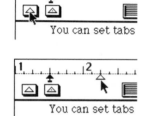

You can set tabs

You set tabs by dragging the little triangles at the left, under the ruler. The triangle on the left is a standard tab; the other triangle (with a dot) is a decimal tab. The decimal tab is used for entering numbers in a column; decimal points will line up on the tab location.

Drag a tab triangle to any position on the ruler.

You must drag the tab triangles to the ruler; the tab icon disappears if you drag it to any other location.

If you press the Tab key while typing text, the insertion point will move to the next tab position, just as on a typewriter. You can drag as many tabs as you need from their boxes.

Drag the tab triangle away from the ruler and release the mouse button.

The tab icon disappears; this clears the tab.

Spacing and justification

The two sets of icons under the ruler in the center and to the right represent pages with different spacing and justification.

Position the pointer in the double-spaced page icon and click.

Spacing and justification. The two sets of icons under the

ruler in the center and to the right represent pages with

Click the single-spaced page icon.

Your document is single-spaced.

Click the page icon with center alignment.

Spacing and justification. The two sets of icons under the ruler in the center and to the right represent pages with different spacing and justification. Position the pointer in the double-spaced page icon and click.

Click the other page icons in turn.

Your text lines change justification instantly on screen: left-justified, centered, right-justified, and both margins justified.

Changing the format within the text

Format
Insert Ruler
Hide Rulers
Open Header
Open Footer
Display Headers
Display Footers
Set Page #...
Insert Page Break
Title Page

A ruler sets the format for any text that follows it, until you insert another ruler. You can insert a new ruler anywhere.

Choose **Insert Ruler** from the **Format** menu.

You can make any changes you wish to the new ruler. If the rulers are too intrusive, you can make them invisible by choosing Hide Rulers from the Format menu.

Editing by Selecting

Editing means changing—anything from correcting a typo to doing a wholesale cut-and-paste operation. Before you can alter text, you must select it. To select text:

Position the pointer just before the text.

Before you can alter text, you must select it.

Drag the pointer across the text you wish to select.

Release the mouse button.

The selected text is highlighted in reverse color. Your next command will affect only the selected text.

You can select an individual word quickly by pointing at it and double-clicking.

You can change the selected text in many ways. Three fundamental editing operations will copy, move, and delete it.

Choose `Copy` from the `Edit` menu.

The selected text is copied into the Clipboard, an electronic scratch pad.

Move the pointer to another part of the text and click.

The blinking insertion point appears in the new location.

Choose `Paste` from the `Edit` menu.

The selected text is copied into the new location; it also remains intact in its original location.

Select another portion of text.

Choose `Cut` from the `Edit` menu.

The selected text is deleted and disappears into the Clipboard.

Move the pointer to another part of the text and click.

Choose `Paste` from the `Edit` menu.

The text is moved from the Clipboard into the new location. The Clipboard can hold one item at a time. Any time you choose Cut or Copy from the Edit menu, you replace the previous Clipboard contents with the new selection. So if you want to get rid of some text entirely, you can simply cut it to the Clipboard and leave it there until it is replaced by something new.

Before you can alter text, you must select it. Before you can alter text,

Choosing Typefaces and Type Sizes

MacWrite lets you choose the typeface, or font, in which your text is displayed and printed; you can also choose the size and style (bold, italic, outlined, shadowed, and so on).

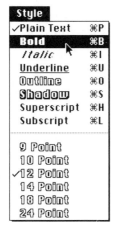

Font choices are stored with the text. Whenever you move the insertion point and add new text, MacWrite automatically uses the font of the adjoining text.

Select some text by dragging through it so it is highlighted.

Choose any font from the Font menu.

The highlighted text is now displayed in that font.

Choose Bold from the Style menu.

The selected text's font doesn't change, but appears bold.

Choose 18 point from the Style menu.

The text now appears in 18-point type. Points are a measure of type size; ordinary printed text is generally 10 to 12 point (see Chapter 26 for more information).

The outlined point sizes in the Style menu indicate choices with the best appearance.

More About Saving a Document

We've already covered saving a document to disk very briefly. I'll go over it again in more detail. As well as saving your files at the end of a session, you should save your work regularly during a session to guard against losing work because of a power failure.

Choose Save from the File menu.

If the file is new, a dialog box will ask you to give the file a name; type in a name and click Save.

You cannot have two files with the same name on the same disk. If the file already exists, MacWrite will replace the original file with the new version.

If you want to preserve both the original version and save the new version, you have to save the new version under a different name. To do this:

Choose Save As... from the File menu.

A dialog box prompts you for the new name.

After you save a file, MacWrite returns you to the place where you were in your document.

To quit MacWrite and close the document you're working on:

Choose `Quit` from the `File` menu.

If you have made changes since the last time you saved your document, a dialog box asks if you want to save the latest version before quitting.

Click Yes.

The document closes and the Desktop clears. You can now open another document or go to another application.

MICROSOFT WORD

Microsoft Word is a more powerful and complex word processor than MacWrite. Word is also more expensive and somewhat harder to learn. It competes with dedicated word processors, offering common features and some unique ones, plus the advantages of the Macintosh interface.

MacWrite Versus Microsoft Word

This comparison is based on initial versions of both programs for the 128-KB Macintosh.

Word has the following major features that MacWrite does not:

- Multiple windows that allow you to see other parts of the same file or of a different file. You can Cut and Paste between windows.

- A glossary function that lets you type short codes in your text in place of frequently occurring words or phrases. For example, you can define a glossary entry so that every time you type MC, Word expands it to Macintosh.

- Horizontal scrolling, which means your document can be wider than the screen width; you

> scroll from one side to the other to see the complete text.

- Mail merge—a program that automatically inserts names and addresses from a mailing list into a form letter.

- Footnotes that are placed at the end of text, or along page bottoms; footnotes are even continued into the next page if necessary.

- Multiple printing formats, including multi-column printing.

Size of file

MacWrite: Limited by RAM; about 8 ½ pages, single-spaced.

Word: Limited by disk capacity; Word reads and writes to disk as necessary. With long documents, disk access time slows operation.

Setting margins and tabs

MacWrite: Visual ruler sets indents, margins, and two types of tabs (left-aligned and decimal).

Word: Visual ruler sets indents, margins, and four types of tabs (left-, center-, and right-aligned, plus decimal); can automatically fill space between tabs with dashes, underlines, or periods.

Visual display of page

MacWrite: Nearly complete page display, including running heads at the top and running footers at the bottom of each page.

Word: Does not show running heads or footers; does not always show exact page-break location. May display complete pages in a preview mode, but you won't be able to make changes during preview; you must go back to the original file.

Printer functions

MacWrite: Stored formatting information works best with ImageWriter or equivalent printers.

Word: Stored formatting information can be adapted to the features of any printer, present and future. Information in the same document will work with two completely different printers.

Learning time

MacWrite: Short; useful operation within an hour.

Word: Word takes a little longer to learn than MacWrite for comparable features. Word's more-advanced features require several additional hours.

Starting Word

The following description of Word starts from the beginning. Many basic steps are shared with MacWrite and are described only briefly here.

Insert a system disk containing Word.

Double-click the Word disk icon.

Double-click the Word icon to open it.

The Word window, labeled Untitled, opens.
Notice the diamond symbol at the upper left. This symbol marks the end of the text.

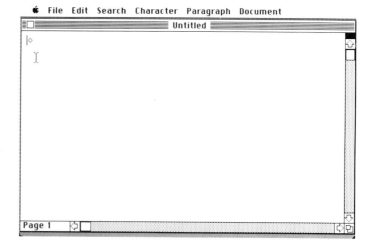

Type in some text—any text.

Backspace and retype to correct minor typing errors.

Keep typing at the end of the line; Word automatically bumps words to the next line without your having to press Return. The only time you have to press Return is at the end of a paragraph.

Inserting and Adding Text

You can add text only at an insertion point within the text or at the end-of-text marker.

Position the pointer between two words and click.

The blinking bar marking the insertion point appears wherever you click within text. The end-of-text marker changes to show that whatever you type will no longer appear there.

Type a few words.

The extra text is inserted at the insertion point between the two words.

Move the pointer to the end of the last line and click.

Type another sentence.

Hit the Return key several times.

You hit the Return key if you want to skip lines.

Type in more text.

If you change your mind you can undo your last step.

Choose Undo Typing from the Edit menu.

Undo reverses your last action, back to the last click of the mouse.

You can get your typing back by undoing the Undo Typing command.

Choose Redo Typing from the Edit menu; *or*

Type Command-z.

Editing by Selecting

Word follows the same conventions as other Macintosh programs for basic editing (see the section Editing by Selecting in the description of MacWrite).

Select an area by dragging though it.

Select a word by double-clicking the word.

Select a sentence by pressing the Shift key and double-clicking the sentence.

Copy, Cut, and Paste work the same way as they do with MacWrite.

Formatting with Word

You can set formats in Word at three different levels: by characters, by paragraphs, and by divisions. You can define a division to be any size; for example, the introduction, body, and appendixes of a book could be defined as divisions, each with a distinct format.

Type in two paragraphs' worth of text.

Click anywhere in one paragraph, placing the insertion point in the paragraph.

Point at Paragraph on the menu bar and pull down the menu.

The Paragraph menu gives you choices for justification and spacing. Try several.

Choose **Formats ...** from the **Paragraph** menu.

Word displays a ruler and a dialog box where you can enter many format choices or parameters, including left and right margins and line spacing. Some of these format choices are also available directly from the Paragraph menu.

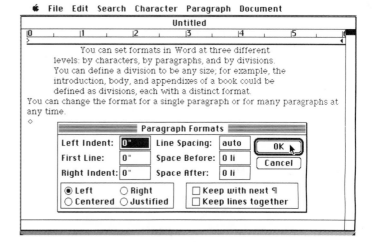

You can change the properties of a single paragraph or of many paragraphs at a time. New paragraphs use the properties of the previous paragraph unless the properties are changed.

The ruler always appears at the top of the window, but the margin settings displayed on the ruler apply to the paragraph containing the insertion point.

Although the ruler is normally displayed in inches, you can reset the measurements to centimeters or printer's points, or turn the ruler into a typewriter-style 10- or 12-pitch counter. Choose Options from the Edit menu to see the choices.

To set margins, drag the small markers to the desired location on the ruler. Or you can enter numerical values directly, such as a 1-inch left margin and 0.5-inch right margin.

Click OK in the dialog box.

Choose Tabs... from the Paragraph menu.

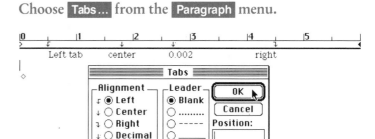

To set tabs, click in the white strip just below the ruler. A small tab marker appears where you click; the position is given in the dialog box. You can set not only the left-justified and decimal tabs, but also a centered and right-justified tab as well.

Click OK in the dialog box.

Choosing Typefaces and Type Sizes

Drag through some text so it is selected and highlighted.

Choose a type style from the Character menu.

The selected text changes to reflect your choice.

Choose Formats ... from the Character menu.

The Character Properties dialog box lets you set the type style, font, and size, as well as normal, superscript, or subscript position.

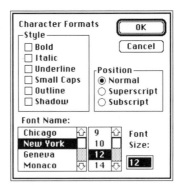

Choose any font by clicking the font name in the list box.

Enter the font size you want in the box labeled "Font size."

Click OK in the dialog box.

Saving Your Work

Choose `Save` from the `File` menu.

If the file is new, a dialog box will ask you to give the file a name.

Type in a name and click `Save`.

If the file already exists, Word will replace the original file with the new version.

If you want to preserve both the original version and save the new version:

Choose `Save As...` from the `File` menu.

A dialog box prompts you for the new name. To quit Word and close the document you're working on:

Choose `Quit` from the `File` menu.

If you have made changes since the last time you saved your document, a dialog box asks if you want to save the latest version before quitting.

Click Yes.

The document closes and the Desktop clears. You can now open another document or go to another application.

Other Word Features

Consult the Word manual for other functions. Word has many powerful features designed for serious word processing; if you work with words, take the time to learn how to get the exact results you want.

Although MacWrite and Word files are not compatible in their formatted form, both programs will read and write pure ASCII text files. Or you can copy text into the Clipboard in one program and paste it into the text in another. The Clipboard will transfer the text without its formatting information.

Word on the Macintosh will read files produced by Microsoft Word on other computers.

THINK TANK

Think Tank, from Living Videotext, is a specialized word processor. It is organized not to deal with a long linear document but to handle outlines.

Any word processor can deal with an outline, of course. But word processors can only show a screenful at a time; most of the time you can only see details in one part of the outline—only the trees in a forest.

```
 ⌘  File  Edit  Extra  FontSize

 +   The States of the Union
      +   New England
           -   Maine
           -   New Hampshire
           -   Vermont
           -   Massachusetts                ▶
           -   Rhode Island
           -   Connecticut
      +   Mid Atlantic
      +   Southeast
      +   Midwest
      +  [Appalachia]
           -   West Virginia
           -   Tennessee
           -   Kentucky
      +   Deep South
      +   Ozarks
      +   Great Plains
```

Think Tank tracks the relative importance of outline entries by the indentation level. The program preferentially keeps the main headings, the most important entries, on the screen. When you look at an outline, you first see only main headings. You can then select any heading, and expand it, showing its subheadings. And, in turn, you can select a subheading and expand it to show the sub-subheadings, and so on. Because only the entries you select are expanded, the major entries remain on screen. In effect, you can always see both the forest and the nearby trees.

You can use Think Tank and a Macintosh word processor together, using each for the task it does best.

Chapter 6 Spreadsheets

Spreadsheet programs are the most popular business application for microcomputers. They are powerful tools for calculation and projection.

For example, suppose we want to calculate the difference in cost between two new cars. One model has better fuel economy but a higher price. Is it cheaper in the long run to buy this model than one that consumes more fuel but costs less? To do this calculation carefully without a computer, we take out a sheet of ledger paper and systematically enter each cost item. To get a total, we must make many assumptions about the cost of gasoline, how many miles we expect to drive each year, the interest rate on the car loan, and so on. Since we can't be sure how many miles a year we will drive, we have to repeat the entire calculation several times for high and low estimates. The process is so laborious that even an accountant would stop calculating and start guessing after one or two calculations.

We can set up the same analysis with a spreadsheet. A spreadsheet works like a ledger sheet; it is organized in rows and columns. We can link the value of any entry to that of any other entry with a mathematical or logical formula. Once we have entered the values, the computer performs all the calculations.

For a single calculation, a spreadsheet may not be faster than a calculator. But for repeated calculations with changing values, called variables, the spreadsheet shines. If we change any number—the number of miles we drive each year, for example—the rest of the calculation is performed automatically. The process is so much easier that we can run dozens or hundreds of calculations painlessly. In the process, we will come to learn the true costs of owning a car—where the money really goes and which costs are essentially irrelevant.

Spreadsheets give you the power you need to plan ahead in your business. You can construct a spreadsheet model of your income and expenses, for example, using formulas to add tax and shipping automatically to each purchased item and to calculate discounts for volume purchases.

Spreadsheets aren't just for calculations. If you need to produce an organization chart or other text material that is arranged in columns and rows, a spreadsheet works much better than a word processor.

MICROSOFT MULTIPLAN

Microsoft® Multiplan™ for the Macintosh is a spreadsheet program. If you have used a spreadsheet program on another computer, you are in for a revelation. To begin with, the screen is far easier to read. Instead of typing endless keystrokes to perform such simple tasks as changing a column width, you simply point at the line dividing two columns, grab it with your mouse, and drag the column wider or narrower. If you want two windows showing different parts of the spreadsheet, you grab a split bar, and drag the column until the windows are set to your satisfaction. It's a lot easier to do than to describe. A conventional spreadsheet on an ordinary computer is archaic and clumsy by comparison.

In this Multiplan profile, we will build a spreadsheet model to analyze the cost of buying and owning a car. Although building the model takes many steps, you should be able to have it running in 20 minutes. I've included the complete model because it shows the power of Multiplan, and because the results are interesting; most car owners don't really know where their money goes.

Starting Multiplan

Multiplan

Put the Multiplan disk into the Macintosh.

Open the disk icon (if it's not open already).

Double-click the Multiplan icon.

An Untitled window opens up, displaying an array of cells. The pointer is shaped like a fat cross when moving over the cells.

Click any cell.

The cell color reverses. Clicking a cell selects that cell.

Each cell has an address: a row number down the left side and a column number across the top; R1C1, for example, is the address of the cell at the intersection of row 1 and column 1. The selected cell's address is displayed in the formula bar along the top of the window. As you click on different cells, the cell address in the formula bar changes.

The formula bar displays not only the cell address but also the contents of the current cell.

Entering Labels

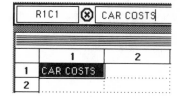

Click the first cell at the upper left (address: R1C1).

Type CAR COSTS.

The label appears in the first cell as you type it. If you make a mistake, backspace and retype.

Press the Return·key.

The next cell down (R2C1) becomes the active cell.

Press the Return key again.

This step moves the active cell down one more (R3C1). You could also have just clicked the next cell down.

Type Price and press Return.

If you make a mistake but don't notice it until after you have pressed Return, you can go back and correct the mistake in the usual Macintosh way:

Click the cell with the mistake.

The formula bar at the top shows the active cell's contents.

Drag through all or part of the contents to select it.

Delete the selection by pressing the Backspace key; *or*

Type a new entry.

Another method: Undo your last step.

Choose Undo Typing from the Edit menu.

If necessary, you can always retrace your steps. For a more complete guide, see the Multiplan manual.

And now, back to entering labels:

Click cell R4C1.

Type Down Payment and press Return.

Continue with:

Loan Value

Monthly Payment

1st Yr Cost

2-3rd Yr Cost

Fixed Costs

MPG

Running Costs

3 Yr Total

Salvage Value

3 Yr Cost.

After each entry, press Return.

Some of the labels may be a little wider than the column. Until you enter something in the cell to the right, you can still read the entire cell's contents; however, entries in column 2 may partially obscure long labels in column 1, so let's widen column 1 now:

Point at the line dividing columns 1 and 2 just above the first row.

The pointer changes to a line with arrows.

Drag the pointer to the right until the column division clears all the labels.

Dragging to the right makes the column wider; dragging to the left makes it narrower. All the other columns move right or left, their widths unchanged.

Now you are done with the first column. If the spreadsheet has scrolled off the top of the window, press the upper arrow of the vertical scroll bar. The top of the spreadsheet will come back into view.

Click the first cell in the second column (R1C2).

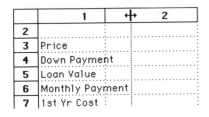

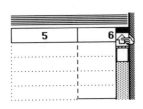

Type Gas Cost and press the Tab key.

If you press Tab after the entry rather than Return, the active cell moves to the right.

Type Miles Yr and press Tab.

Type Interest and press Tab.

Type Loan Term and press Return.

Entering Variables

Click the cell under Gas Cost (R2C2).

Type the cost of gasoline, say 1.30, and press Enter.

The entry appears as 1.3. Since most of this spreadsheet will show dollar values, you can change the format of column 2 to display in dollars.

Select the entire column of cells by clicking the column heading.

The entire column is highlighted.

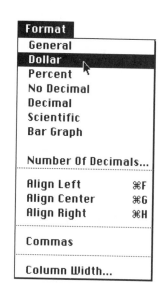

Choose Dollar from the Format menu.

Now all numeric values in the second column will appear with a dollar sign and two decimal places.

Click the cell under Miles Yr (R2C3).

Type 12000 and press Tab.

We'll use 12,000 miles driven in a year as a starting point. Because this cell was not selected for the dollar format, there is no dollar sign.

Type 0.14 and press Enter.

0.14 is 14 percent interest. As with the other variables, we can change the loan interest later. To display it in percent format, make sure that R2C4 is still the selected cell (pressing Enter doesn't move the selected cell):

Choose `Percent` from the `Format` menu.

The entry now reads 14.00%.

Click the cell under Loan Term (R2C5).

Type 36 and press Enter.

This sets a three-year, or 36-month, loan term.

	1	2	3	4	5
	CAR COSTS	Gas Cost	Miles Yr	Interest	Loan Term
		$1.30	12000	14.00%	36
	Price				

Naming Variables

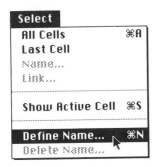

For convenience, name the four variables you have just entered. You can then build up formulas with easy-to-understand names instead of cell addresses like R2C2.

Click the cell containing $1.30 (R2C2).

Choose `Define Name` from the `Select` menu.

A dialog box asks you for the name of this cell.

Press Enter.

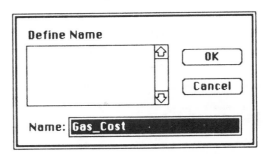

This names the cell value. Pressing Enter or Return does the same thing as clicking the OK button in the dialog box.

Multiplan proposes the name Gas_Cost, so you don't have to type it. When you choose Define Name for a particular cell, the program will automatically look at adjacent cells for possible names.

Click the cell containing 12000 (R2C3).

Choose **Define Name** from the **Select** menu.

Press Enter.

Click the cell containing 14.00% (R2C4).

Choose **Define Name** from the **Select** menu.

Press Enter.

Click the cell containing 36 (R2C5).

Choose **Define Name** from the **Select** menu.

Press Enter.

> Now you can start building up the formulas for the main calculation.

Entering Formulas

Click the cell to the right of Price (R3C2).

Type 6000 and press Return.

> $6000 is the price of an economy car.
> The active cell is now R4C2, the cell to the right of Down Payment. The down payment is a quarter of the price. In the following instructions, use the mouse to perform the action given in [brackets].

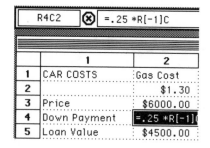

Type = .25 * [click R3C2, the cell above] and press Return.

> You have told Multiplan to multiply (computers use * instead of × to avoid confusion with the letter X) the price in R3C2 ($6000) by 0.25 and put the result ($1500) in R4C2.
> For the loan value, subtract the down payment from the price:

Type = [click R3C2, price]−[click R4C2, down payment] and press Return.

The monthly payment formula is the most complex:

Type = ([click R5C2, loan value] ∗ Interest / 12) / (1 − (1 + Interest / 12) ˆ (− Loan_Term)) and press Enter.

R7C2	=(R[-1]C*Interest/12)/(1-(1+Interest/12)^(-Loan_Term))

Untitled

	1	2	3	4	5	6
1	CAR COSTS					
2		Gas Cost	Miles Yr	Interest	Loan Term	
3		$1.30	12000	14.00%	36	
4	Price	$6000.00				
5	Down Payment	$1500.00				
6	Loan Value	$4500.00				
7	Monthly Payment	$153.80				

This is the standard formula for monthly loan payments; your bank may use a slightly different formula. The ˆ symbol indicates an exponent.

Check the entry for accuracy.

The formula bar should show: = (R[− 1]C ∗ Interest / 12) / (1 − (1 + Interest / 12) ˆ (− Loan_Term)).

If you put in spaces around the symbols, Multiplan removes them. The R[–1]C is the address of the loan value cell you clicked relative to the address of the cell where you were entering the formula (up one row, same column).

Edit the line if necessary to correct mistakes.

The first year cost of the loan is the down payment plus 12 monthly payments:

Click the cell to the right of 1st Yr Cost (R7C2).

Type = [click R4C2, down payment] + 12 ∗ [click R6C2, monthly payment] and press Return.

If you see # # # # # in the cell, the column is too narrow. Open it up as described above, dragging the divider between columns 2 and 3 to the right.

The selected cell (R8C2) is now the one to the right of 2-3rd Yr Cost.

Type = 24 ∗ [click R6C2, monthly payment] and press Return.

The next item, Fixed Costs, includes car registration, insurance, and maintenance.

Type 800 and press Return.

The next item is MPG—miles per gallon.

Enter 30 and press Enter.

Since miles per gallon isn't a dollar value, you need to delete the $ sign. Make sure the cell R10C2 is still selected:

Choose **General** from the **Format** menu.

The cell contents changes from $30 to 30.

For Running Costs, click R11C2, type = Gas_Cost ∗ Miles_Yr/[click R10C2, mpg], and press Return.

For 3 Yr Total, type = [click R7C2, 1st yr cost] + [click R8C2, 2-3rd yr cost] + 3 ∗ [click R9C2, fixed costs] + 3 ∗ [click R11C2, running costs] and press Return.

The next item, Salvage Value, is the expected selling price of the car after three years. A $6000 car might sell for $4500 after three years.

Type 4500 and press Return.

For 3 Yr Cost, type = [click R12C2, 3 yr total] − [click R13C2, salvage value] and press Enter.

	1	2
1	CAR COSTS	Gas Cost
2		$1.30
3	Price	$6000.00
4	Down Payment	$1500.00
5	Loan Value	$4500.00
6	Monthly Payment	$153.80
7	1st Yr Cost	$3345.59
8	2-3rd Yr Cost	$3691.18
9	Fixed Costs	$800.00
10	MPG	30
11	Running Costs	$520.00
12	3 Yr Total	$10996.78
13	Salvage Value	$4500.00
14	3 Yr Cost	$6496.78

What If ...

Now you're ready to see the power of a spreadsheet. You can change any variable—the price of gasoline, the price of the car, the interest rate—and all the affected numbers will change. What if the price of gasoline were to decrease or, more likely, increase dramatically? Click R2C2, gascost; vary the gas cost from $1.00 to $4.00 and watch how the 3 Yr Cost changes. The total cash outlay for a car at the end of three years (3 Yr Total) is sobering; think how many Macintoshes you could buy.

Duplicating the Model

If you want to compare several cars, you can change the price and other entries, but then you won't be able to compare two cars directly because the new entries will erase the old.

The better way to make a comparison is to build up a second column. You could retype everything, but Multiplan lets you duplicate a column quickly.

Drag in the second and third columns starting at R3C2 (price) and going down to R14C3 (3 yr cost).

	1	2	3
1	CAR COSTS	Gas Cost	Miles Yr
2		$1.30	12000
3	Price	$6000.00	
4	Down Payment	$1500.00	
5	Loan Value	$4500.00	
6	Monthly Payment	$153.80	
7	1st Yr Cost	$3345.59	
8	2-3rd Yr Cost	$3691.18	
9	Fixed Costs	$800.00	
10	MPG	30	
11	Running Costs	$520.00	
12	3 Yr Total	$10996.78	
13	Salvage Value	$4500.00	
14	3 Yr Cost	$6496.78	

This selects the cells in column 2 that you want to copy and tells Multiplan where to put them. If you wanted to copy column 2 more than once, you would simply select more columns.

Choose **Fill Right** from the **Edit** menu.

Voila! The contents of column 2 are cloned into column 3.

Now change the appropriate figures—price, fixed costs, mpg, and salvage value—for a second car.

2	3
Gas Cost	Miles Yr
$1.30	12000
$6000.00	$6000.00
$1500.00	$1500.00
$4500.00	$4500.00
$153.80	$153.80
$3345.59	$3345.59
$3691.18	$3691.18
$800.00	$800.00
30	30
$520.00	$520.00
$10996.78	$10996.78
$4500.00	$4500.00
$6496.78	$6496.78

You can repeat this duplication for as many columns as you like. You can then see what happens if the price of gasoline goes up to $5.00 per gallon. Or if you drive 30,000 miles a year. Or the interest rate drops to 10 percent. If you are interested in what your present car is costing you, you might as well treat its current value as its price. This strategy adds interest charges to the cost and thus reflects true costs, since if you had the money instead of the car, you could invest the money and earn interest on it.

With the model you've created, you can calculate the real difference between a $6000 car with 30 miles to the gallon and a $9,000 car with 40 miles to the gallon. The model will tell you what the break-even point is for holding on to an older gas guzzler and buying a new econobox.

	1	2	3
1	CAR COSTS	Gas Cost	Miles Yr
2		$1.30	12000
3	Price	$6000.00	$9000.00
4	Down Payment	$1500.00	$2250.00
5	Loan Value	$4500.00	$6750.00
6	Monthly Payment	$153.80	$230.70
7	1st Yr Cost	$3345.59	$5018.39
8	2-3rd Yr Cost	$3691.18	$5536.78
9	Fixed Costs	$800.00	$1150.00
10	MPG	30	40
11	Running Costs	$520.00	$390.00
12	3 Yr Total	$10996.78	$15175.16
13	Salvage Value	$4500.00	$7000.00
14	3 Yr Cost	$6496.78	$8175.16

To make this model easy to enter, I've kept it all on one screen. To enlarge your model, read the Multiplan manual about how to freeze the labels (titles) and make a split window. You can then elaborate the fixed costs to include license fees, use taxes, and insurance, and have the maintenance costs go up year by year. You can also add more entries with your projected earnings and tax rate, and deduct the car-loan interest from your income tax.

Making a Table

Although ordinarily used for numerical calculations, a spreadsheet such as Multiplan works much more effectively than a word processor for creating tables of text.

Moving an entry from one portion of a table to another is difficult with a word processor, but easy with a spreadsheet.

Multiplan distinguishes between text and values by the characters you type; it treats entries as text unless they consist of numbers only or numbers plus the letter E (for exponent) and a period (decimal point). Multiplan will treat a number as text if you first type a space and then the number, or if you put quotes around the number.

You can choose Align Left, Align Center, or Align Right from the Format menu to position entries within cells.

When you are done, you can copy the table to the Clipboard and then paste it into a word-processing document.

Other Features

Multiplan has many other features. You can enter continuous text; you can set password protection for selected cells, make simple bar charts, or use the desk-accessory calculator and paste the result into the spreadsheet. Printer controls let you set page breaks, headers, and footers. A paste-and-link option lets you put the results into Microsoft Chart to produce classy graphs. Learn about these and other functions in the Multiplan manual.

Chapter 7 Business Graphics

n the business world, much of the information we work with comes to us as numbers—costs, interest rates, discounts, and so on. We saw in Chapter 6 how to manipulate numbers almost effortlessly with spreadsheets. Spreadsheets produce the tables of numbers we've all seen in annual reports and statistical summaries. But the meaning of numbers is all too often obscured when they are printed in tables.

We can recognize and interpret graphics much more easily than numbers. For the same reason that the icons in the Macintosh Finder work more effectively than the massed text that passes for file directories on other computers, spotting trends or comparing two numbers is much quicker on a graph than in a gray column of numbers.

To turn numbers into graphics, we have in the past relied on graph paper and sharp pencils. If a number changed, we had to find an eraser. If several numbers changed, we had to find a wastebasket.

The microcomputer began changing traditional graphing methods about 1979, giving professionals the tools to create graphs with only moderate effort. Increasingly powerful micros and more sophisticated software produced better charts. Macintosh has ushered in a new era, giving us not only higher-quality charts but the ability to modify and annotate them and even include them within text.

You could use a program like MacPaint to draw charts, but MacPaint is a free-form drawing program, unable to take numerical input and automatically turn it into charts. A business graphics program takes numerical input, either from another program or from the keyboard, and generates charts in standard formats—bar graphs, pie charts, line graphs, and so on.

When selecting a business graphics program, you should consider two major issues: how information can be entered into the program, and the quality of the results.

Information entry is mainly a question of which files the program can read. Keyboard entry for all business graphics programs is roughly the same; the primary difference is file compatibility. If you have already constructed a spreadsheet model, the graphics program should be able to read selected cells and create a graph. Under no circumstances should you have to retype any information. A graphics program should also be able to create charts from numerical information in a data base or any other structured file. You may need to chart sales from information in an accounting program, for example.

The quality of the charts is not only a matter of personal taste. A presentation-quality chart not only pleases the eye but is easier to understand. Different data values must be easy to discriminate; you should be able to add numerical values to a graph for convenient reference. A good charting program gives you many choices; programs with limited choices force you to accept a few rigid notions of what a graph should look like.

MICROSOFT CHART

Microsoft® Chart can plot numbers from a Multiplan spreadsheet, from SYLK files, from data entered by the user, or from the Clipboard. Chart uses the Macintosh graphics capabilities to turn out presentation-quality graphs with far more flexibility and ease than older graphing programs. You can make a graph, change its appearance, annotate it, and incorporate it into a report. You always see on screen exactly what you will get on paper.

In the sample chart you will create in this chapter, you will use keyboard entry for data input, since you may not yet have a program whose files Chart can use. The chart will be a comparison of consumer costs over the past decade for three sets of values, called data series. The three are food, energy, and home electronics.

Starting Chart

Insert the Chart disk.

Double-click the disk icon, if the disk window is not already open.

Microsoft Chart

Double-click the icon labeled Microsoft Chart.

The Chart program is loaded into memory and displays two windows. The window labeled Untitled will show the finished chart; the New Series window gives you a table in which to enter data.

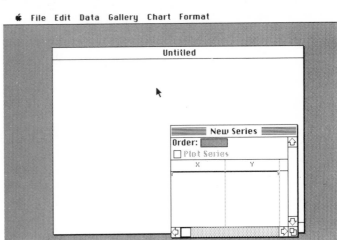

Entering the First Data Series

Choose **Date ...** from the **Data** menu.

A dialog box asks for the type of data you want to enter, in this case data organized by date.

Date Series

Series Name: Food

Category Name: Year

Value Name: Price

First Category: 1974

Increment Each Category By

[2]   ◉ Years ○ Months ○ Days ○ Weekdays

[OK]   [Cancel]

Type Food for the Series Name and press Tab.

This will be the name of your chart.

Type Year for the Category Name and press Tab.

The category entries are normally plotted horizontally (x-axis), and will be calendar years.

Type Price for the Value Name and press Tab.

The value entries are normally plotted vertically (y-axis), and will be the prices.

Type 1974 for the First Category and press Tab.

1974 is the first year of your data.

Type 2 in the category Increment box.

You are going to plot even-numbered years, from 1974 to 1982.

Click the button beside Years.

The button is filled in to indicate your selection. Most likely, this button is already selected.

Check for mistakes; use the Tab key to cycle through the typed entries and type over any mistakes.

Click the OK button.

If you click OK and then find you've made a mistake, you can choose Date... from the Data menu again, and redo any wrong entries.

A new window, labeled Food, appears with two columns labeled Year and Price.

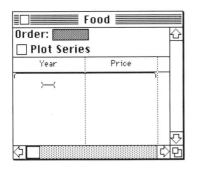

Type 177 and press Enter.

177 appears in the Price column. The first date, 1974, automatically appears in the Year column, and the program advances to the next line.

Type 183 and press Enter.

Continue with:

206

245

255, pressing Enter after each entry.

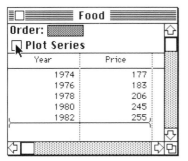

The Year column is automatically incremented by two years for each entry. The last entry is for 1982.

Click the Plot Series box in the Food window.

Chart now draws a chart on the screen. Unless you tell it otherwise, Chart will always draw a column chart, but you can change the form of the chart at any time.

Pull down the Gallery menu.

You can select among seven chart types.

Choose Column... from the Gallery menu.

Eight little column charts appear; one of them is highlighted.

Click the column-chart type of your choice.

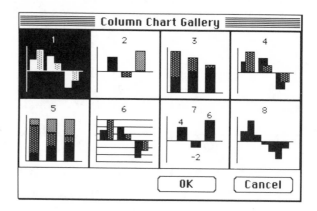

Click the OK button.

Chart draws a new column chart following your wishes.

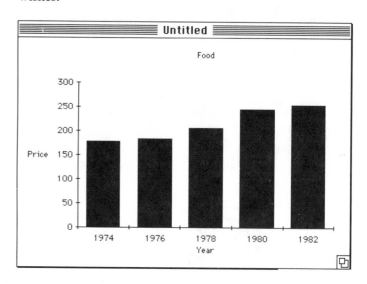

Entering a Second Data Series

Click the New Series window to make it the top window.

Choose Date ... from the Data menu.

Again you get the Date dialog box.

Type Energy

Click the OK button.

> A new series window, labeled Energy, opens up.

Type 208

> 265

> 322

> 574

> 677, pressing Enter after each entry.

Click the Plot Series box.

> Chart now plots the second series next to the first series. How can you tell the two entries apart?

Click the chart window.

Choose Add Legend from the Chart menu.

> A small legend appears, keyed to the series shading.

Entering a Third Data Series

Click the New Series window.

Choose Date ... from the Data menu.

Type Electronics

Click the OK button.

> The Electronics series window opens up.

Type 93

> 91

> 90

> 91

> 88, pressing Enter after each entry.

Click the Plot Series box.

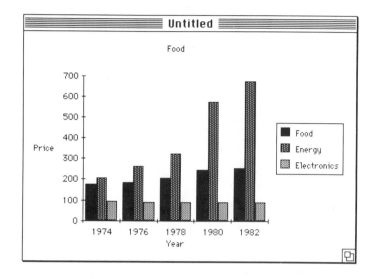

This completes your graph data. You now have three series plotted side-by-side, with a legend identifying the Food, Energy, and Electronics columns.

Customizing Your Chart

You can improve the appearance of your graph in many ways, adjusting the labels and changing the column patterns to suit your own taste. To change the word Food above the chart:

Click Food.

Black squares surround the word. To widen the label space:

Drag the square on the right.

Select the word Food by dragging through it and type Price Index.

Click the Food series window to bring it to the top.

Choose `Categories ...` from the `Format` menu.

Select the features you want for labeling along the x-axis. I suggest that you click Year for Show and Short for Date Format. When you are satisfied:

Click the OK button.

Chart relabels the axis to your specifications.

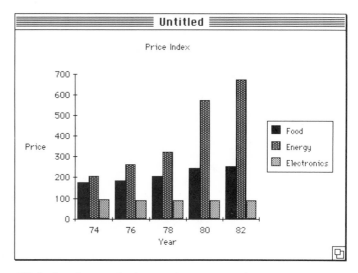

Click the chart window to bring it to the top.

You can change the column shading for each data series.

Click in one data column.

Small white circles appear in some of the columns of the selected series.

Choose `Patterns ...` from the `Format` menu.

A dialog box gives you a palette of patterns, for both the column and the column border. Make some selections.

Click the OK button.

The columns in the chart change according to your choices.

The producer price information you have plotted comes from the United States Statistical Abstracts (1982-1983 edition). Home electronics is the only producer price category that shows a drop over the period you have charted. The price information does not have a separate category for computers, but personal computers have dropped in price even more than home electronics in general.

Microsoft Chart has many other features; consult the manual for more information.

For insight into preparing quality graphics, see *Presentation Graphics on the Apple Macintosh*, by Steve Lambert (Microsoft Press, 1984). Here is a sample chart prepared by Steve Lambert with Microsoft Chart and MacPaint.

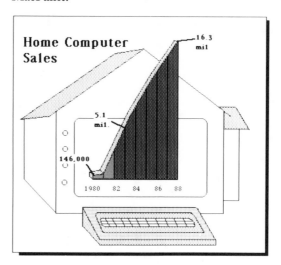

Chapter 8 Business Programs

This chapter takes a brief look at several types of business software. When it was written, software in many categories was not yet complete.

Among Macintosh programs, word processors, graphics programs, and spreadsheets will clearly take full advantage of the Macintosh interface. Some business programs may not embrace the interface as thoroughly. Business software has been the most conservative category of microcomputer software; using the Macintosh interface requires a more innovative attitude than many companies have exhibited so far.

Many business programs will be derived from versions written for conventional microcomputers. If you are considering buying a program that works much as it did on earlier microcomputers, think carefully about whether you can live with the program for the long term. Do competing programs take more advantage of the Macintosh interface? Are they easier to use?

DATA BASES

A data base is an organized collection of information, or data; for example, an address book is a data base. A specific database file is made up of records (such as a complete address), each of which is in turn made up of fields (name, street address, zip code, and so on). You index a data base by a field; for example, most address books are indexed by name, as are telephone directories.

The power of a computerized data base is that you can change the index field; you can index on zip codes, for example, when you are preparing a mailing. You can also index on more than one field. You see only those records with fields that meet specific criteria; for example, you can request all the Jacksons who live in Chicago.

A database program lets you enter, sort, update, find, and print your data quickly and easily. Although the idea of a data base is simple, database programs are the most complex of the common microcomputer applications. The most powerful go far beyond simple functions, letting you define relationships between data entries, perform statistical and accounting calculations, extract and reorganize the data, and much more.

Traditionally, the problem for the user has been deciding how much power to buy; the more powerful the database program, the more difficult it has been to use. With the Macintosh interface, this problem should ease; important and common functions will be available quickly through pull-down menus; more complex choices will be chosen in a dialog box. (Completed database programs for the Macintosh were not yet available when this overview was written.)

Selecting a Data Base

Ask yourself these key questions when looking at database software:

- Does the program have sufficient power for potential future needs? Will your address book grow into a professional clients list with billing information, for example?

- Can you restructure the data base for sophisticated operations such as numerical calculations on entries?

- Can you extract information from the data base and move it easily into a word-processing document?

- Can information travel back and forth between the data base and your spreadsheet program?

Microsoft File

Microsoft® File, described here in its preliminary form, is a database program of moderate power. It offers all the essential features of a data base, including sorting, queries, and report generation. File does not work with two files at once or establish relationships between two files.

Because of the Macintosh interface, arranging and looking at your data is far easier than on older computers. File works with two principal windows: The Datafile window shows the actual data, and the Form window shows the structure underlying the data base. You can change a data entry by clicking the record. Here is an address-book sample.

♦ File Edit Form Organize				

			Addresses		
	first name	last name	street	city	not
1	Barry	Ackerley	40 NE 37th Plac	Blantyre, Malaw	Call on
2	Elaine	Anderson	1820 Elm Stree	New York, NY	Send cop
3	Bob	Armstrong	2840 Jefferson	Atlanta, GA	Meeting
4	Gene	Baker	585 Mt. Index P	Riverside, CA	Architec
5	Chin-wu	Bao	Box 12	Gusong, Sichuan	Send Tel
6	Peter	Bowen	14 Lummi Key	South Head Is.,	Sailing
7	Mike	Burbridge	1758 Third Ave	Winnipeg, Manit	Makes de
8	Robin	Campbell	2 Bay Road	Port Mathurin, R	Sailing
9	Jeff	Chabot	325 Divison Ro	Fremantle, Wes	Sailing

		Form			
0	first name	last name	street	city	notes
View 1					
9/9					

The first sample shown here has each record in a small cubbyhole so that as many records as possible are on the screen at one time. To change the format, point at the thin line under the field entries in the Form window and drag the line downward. This creates more vertical space for each field and the records in the Datafile window immediately follow suit. Drag the small box in the lower right corner of a field box to increase its size. Again, the data follow suit, wordwrapping within the box when possible.

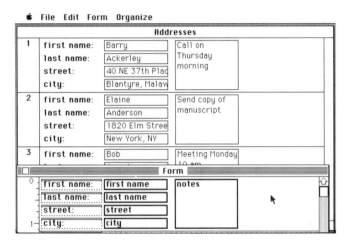

To change the relative position of each field, point at the strip along the top of each field box. The pointer changes to a four-way arrow; drag the box to any desired location.

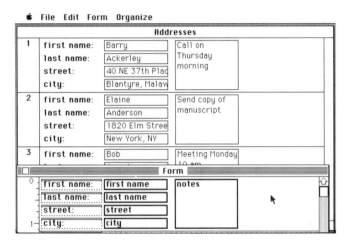

To display data in stacked fields, choose Vertical Form from the Form menu.

To find information within your data base, choose Find... from the Organize menu. A dialog box lets you fill in what information you know, such as a last name, and File goes off and finds all the matching records.

You can put your data in order by choosing Sort from the Organize menu. A dialog box lets you select which fields to sort on and whether in ascending or descending order; for example, you could sort alphabetically on last name, or in ascending numerical order on zip code.

File stores information in fields as text, numbers, or dates. You specify the field type when you initially build up the data base. You can also specify if you need fast access to the field or not. Fast access tells the program to keep the field in sorted order, so that when you query the data base, it can find your information quickly without reading a lot of data.

ACCOUNTING PACKAGES

If you are considering using a commercial program for accounting, you should examine the packages with the advice of a qualified accountant. Many general-purpose accounting programs are too general, unable to meet the needs of particular businesses. An increasing number of accounting programs serve a specific business, such as medical offices or auto dealerships.

Many accounting programs, including specialized ones, can be modified to meet your needs. Most often you will need a programmer to assist in making the changes.

Besides your accounting needs, see if the program will work with the other software you use. Can you generate graphs from the data? Can you move the data to a spreadsheet to make financial projections? Can the program grow with the company? Can your accountants use your files on their computer to perform audits?

Except perhaps for the smallest business, any computer used for accounting will probably need a hard disk to store comprehensive files.

FINANCIAL MODEL BUILDERS

For many business computations, the formulas are well established. Everyone uses the same formulas to calculate depreciation or financial ratios, for example. A computer program can therefore speed up analysis of common situations by building a financial model for you. You only have to answer a series of questions, and the model builder creates a file. The file can then be read by a spreadsheet or other program and you can devote your time to analyzing the results rather than reinventing the wheel.

For the Multiplan program, Microsoft has a series of model builders, called the Multiplan™ Applications Products, that construct spreadsheets for budgets, financial statements, cash flow analyses, and personal finance.

The first model builder available for Multiplan is the Microsoft® Budget package. When you start the program, a series of screens asks you to enter information. You respond to questions about the time intervals for the budgets, the starting year, and how many years are in the budget, and then you enter the sales and costs budgets for each product you produce.

After you have entered all your data, the program builds up a SYLK file, a file format compatible with Multiplan. You can then start Multiplan and read in the Budget file. All your information appears laid out in the proper form, ready for your analysis.

Other such programs will undoubtedly be available for the Macintosh in the near future, making it a flexible and powerful business machine.

Chapter 9 Introduction to Communications

Computers can help make your own work easier and more efficient, and they should make exchanging work with others easier and faster, too. With a telephone line and the proper hardware and software, you can connect your Macintosh with public information services and data bases, electronic mail services, and anyone else who also has the proper equipment.

In advertisements, computer communications seem easy—sometimes too easy; in reality, communications can be the most frustrating operation you attempt with your computer. This chapter deals mainly with communications software and only covers the information essential to getting you started. For more information about modems, see Chapter 19; for a complete discussion of communications protocols, see Chapter 27.

WHAT YOU NEED

To use your Macintosh to talk to another computer, you will need:

- Communications software—MacTerminal from Apple or the Microcom Communications package, for example.

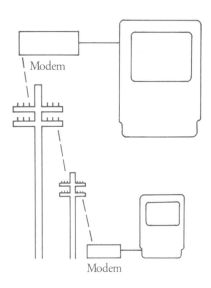

Modem

Modem

- A modem. Many modems will work with the Macintosh; make sure that the communications software you choose is compatible with the modem hardware.

- A telephone line (not a party line).

You will also need some information, called communications parameters, about the computer you want to communicate with and its modem:

- Baud rate—the modem's operating speed (300 or 1200 baud in most cases, corresponding to roughly 30 or 120 characters transmitted per second).

- Character width—how many bits make up each of the characters being transmitted (seven or eight); also called data bits.

- Stop bits—how many bits mark the end of each character (one or two), so that the computer knows when one character stops and another begins.

- Parity—a simple form of error detection (even, odd, or no parity).

- Handshake—a way for the receiving computer to tell the sending computer to pause (XON/-XOFF, clear to send, or no handshake). This parameter is not always needed for short messages or files.

GETTING READY TO COMMUNICATE

Connect your modem to the Macintosh and to a telephone jack according to the instructions in the modem manual. Insert a disk with the communications program into the disk-drive slot.

Specific set-up instructions will vary among different communications programs, although general procedures

are similar; the following instructions apply to the preliminary programs from Apple (MacTerminal) and
Microcom.

Choose Communications ... from the Settings menu.

A dialog box appears.

```
Communications

Baud Rate   ○ 50      ○ 75     ○ 110    ○ 134.5
            ○ 150     ○ 200    ○ 300    ○ 600
            ● 1200    ○ 1800   ○ 2000   ○ 2400
            ○ 3600    ○ 4800   ○ 9600   ○ 19200

Bits per Character   ○ 7 Bits      ● 8 Bits

Parity        ○ Even  ○ Odd   ● None

Handshake     ● XOn/XOff    ○ None

Connection    ○ Modem       ● Another Computer

Connection Point    ○ Printer Port   ○ Phone Port

                                    [ OK ▶ ]  [Cancel]
```

Click the appropriate baud rate, character width, parity,
and handshake.

If you have control over the setting of both the sending and receiving machines, the choice of character width,
parity, and so on aren't important so long as the two
computers agree.

If you are trying an information service for the first
time and you don't have its parameters, start with:

8 bits character width

no parity

XON/XOFF handshake.

This combination often works. Check the manual;
a character width of eight bits will probably generate one
stop bit, and a character width of seven bits probably two
stop bits.

From another menu, a dialog box asks you for the
terminal type, which is not critical for many situations.

113

```
┌─────────────────────────────────────────────────────────┐
│ Terminal Settings                                         │
│                                                           │
│ Terminal        ◉ VT100   ○ TTY      ○ IBM 3278           │
│ Compatibility   ◉ ANSI               ○ VT52               │
│ Cursor Shape    ○ Block              ◉ Underline          │
│ Character Set   ○ United Kingdom     ◉ United States      │
│ Line Width      ○ 132 Columns        ◉ 80 Columns         │
│ Protocol Conv:  ○ AppleLine          ○ Cluster Ctlr.      │
│ ☒ On Line       □ Local Echo         ☒ Show LEDs          │
│ ☒ Auto Repeat   □ Auto Wraparound    □ New Line           │
│ □ Rpt. Controls □ Transparent        ( OK )  ( Cancel )   │
└─────────────────────────────────────────────────────────┘
```

If you don't know the type, start with TTY or VT52. The wrong choice will lead to problems only if the other computer expects you to have full-screen editing or other features not commonly used in the average micro-computer communications link.

Another dialog box asks whether your computer is originating or answering the call. When your Macintosh talks to another microcomputer, one computer/modem must be set to originate and the other set to answer. By convention, the person who makes the phone call origi-nates. The person who receives the call should set the receiving modem to answer the call automatically.

Pull down the `Phone` **menu to set the telephone number.**

Enter the number—say 555-1234—in the dialog box. If your phone line requires you to dial 9 first, enter 9555-1234. If you must usually wait a moment to get a second dial tone after you dial 9, enter a comma after the 9 (9,555-1234); the comma inserts a two-second pause in the automatic dialing sequence of an Apple or Hayes™ modem; for longer delays, use more commas.

You can put in hyphens to make your number more legible; the modem will ignore them.

Make sure no one else is using your phone line.

The Apple modem and other modems connected directly to your computer and to the phone jack don't need a telephone for operation. You may, however, want to keep a telephone connected to the line for voice operations.

Make sure all your phones are on the hook (that is, hung up) before making the connection.

MAKING THE CONNECTION

With all that preparation out of the way, you are ready to make the connection with the other computer and start transmitting your data.

Choose `Dial` from the `Phone` menu.

The Apple modem contains a speaker; you will hear the modem dialing the number and then the shrill answering tone from the other computer's modem. Your modem then switches automatically from voice mode into data mode and silences its speaker. You can proceed with transmitting your data.

If you hear a busy signal instead of the other modem's answering tone:

Choose `Hangup` from the `Phone` menu.

If you hear a person's voice:

Pick up a telephone before choosing `Hangup`.

Once the two computers are connected, whatever you type at Mac's keyboard will be transmitted to the remote computer. For many computer systems, you must send a Return or Command-c (Control-c)—sometimes more than one—to elicit a response.

When you are done:

Choose `Hangup` from the `Phone` menu.

With luck, everything will work and you can enjoy computer communications.

COMMUNICATING BETWEEN MACINTOSHES AND LISAS

Moving information between identical computers is usually easy: If the computers are within walking distance, you simply swap disks. You can swap Macintosh disks with those of Lisa 2s running Macintosh software. Between computers, you can also use a direct wire connection (called a "null-modem" because the wire replaces two modems), or telephone lines.

In any case, you should use the same communications software at each end, set up with identical parameters. On a telephone line with modems, one Mac must be set to originate, the other to answer.

SO MUCH FOR THE EASY PART ...

Because communications involves so many steps, finding the exact source of a problem can be difficult. You can test your own hardware and software by calling another computer, but even a successful connection won't rule out subtle problems in data transfer.

For more information about communications, including an explanation of what happens at each step, read Chapter 27. You'll probably find that chapter easier to read after you have had some experience with communications.

Chapter *Programming* 10 *Languages*

T his chapter discusses the programming languages available for the Macintosh. It does not take as much of a step-by-step approach as the other chapters dealing with software, although it does offer two sample programs to illustrate the Macintosh programming process.

If you want to write programs for Mac, the first languages available are BASIC, Pascal, and Logo. All three were originally developed for teaching purposes. Each language has its strengths and weaknesses; each also has strong advocates who insist that no other language is worthy of attention. Recognizing that others may not agree with my opinions, I offer this brief guide to computer languages in general and to these three languages in particular.

AN OVERVIEW OF LANGUAGES

Computer languages are either high-level or low-level. Although the boundary is not well defined, high-level languages, such as BASIC, Pascal, and Logo, contain elements of English to make them easier for people to use. Low-level, or machine, language on the other hand, deals directly with the microprocessor instructions and consists almost entirely of cryptic abbreviations or numbers.

Interpreters and compilers take high-level language instructions (source code) and turn them into low-level machine instructions. A language interpreter takes one line of high-level instructions and converts it into the low-level form the microprocessor can understand. The microprocessor carries out that line of instructions and hands control back to the interpreter, which converts the next line, and so forth.

Working a line at a time, an interpreter is less efficient than a compiler, which translates the entire high-level language program into a machine-language program. A compiled program will usually run much faster than an interpreted one. However, developing and debugging a program is much faster with an interpreter because you don't have to write the whole program in order to find out if it works.

Because compilers take considerable memory space to operate, many more compiled languages will be available for the 512-KB Macintosh than for the initial 128-KB version. The BASIC, Pascal, and Logo available for the first Macintosh are all interpreted versions of the languages.

BASIC

BASIC is the most common microcomputer language and remains the best choice for short, relatively straightforward jobs. BASIC was originally written by John Kemeny and Thomas Kurtz at Dartmouth College in 1964 as a simplified form of FORTRAN, the traditional computing language for scientific work on large computers. It is considered the easiest of the three languages to learn.

BASIC works somewhat like a stream-of-consciousness process—quick and intuitive, but often a little untidy in actual execution. You will probably find it difficult to follow a BASIC program written by someone else, or even a program you wrote some time ago, unless you include unusually clear annotations. BASIC is a moderately well-specified language; there are industry standards for the instructions and syntax. Once you have learned a particular version, or dialect, others are easy to pick up. After you have learned BASIC, you'll find it easy to move on to FORTRAN, a slowly dying language that is now most useful at large corporations or research centers.

BASIC for the Macintosh

There are two versions of BASIC presently available for the Macintosh: one from Apple, the other from Microsoft. Both are interpreted BASIC. You will find both much easier to use than the BASICs for earlier microcomputers. On Mac, you can write the BASIC program in one window and see the program's output in another window.

Macintosh BASIC, from Apple, differs from other BASIC languages. It has no line numbering and features additional procedures to add some structure. Several small BASIC programs can run concurrently; a new window is opened for each new program's output.

Microsoft® BASIC has the advantage of being widely known. The Macintosh version is compatible with Microsoft BASIC versions for other computers except for some instructions that are specific to a particular microcomputer design—mainly variations in graphics and sound generation. Specific features of Microsoft BASIC are discussed later in the chapter.

Pascal

Pascal was designed by Nikolas Wirth, who based it in part on Algol, a language more popular in Europe than in North America. Pascal comes much closer to the academic concept of what a good programming language should be. Its structured design almost forces you to think in an orderly way. The same structure makes Pascal harder to learn than BASIC, but also makes it easier for other people to follow the logic of your program and figure out how it works.

Pascal standards are spelled out by the International Standards Organization (ISO). Although several variations exist, the presence of clear standards inhibits the dialects from straying too far. With Pascal programming experience, you have a head start learning C, now the most popular development language for commercial microcomputer programs.

The first Pascal language for the Macintosh is inter-pretive. It was developed by Think Technologies, and is sold by Apple as Macintosh Pascal. The first commercial Pascal to appear in interpretive form, Macintosh Pascal is ideally suited for teaching the language. As with other Macintosh languages, the ability to put your program in one window and see the output in another will make traditional Pascal programming seem archaic.

Logo

Logo is best known as a language for children because its graphics are very easy to learn. However, for more complex programs, Logo is the hardest of Mac's first three programming languages to learn; progressing beyond the simplest steps is difficult. Because Logo is an extendable language (you can define new procedures within the lan-guage), there is no standard form.

Logo was written at MIT by a group headed by Seymour Papert. Experience with Logo can be applied to Lisp (the language from which Logo is derived), though Lisp has thus far been mainly limited to academic and industrial research into artificial intelligence.

Macintosh Logo was written by Logo Computer Sys-tems, Inc. of Montreal, the company founded by Seymour Papert that also developed Apple Logo for the Apple II. The language has been changed somewhat to take advan-tage of the Macintosh's features.

Digital Research, Inc. plans to release a second ver-sion of Logo, called DR Logo.

PROGRAM DEVELOPMENT
WITH ASSEMBLY LANGUAGE

Because high-level languages are so different from the machine code that a CPU can execute, programs written in high-level languages often can't take full advantage of a CPU's power and they often run slowly. Programs written directly in machine language would be optimum, but machine code is much too hard for most people to write.

Assembly language, a primitive language close to machine language and easier for humans to work with, offers a solution.

The Macintosh Assembler/Debugger from Apple gives the assembly-language programmer access to the software tools in ROM. For efficient operation with the 128-KB version of the Macintosh, the Assembler and Debugger can operate with two Macintoshes connected together. One runs the program under development; the other runs a diagnostic program to track the operation of the first machine.

For adequate speed and flexibility, most commercial programs for Macintosh will be written in a combination of compiled code and assembly language, although many business packages are in Microsoft BASIC. If you want to write serious programs for sale, you will probably need more powerful development tools; the Mac itself does not have sufficient power. Apple provides Mac development tools in compiled Pascal for the Lisa; Lisa's extra power makes program development considerably easier. Many companies developing Macintosh software are using Lisas; others are using minicomputers, such as Digital Equipment Corporation's VAX™.

MORE ABOUT MICROSOFT BASIC

Microsoft BASIC is by far the most common BASIC used with microcomputers. (Applesoft BASIC on the Apple II is a version of Microsoft BASIC.) Although Microsoft BASIC has grown over the years with the microcomputer industry, the language structure has remained essentially the same. Current versions on different microcomputers differ principally in the extra commands for special hardware features. The commands that draw graphics on the screen, for example, must be adapted to each individual computer type.

You should get Microsoft BASIC if you want to write programs in BASIC that can be adapted easily for other machines, or if you want to run programs written by others. If you have used other versions of Microsoft

BASIC, you may want to try out the special features
of the Macintosh version:

Graphics support. All the graphics functions in the
IBM PC version are included except for PAINT and
DRAW. Compared to the IBM PC, the Mac resolution is
higher and the processor faster, so animation is better. On
the other hand, Mac doesn't have color.

Mouse support. Detection of mouse movement and
button operation are included in one function call.

A decimal math package. Accurate accounting
calculations are now possible.

Device independent input/output. The screen,
keyboard, printer, and Macintosh Clipboard can be
treated as disk files.

Microsoft BASIC uses three screen windows:

The command window. This is where you can enter
instructions. (The command window serves the same
purpose as the OK prompt in other Microsoft BASICs.)

The output window. This window shows the results
of the BASIC program, whether text or graphics. Its size
can be changed, but it does not have scroll bars, so you
can't bring different parts of the output directly into view.

The list window. The source code or BASIC language
statements are displayed here. You click in the list window
to make it active. If you click anywhere in a line of source
code, the line appears in the command window and you
can edit the line using the standard Macintosh editing
techniques. When you press Return, the lines pop back
into the list window.

The list window contains both scroll bars and a size
box; you can scroll through the source code easily and
pick out lines for editing.

The menu bar contains three menus:

The File menu. The normal functions for opening,
closing, and saving files, and for quitting are included in
this menu.

The Edit menu. You can copy, cut, and paste to the Clipboard.

The Control menu. You are given menu control of commands that you can also enter in the command window, such as stop execution, continue, suspend, list, run, and trace on or off.

The initial version of Microsoft BASIC for the Macintosh is about 40 KB long, leaving about 30 KB for the BASIC program and data. It runs one program at a time.

A Sample Microsoft BASIC Program

This program draws a balloon that moves about the output window.

Double-click the MBASIC icon in the disk window. Type the BASIC program source code.

```
10 REM *** Program to move a balloon around
20 DEFINT A-Z
30 CLS
40 DIM A(250)
50 REM *** Draw balloon
60 FOR A#=0 TO 1.4 STEP .15
70 CIRCLE(100,100),20,,,,TAN(A#)
80 NEXT A#
100 LINE(115,100)-(105,130)
110 LINE(85,100)-(95,130)
120 LINE(95,130)-(105,134),,BF
130 CIRCLE(100,125),2
140 LINE(98,127)-(102,133),,BF
150 GET(75,80)-(125,135),A
170 REM *** Define object and put it on the screen
180 XMAX=420: YMAX=160
230 X=75: Y=80      'Set initial coordinates for balloon
240 XD=RND*20-10: YD=RND*20-10  'Set direction
310 REM *** Repeatedly erase and redraw object
330 X0=X: Y0=Y
350 X=X+XD: Y=Y+YD
370 IF X<0 OR X>XMAX THEN XD=-XD
380 IF Y<0 OR Y>YMAX THEN YD=-YD
390 PUT(X0,Y0),A
400 PUT(X,Y),A
410 GOTO 330
```

The command window automatically opens up; as you press Return at the end of each line, the line moves to the output window. When you have finished entering the program:

Choose **List** from the **Control** menu.

The list window opens up to display the source code you have just typed. Make the window as large as needed with the size box and scroll through the listing to check your work. If you find any errors, click anywhere on the offending line and move to the command window to correct your mistake.

When you're satisfied with the source code:

Choose **Run** from the **Control** menu.

The balloon appears in the output window.

Choose **Stop** from the **Control** menu.

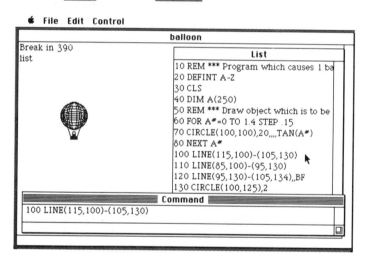

The program stops executing, and the output window shows the source-code line where it stopped.

If you are used to typing Control-c to stop a Microsoft BASIC program on other computers, you can do the same on a Macintosh with Command-c.

Choose Save from the File menu.

This command saves your program on the disk. If you prefer, you can still use traditional MBASIC commands, entering RUN, SAVE, and SYSTEM in the command window.

Microsoft BASIC Notes for Programmers

Microsoft BASIC on the Macintosh can call the QuickDraw graphics routines in ROM. It can also write directly to memory with PEEK and POKE.

If you want to move a program written in Applesoft BASIC to Microsoft BASIC on the Macintosh, you must write replacement graphics instructions for the following Apple II-specific statements: HTAB, VTAB, HGR, GR, HLIN, VLIN, HPLOT, HCOLOR, COLOR, HGR2, and PDL. Any PEEKs and POKEs in Applesoft BASIC will not work on the Macintosh.

If you want to move a BASIC program from the IBM PC, here are the statements in IBM BASICA (version 1.0) not supported by the Mac version: BLOAD, BSAVE, COLOR, COM(n) ON/OFF/STOP, DEF SEG, DEF USR, DRAW, KEY, LOCATE, MOTOR, ON (event) GOSUB, OUT, PAINT, PEN, PLAY, SCREEN, SOUND, STRIG, and WAIT. Similarly, the following IBM BASICA intrinsic functions are not in the Mac version: CRSLIN, INP, SCREEN, STICK, and USR. Finally, these machine-specific statements/intrinsics will need modification: CALL, CLEAR, PEEK, POKE, and VARPTR.

MORE ABOUT MACINTOSH PASCAL

This sample Macintosh Pascal program produces an array of lines on the screen.

Double-click the MacPascal icon.

The Pascal interpreter program loads into memory. Three windows come up on screen, one for the Pascal source code (Untitled) and two for the output: the Text window receives the character output; the Drawing window receives graphics output.

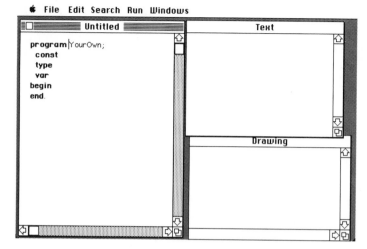

You can, of course, adjust the window size and location to your own preferences.

If you want to use a Pascal program that is already on the disk:

Choose `Open` from the `File` menu.

Otherwise:

Type the Pascal program source code.

```
program Rays;
  const
    topEdge = 20;
    bottomEdge = 80;
    leftEdge = 20;
    rightEdge = 160;
    raySpacing = 8;
  var
    ray : integer;
    numberOfRays : integer;
  begin
    numberOfRays := (rightEdge - leftEdge) div raySpacing;
    for ray := 0 to numberOfRays do
      begin
        Moveto(leftEdge + (ray * raySpacing), topEdge);
        Lineto(rightEdge - (ray * raySpacing), bottomEdge);
      end
  end.
```

126

While you enter the Pascal source code, the interpreter automatically checks the code, putting in indents and rendering the major instructions, such as Begin, For, and End, in boldface.

You can also use a word-processing program to generate the Pascal source code, but you will then lose the indenting and boldface features.

All the usual Macintosh text-editing techniques are available. If the program contains an error that the interpreter does not understand, a hand icon will point at the offending line at run time.

When you are ready to run the program:

Choose `Go` from the `Run` menu.

To debug a program:

Choose `Step` or `Trace` from the `Run` menu.

With Step, you can click the mouse button to step through the program line by line, with a hand icon pointing at each line. With Trace, the lines step automatically, as if you had chosen Step and were holding down the mouse button.

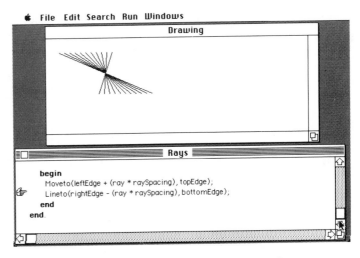

To clear the output windows and restart the program:

Choose `Reset` from the `Run` menu.

To make changes:

Choose `Stop` from the `Run` menu.

You can then use the normal editing techniques to change the source code. To see the results of your changes:

Choose `Go` from the `Run` menu.

Macintosh Pascal Notes for Programmers

Macintosh Pascal adheres to the standard for Pascal and provides all the features of ISO Pascal, except conformant arrays. As with other Pascals, Macintosh Pascal adds many features to ANSI Pascal to take advantage of specific hardware features. It has access to the mouse, QuickDraw graphics, the Mac file system, and some window features. Macintosh Pascal also has PEEK and POKE for direct memory access and IEEE numerics.

Macintosh Pascal programs can be up to 1000 lines long. The initial version permits just one program to be running at a time, and there is no access to assembly-language subroutines or linkers to other program modules.

Programs written in Macintosh Pascal will run in Lisa Pascal with few modifications. The problems of moving source code between computers is partly an issue of program practices; well-designed programs will need only minor work to adapt to another computer. Think Technologies, the company that wrote Macintosh Pascal, will offer versions for other microcomputers.

Chapter 11 Dealing with Disks

iving with a Macintosh means having to learn basic housekeeping with disks. You'll find that disks are much easier to manage than paper files.

This chapter reviews basic disk procedures and gives some hints for setting up your disks. It also tells you what you have to do to move information between different Macintosh programs—between a spreadsheet and a word processor, for example.

EVERYDAY MANEUVERS

We'll start by briefly covering how basic disk operations—duplicating, renaming, erasing—and equally basic file operations—moving, copying, grouping—are performed.

Duplicating Disks

Before you do anything with a brand new system or program disk, you should make a duplicate copy to work with; then, if anything happens to the disk or its programs, you will have the original to go back to. (If a program disk is copy-protected, it will say so; follow the instructions accompanying the program.)

Duplicating with one disk drive

Insert a system disk containing an application program you'd like to duplicate.

Double-click the disk icon to open it.

Choose **Eject** from the **File** menu.

After a pause, the Macintosh pushes the system disk out of the disk drive.

Insert a blank new disk.

When the disk you insert is brand new or has come from another type of computer, the Macintosh cannot read it and responds with a dialog box asking if you want to eject or initialize the disk. Initializing, or formatting, the disk lays down the markers that tell the Macintosh where to record information on the disk. If the disk contains information stored by another computer, initializing will erase the information.

```
┌──────────────────────────────────────────┐
│  ┌────┐   This disk is unreadable:        │
│  │    │                                   │
│  └────┘   Do you want to initialize it?   │
│                                           │
│  ┌──────────────┐      ┌──────────────┐   │
│  │   Eject      │      │  Initialize  │   │
│  └──────────────┘      └──────────────┘   │
└──────────────────────────────────────────┘
```

If you inserted the wrong disk and don't wish to erase its contents, or if you're not sure, click Eject; otherwise:

Click Initialize.

The disk drive formats the disk for recording.
Once your disk has been initialized, the Finder asks you to name the disk and creates a disk icon for it.

```
┌──────────────────────────────────────────┐
│  ┌────┐   Please name this disk:          │
│  │    │   ┌────────────────────────────┐  │
│  └────┘   │ new disk                    │  │
│           └────────────────────────────┘  │
│           ┌──────────────┐                │
│           │     OK       │                │
│           └──────────────┘                │
└──────────────────────────────────────────┘
```

Now you're ready to copy the contents of the original disk (the one you ejected) onto the newly initialized disk.

Drag the original disk's icon so it lies directly over that of the new disk and release the mouse button.

An alert box asks if you really want to copy the contents to the new disk.

Click OK.

Disk Copy

Macintosh then responds with a series of requests to insert first the old, then the new disk.

For quicker copies with a single disk drive, insert a disk containing the Disk Copy utility program. Double-click the Disk Copy icon and follow the instructions.

Duplicating with two disk drives

With one disk drive, you must swap disks many times for a complete copy; the entire procedure takes a few minutes. You will soon tire of swapping disks; a second disk drive helps tremendously.

With two disk drives, you can put the original disk in the internal drive and the new disk in the external drive. To make a duplicate:

Drag the original disk's icon over the new disk's icon and release the mouse button.

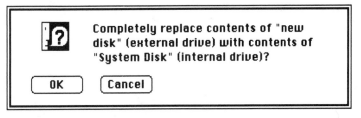

Completely replace contents of "new disk" (external drive) with contents of "System Disk" (internal drive)?

OK   Cancel

An alert box asks if you really want to copy the contents to the new disk.

Click OK.

Renaming Disks

Click the disk icon to select it.

The icon will be highlighted.

Type in a new name and press Enter.

The new name will appear in the title bar of the disk window the next time you open that window and will be changed on the disk itself before ejection.

Changing Disks

Most Macintosh application programs let you change disks when you are saving or reading a file; for example, you may have written a letter to a customer with MacWrite and want to save the letter on a data disk reserved for transactions with that customer rather than on the MacWrite disk.

You don't even need to keep initialized disks on hand for data. If necessary the Macintosh operating system will initialize a disk before putting data on it without disturbing the application program you are using.

Always keep a few nearly empty data disks around in case you need to store information that won't fit on your system disks.

To change disks:

Click **Eject** in the mini-finder.

Dialog boxes will prompt you through a series of disk swaps until the process is complete.

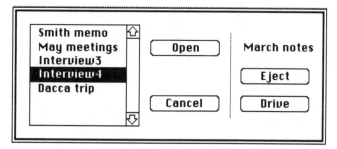

If you have two disk drives, you won't have to swap disks; instead just click Drive in the mini-finder and the

132

system will switch disk drives and then read or save the file.

Ejecting Disks

Whenever you have finished working with the Macintosh:

Choose `Quit` from the `File` menu.

A dialog box will prompt you to save your work on disk if appropriate.

Choose `Close All` from the `Edit` menu.

The disk inside the computer should still be selected.

Choose `Eject` from the `File` menu.

The disk drive ejects the disk.

Moving Files from Disk to Disk

You can move individual files by dragging the file's icon to the destination you want. In all cases, you are moving a copy of the file; the original file remains intact on the first disk. If you want to erase the original file to make space on the first disk, you must move it to the Trash icon.

If you move a file to a disk that already has a file with the same name, an alert box notes the name conflict and asks if you want to replace the file on the destination disk. Click OK if you do.

If you don't want to replace the file, click Cancel. Then to get around the problem, rename the file on the disk before moving it. Or you can select the file on the first disk, choose Duplicate from the File menu, then rename and move the duplicate file.

Moving files with one disk drive

Start with the disk containing the file you want to move. I assume that this disk is inserted in the drive and that its disk window is open.

Click the disk icon.

The disk icon's color changes to dark gray to show that it's selected.

Choose **Eject** from the **File** menu.

The disk is ejected, but the disk window remains open.

Insert the disk that will receive the file.

Double-click the new disk's icon to open it.

The new disk window is displayed on the screen.

Move, size, and scroll in the two disk windows so you can see the icon of the file you want to move.

Drag the file icon from the first disk window into the second disk window.

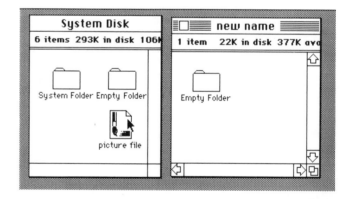

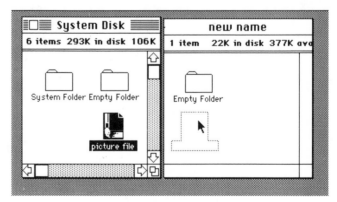

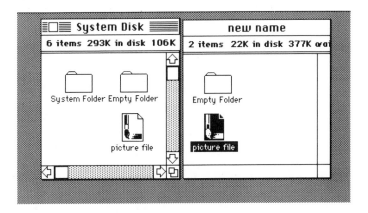

You will then get a series of prompts on screen asking you to swap disks until the file transfer is complete.

It's a good idea to have both disk windows open for this operation, so you can see the contents of both disks. It isn't essential, however; you can drag a file to the receiving disk's icon.

Moving files with two disk drives

If you have a two-drive system, the process is simple.

Put the first disk in the internal drive.

Put the second disk in the external drive.

Open both disk windows.

Drag the file icon from one window to the other.

Again, you don't have to open the receiving disk window; drag the file icon to the disk icon.

Erasing Files

There are two ways to erase files from your disks: The first uses the Trash icon to erase individual files; the second uses a command to erase the whole disk.

Moving files to the trash

You can erase a file by moving it into the trash the same way you would move the file anywhere else.

135

Drag the file icon from the disk window to the Trash icon.

The Trash icon reverses color, becoming highlighted.

 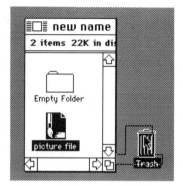

Release the mouse button.

The icon disappears from the disk window.

If you want to store new information on the disk and there is not enough space, files you have put in the trash will be erased to make room. Files will also be erased if you choose Empty Trash from the Special menu. Until then, you can recover a file from the trash. To do this:

Click the Trash icon to open it.

Drag the file icon from the Trash window to a disk icon.

Release the mouse button.

Erasing the whole disk

Choosing Erase Disk from the Special menu will erase all the files on the disk. Use the Erase Disk option only if you want a blank disk; the disk will retain only its initializing information.

Organizing Files in Folders

In every disk window there is an icon labeled Empty Folder. A folder lets you group files together for convenience. You don't have to use folders, but you will find

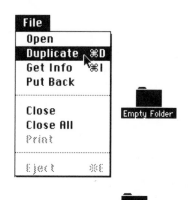

File
Open
Duplicate ⌘D
Get Info ⌘I
Put Back

Close
Close All
Print

Eject ⌘E

Empty Folder

Copy of Empty Folder

them handy if you have many files on a disk. To use a folder:

Select the Empty Folder icon by clicking it.

Choose **Duplicate** from the **File** menu.

The system creates a new icon, Copy of Empty Folder.

Change the new folder's name by typing the name while the folder is selected and pressing Enter.

Choose a name that will reflect the contents of the files you are going to place in the folder.

Open the new folder by double-clicking it.

Move the desired files from the disk window to the folder's window.

If you open the folder's window before moving files, you see the move take place. You could also simply drag a file icon over the folder icon, wait until the color of the folder changed to black, and release the mouse button.

Folders do not change the contents of a disk, they merely reorganize the way you can see the contents.

SETTING UP YOUR DISKS

Disks come in two main types: system disks and data disks. System disks contain the information, or system files, necessary to start Macintosh. You can start a Macintosh from the internal or external disk drive. In most cases, system disks also contain one or more application programs. You can store data on a system disk, if there is enough space.

Data disks store only data; you cannot use a data disk to start the computer.

If you have two disk drives, you can also use program disks, which contain application programs but no system files. A program disk can be inserted in the external disk drive if a system disk is in the internal drive. Since a program disk does not contain system files, it has much more room for data.

Which Files Belong on Which Disks?

The amount of information contained in a file is measured in thousands of characters, or kilobytes (KB); for example, a double-spaced page of a report is about 1500 characters long. (See Section Four for more information about kilobytes and disk storage space.)

Single-sided Macintosh disks hold 400 KB. Long files take up a lot of disk space, so it's best to keep only essential files on any working system or program disk. If your Macintosh has only one built-in disk drive, you have to plan your disks carefully to avoid running out of disk space.

System files

The System and Finder files are essential for nearly all Macintosh operations, both to start the computer and to run an application program. In most cases on a single-drive system, these files must be on the same disk as the application program.

The System file takes considerable storage space—up to 140 KB. The Finder, a key program that manages the Macintosh Desktop with its menus and windows, is stored in a file about 42 KB long.

Printer files

The ImageWriter file (or an equivalent file for another printer; see Chapter 18) must be on the disk if you wish to print from the disk.

If you need several application programs on a single disk and don't need to print while actually using your applications, you can delete the ImageWriter file to save space on that disk. When you want to print your work, save it and move that file to a disk that contains the relevant application program and the ImageWriter file, and print from this disk.

In a few cases, a program may write directly to the printer, bypassing the ImageWriter file; if it does, the program's manual should say so. Such programs probably won't offer any fancy printing abilities.

Creating Space on a Disk

The System, Finder, and printer files take up half a single-sided disk, leaving about 190 KB for your application programs and their data. MacPaint and MacWrite are each 50 to 60 KB long. If you keep both on one disk, you will have only 70 to 80 KB left for your work. MacPaint won't even start unless there is enough space to save a complex image, so you can't have many images or much text stored on the disk in a one-drive Macintosh. You can create more space in several ways.

Trimming the System file

A significant portion of the System file is taken up by the character fonts. To make more space available, some application programs come with a smaller, alternate System file containing only those fonts Macintosh and the application need to operate.

If necessary, you can use the Font Mover program to reduce the size of the System file yourself. With Font Mover, you can copy any unneeded fonts from the System file to a new file called Fonts; you can then move the Fonts file to another disk, freeing space on the disk in use. Later, you can restore the contents of the Fonts file to the System file. Open the Font Mover program and select Help to find out exactly what you can do and how.

The minimum System file size is about 64 KB. You cannot reduce the size of the Finder file.

Trimming files created by the system

The Clipboard file is used to store transient Clipboard information if the information won't all fit in memory. You can erase a Clipboard file in the trash, but the next time you do any work with the Clipboard, the system will create the file again.

The Scrapbook file contains all the information you have pasted into the Scrapbook. You can move the Scrapbook file to another disk; if the second disk already has a Scrapbook file, an alert box notes the duplicate name. As with any other file, you can change the name before moving the file. You will still need to put the original Scrapbook file in the trash and choose Empty Trash from the Special menu to increase the disk space. Later, you can move the old Scrapbook file back, restoring its name.

The NotePad file contains entries you have made in the NotePad desk accessory. This file can also be put in the trash and erased with Empty Trash.

In a two-drive system, the active Scrapbook and NotePad files are the ones on the disk whose window is currently active.

The Clipboard and NotePad files will use from about a few hundred to a few thousand bytes of space, the Scrapbook file potentially more. If you run out of space, you can move as many of these files as possible to another disk.

The Best Solution ...

The only satisfactory solution to disk storage limitations is a second disk drive (or the future double-sided disk drives). A second disk drive improves storage dramatically, giving you another 400 KB of data or program storage. The System, Finder, or printer files don't need to be in the second disk drive in most cases (a few programs will expect to find these files on the same disk).

MOVING INFORMATION BETWEEN PROGRAMS

When working with most Macintosh programs, you can save information in the Clipboard and the Scrapbook so another program can read and use the information.

The Clipboard

When you choose Cut or Copy from the Edit menu, the selected information goes into the Clipboard. You can see the Clipboard contents by choosing Show Clipboard from the Edit menu. To move the information into another program:

Cut or **Copy** the desired information in the first application program.

The information goes into the Clipboard.

140

Choose `Show Clipboard` from the `Edit` menu to see the Clipboard contents.

Not all programs have a Show Clipboard option.

Choose `Quit` from the `File` menu (Save the file if necessary).

Open the second program icon.

Find the place where you want to insert the information.

Choose `Paste` from the `Edit` menu.

The Clipboard contents reappear in the second program.

The Clipboard can only contain one piece of information at a time. Any time you Cut or Copy, you replace whatever you might have put in the Clipboard earlier. To avoid changing the Clipboard, some programs give you the option Clear in the Edit menu, which is similar to Cut, but does not change the Clipboard (Clear may not work exactly the same way as Cut, however).

The Scrapbook

For more flexible operation, put the Clipboard contents into the Scrapbook so they will not be erased by an interim Cut or Copy.

`Cut` or `Copy` the desired information.

Choose `Scrapbook` from the Apple menu (far left).

The Scrapbook window opens up, showing earlier contents, if any.

Choose `Paste` from the `Edit` menu.

The Clipboard contents now appear in the Scrapbook window.

At the bottom left, the Scrapbook window shows the number of items it contains (the number is automatically incremented as you add to the Scrapbook); at the bottom right, the data type appears (TEXT, PICTure, and so on).

Select Scrapbook items by clicking the ends of the scroll bar.

Close the Scrapbook window by clicking its close box.

Choose `Quit` from the `File` menu (Save the file if necessary).

Open the second program, and find the place where you want to insert the Scrapbook information.

In many cases, you will need to click this location to place an insertion point there.

Choose `Scrapbook` from the Apple menu.

Select the desired Scrapbook item by clicking the arrows.

Choose `Copy` from the `Edit` menu; *or*

Choose `Cut` if you won't need the item again.

After you cut the item, it will disappear from the Scrapbook.

Close the Scrapbook window by clicking its close box.

Select `Paste` from the `Edit` menu.

The Scrapbook item appears in the second program.

Not all information can pass between any two programs; there are restrictions related to both the source program and the receiving program. For more information, see Chapter 20.

Understanding
Macintosh

Three

How does the Macintosh hardware and software work? These chapters include descriptions of the inner workings of a Macintosh and its accessories, along with a comparison of the Macintosh and the IBM PC and a look into the future.

Chapter 12 How Macintosh Works

Computers process information—numbers, words, graphs, or nearly anything we would call information. To be practical, a computer must: take information in (input); manipulate the information in some way (processing); get the information out (output); and save the information (storage).

If you're curious about how the Macintosh does these things, you should read this chapter. Although the material is not essential to working successfully with your Macintosh, much of the terminology will appear in later chapters. Here we'll discuss the basic functions of the key hardware components and the software that tells them what to do. Once you have a general idea of how these elements work together, you can find more detail about specific hardware and software in the following chapters. If you know how other computers work, you should still read this chapter, because the Macintosh works differently.

BUILDING UP A MACINTOSH

Let's start with the most basic components:

a keyboard to enter information, a microprocessor to manipulate it, and a video screen to display the output.

Suppose you want to type the letter A. When you press the A key, the keyboard generates an electrical signal corresponding to the letter A. This signal is sent to the microprocessor, which, with associated components, turns it into a different electrical signal and sends it on to the screen. These steps are physically accomplished by Mac's hardware: the keyboard, microprocessor, video screen, and connecting wires.

Computer programs, or software, control all the hardware. Software is nothing more than a set of instructions for the microprocessor; it enables the microprocessor to understand the keyboard's signal for the letter A and to create the dot pattern that makes an A on the screen.

Adding Storage

The hardware and software discussed so far constitute no more than a video typewriter—interesting perhaps, but not very useful. A computer needs to be able to move, copy, and otherwise work with the keyboard entries. To do this, it requires a kind of scratch pad—a place to keep the keyboard characters while manipulating them.

Random access memory (RAM)

The computer's scratch pad is an electronic storage area called random access memory, or RAM. RAM is fast; characters can be stored or retrieved in a microsecond (a millionth of a second). Random access means that the microprocessor can go instantly to any spot in the storage area for information, without having to look at any other

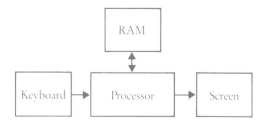

part of memory first, and can then jump forward or backward to another spot without having to read any information in between. RAM has a major limitation; it is transient. When the power goes off, anything stored in RAM disappears.

A special area, called video RAM, is set aside as a map of the screen. Software controls this area to produce the images you see.

Read-only memory (ROM)

Programs must be in electronic memory to instruct the microprocessor, but not all software operates from random access memory. Because RAM only offers temporary storage, some instructions—such as the program that tells the microprocessor what to do when the power comes on—can't stay there. These programs are held in another form of electronic memory called read-only memory, or ROM. ROM is permanently stored on a wafer of silicon called a chip.

In all computers, ROM contains the initial instructions for starting the computer. The Macintosh's ROM also contains essential programs for controlling how a disk drive works, for interpreting input from the keyboard and mouse, and for drawing graphics or text on the screen.

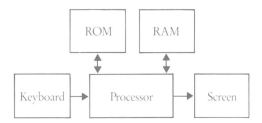

From the microprocessor's standpoint, ROM is simply another information source, just like RAM and just as fast. But whereas RAM is transient, ROM is fixed. Once the computer leaves the factory, its ROM is permanent, whether the power is on or off; the only way to change it is to replace the ROM chip itself. Because ROM is thus not as permanent as hardware, ROM programs are sometimes called firmware.

Long-term storage

To store large amounts of information permanently, or at least for long periods, microcomputers use disk drives that can read and write the information on magnetic disks, just as a tape recorder can play and record sound on tape. Like a tape recorder, a disk drive stores information as a series of magnetic pulses, except that on a disk the pulses are arranged in concentric circles.

Although a disk drive can read and write much faster than a human, it is far slower than RAM; finding a character on disk can take a disk drive a few seconds, compared to RAM's microseconds.

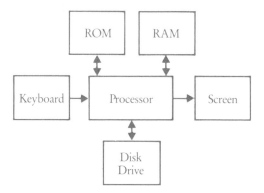

Because of this tremendous speed difference, all microcomputers normally use RAM for active work and disks for permanent storage, exchanging information between the two as needed. When you finish working with one block of information, or file, you tell Mac to store it on disk so that its RAM is free to work with another block of information. Once a disk location is found, a disk drive can read and write continuous information at the rate of 60,000 characters a second.

Like text or graphics information, computer programs may also be stored in disk files. Before a program can be used, it must be read (temporarily copied) into RAM for fast, effective operation. When you insert a Mac-Write disk, for example, and use the mouse to select the program, the computer transfers a copy of the MacWrite instructions from the disk into RAM. If you quit MacWrite and change to MacPaint, the MacWrite instructions are replaced with a copy of the MacPaint instructions. In both cases, the programs also remain permanently stored on the disk.

Now let's look briefly at how information is coded and how it travels through the computer.

BITS AND BYTES

A computer can only process information it understands. Computers understand electronic signals with just two states: on and off. They process information as individual on/off signals, or bits, coding each bit as 1 (on) or 0 (off). (In some cases, 1 is off and 0 is on, but the principle remains the same.)

One bit can't convey much information, so a computer strings many bits together to create something useful. A single character (a letter of the alphabet, number, or punctuation mark) is coded by eight bits in sequence, or one byte. The letter A, for example, is 01000001, B is 01000010, and so on. Each hardware component—keyboard, memory, disk drive—codes the letter A the same way.

The information content of a single byte is still limited, so much of the time we talk in terms of kilobytes. A kilobyte, or 1 KB, is 1024 bytes. Although "kilo" ordinarily means 1000, a kilobyte isn't an even 1000 bytes because the computer's counting system is based on the number two, not the number ten. Two multiplied by itself ten times gives 1024.

Disk file size is customarily measured in kilobytes. A file 6 kilobytes long contains about four pages of text, or 6144 characters (a typical double-spaced typewritten page holds about 1500 characters). A 6-kilobyte file doesn't have to consist of characters, though; it can be a program or a picture of equivalent length.

A few other measures: 1024 kilobytes equal 1 megabyte; 1024 megabytes equal 1 gigabyte. Usage is erratic, however; a megabyte is sometimes defined as 1000 kilobytes, a gigabyte as 1000 megabytes. In most cases, the difference is minor.

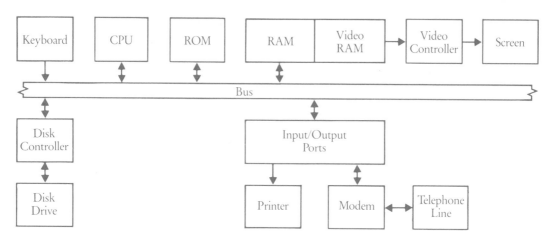

THE BUS

Coded information travels through the computer on a bus, a set of wires serving as a data highway that links the computer's components together. (This internal bus should not be confused with the external AppleBus, an electrical connection that ties separate computer units together to exchange information.) Each component communicates with the microprocessor via the bus.

The bus carries two main kinds of information: One group of wires conveys the actual data, such as the coded letter A; another group of wires carries the address of the component to which the data are headed. Each component accepts only information addressed to it; for example, information intended for the printer will not inadvertently go to the disk drive.

Most of the action on the bus is orchestrated by the computer's central microprocessor; we'll take a quick look at that next.

THE CENTRAL PROCESSING UNIT

The heart of every microcomputer is a single integrated circuit chip—the microprocessor, or central processing unit (CPU). The Macintosh's CPU chip is a Motorola 68000®.

A CPU's power depends on three factors:

- How much information it can work on at once, measured two ways:

    How many bits (called input/output, or I/O, bits) the CPU can take from and put onto the bus at a time—16 bits in the 68000.

    How many bits the CPU processes internally at one time—32 in the 68000.

- How many different kinds of instructions it can perform.

- How fast it operates—how much time each instruction takes.

By current standards, the 68000 is a more powerful chip than others commonly used in microcomputers, but the differences among chips are less important than advertisements claim.

The CPU is powerless by itself. To do anything useful, it carries out, one at a time, the step-by-step instructions provided by software. An instruction might read: "Take the information stored in memory location 125, add 1, and put the result in location 240." Or: "Take the character placed on the bus by the keyboard and put it in memory location 300." Each step is simple; computers do useful work because they can perform millions of steps in rapid succession.

THE MANY FORMS OF SOFTWARE

You can already see that software comes in many forms, some built-in and some available on disks. Some essential software tells the microprocessor how to read a disk drive; other software can draw a picture of a disk drive. The next several sections describe the differences.

ROM Software: Key to the Visual Interface

Mac's 64-KB ROM contains the key to its operation. Among current microcomputers, only Apple's Lisa and

Macintosh have such a comprehensive collection of programs in ROM. These programs make Lisa and Macintosh what they are: the first microcomputers with a powerful visual interface.

The ROM software controls the interface; it draws most of what you see on the screen, monitors the mouse, and much more. It therefore defines the way that you deal with application programs—the word processors or spreadsheets you use for your work. ROM programs make up a kind of programmer's tool kit, to be used by both professional and amateur programmers. This unique interface is the reason different Macintosh applications work much the same way.

The ROM programs include the following:

- QuickDraw draws complex graphics on the screen quickly.

- The Font Manager uses QuickDraw to create typefaces on the screen.

- The Event Manager keeps track of what you do with the mouse and keyboard.

- TextEdit is a basic text entry and editing program.

- The Window Manager draws and controls windows on the screen.

- The Control Manager creates and monitors the dialog boxes and your choice of buttons within the boxes.

- The Menu Manager creates and monitors the pull-down menus.

- The File System creates and controls files in memory and on disk.

Other programs control other essential operations.

The Operating System: A Traffic Cop

A fundamental program called the operating system acts as traffic cop, keeping track of and directing all Macintosh operations. It manages everything in memory and keeps track of information going to and from each component, whether disk drive, printer, keyboard, or screen.

In conventional microcomputers, the operating system is read in from a disk and stays mostly in RAM when the computer is working. Some popular operating systems are Apple DOS (Disk Operating System) for the Apple II; CP/M-80™ (Control Program for Microprocessors); and MS-DOS™ (Microsoft Disk Operating System).

In contrast, most of the Macintosh operating system (which has no name) resides in ROM. The rest is stored in a file named System on the disk you use to start Mac. This file is read from the disk into RAM when you first turn the computer on; it adds to or modifies the ROM instructions.

The System file contains information such as specific keyboard layout. Storing this information on disk makes changing to a foreign-language keyboard easy; Apple merely changes the System file used with foreign versions of the Macintosh.

The System file contains many other programs, including:

Utility programs. Some of these are nearly as important as the operating system; others are simply handy to have available. When you select a file icon and then choose Get Info from the File menu, for example, you are actually starting a small utility program that checks that file and displays information about it.

Desk accessories. The menu under the Apple symbol (far left on the menu bar) lets you choose functions such as a clock, a calculator, or a note pad. Because these programs are short, they can usually share RAM space with an application program.

Font data. This information dictates the font—the actual shapes of the letters you see on screen. Several fonts are essential to Mac's operation—the ones you see in the Finder and main menus, for example. Many additional

fonts and type sizes are also available from this file when
you are using MacWrite, MacPaint, and other programs.
To create these fonts, the operating system transfers the
information from disk to RAM. If you change fonts or
greatly change the type size, you may have a short wait
while the Font Manager program (in ROM) goes back
to disk to bring the new information into RAM.

Because information about each font takes up
considerable disk space, you may want to use the Font
Mover program to store rarely used fonts on a separate
disk.

Messages. Both warning and advisory messages
also reside in the System file. For foreign versions of the
Macintosh, Apple changes this file to give messages in
another language. (The ROM programs contain no text
in any language.)

The Finder: Keeping Track of Disk Files

Another important program stored on disk and read
into RAM when you first turn Mac on is the Finder. The
Macintosh Finder includes many functions traditionally
performed by a computer's operating system. It handles
most operations that involve disks: creating the disk window with its file icons, copying files, copying disks, and
so on. The Finder doesn't work alone; it uses many programs in ROM for actual disk access, in effect acting as
liaison between you and the ROM programs that control
the disk drive.

Each disk has a directory that functions as its table of
contents. The directory contains a list of files on that disk,
along with each file's icon and other attributes. When you
insert a disk, the Finder puts this directory information
into RAM where it remains, even if you change disks.
You can display the directory from an ejected disk on the
screen, but if you want to use a file from it, the Finder
asks you to change disks.

The Desktop file

For each disk, the Finder creates a hidden Desktop file to hold information about each of the files on the disk. The Desktop file notes whether a file is an application program or data file; if it's a data file, the Desktop file records which application program created it, and keeps track of the associated icon images. Because the Desktop file stores which application created a data file, the operating system loads that application if you merely open the data file.

Clock/Calendar

Mac has a battery-operated clock/calendar whose time and date are read into RAM. Every time you create or modify a disk file, the date is automatically stored with the directory entry. This time-and-date keeper drives the desk-accessory clock as well.

Application Programs: Your Primary Tools

You use application programs for doing work—Mac-Write to produce written documents, MacPaint to create illustrations, and Microsoft Multiplan for financial calculations. Permanently stored on disk, application programs are read into RAM when you need them. Because these programs are large and complex, only one will fit in RAM at a time. If necessary, the operating system moves programs or files from RAM to disk to make space for your application.

Even such maneuvering cannot free enough space for some programs. Many sophisticated applications are simply too large to fit into RAM all at once. These programs operate with a core program that stays in RAM, plus subsidiary components, called overlays, that remain on the disk until needed. As you select functions—a sorting routine or trigonometric calculation, perhaps—the core program brings needed overlays into RAM; each new portion replaces other overlays not currently in use.

Although the overlay procedure lets you use powerful programs, it also slows operation. On a Macintosh with more memory, overlays would usually be unnecessary; RAM could contain an entire application, and the programs would run much faster. With enough memory, several application programs could be in RAM at the same time, and you could switch applications instantly, without waiting for disk drives to read the new program into RAM. Apple's Lisa works this way.

THE MANY USES OF RAM

A Macintosh has far more activity going on in RAM than a conventional microcomputer. RAM holds a lot of software:

- The video memory.
- Parts of the operating system.
- Utility programs.
- Desk accessories.
- Current font data.
- Icon images.
- The Finder.
- Disk directories.
- The clock/calendar.
- An application program.

RAM also contains two forms of your data:

- Data used in the application program.
- The Clipboard.

Data: Your Information

The point of all this software, of course, is to do something with your information.

You can enter data into the computer through several routes:

- The keyboard.

- The mouse.

- From disk.

- From another computer, either over a telephone line or through a network linking computers together.

From an application program's standpoint, the source of the data doesn't matter because in most cases, the program will put the data into RAM before beginning work. If the data won't fit in RAM, the program will read some into RAM and leave the rest on disk, swapping chunks as needed.

The Clipboard

Whenever you Cut or Copy anything from the screen, that information goes into the Clipboard, an area of RAM set aside for information exchange between programs. For example, you may want to cut a series of numbers from a Multiplan spreadsheet and paste it into a MacWrite document, so you can include a financial statement in a memo.

You can store text, a drawing, or numbers in the Clipboard, but you can only store one item at a time. If you need to store more items, Paste the Clipboard contents into the Scrapbook; this frees the Clipboard for another item.

WHAT HAPPENS WHEN YOU START A PROGRAM

To tie all these software components together, here is a brief outline of what happens when you start MacWrite. The outline is not complete and events don't occur quite so linearly, but you'll get an idea of how the Macintosh system works.

When you turn Macintosh on, a ROM program called Boot tells the microprocessor to check whether a disk has been inserted in the drive. (The term boot comes from the idea that the computer is pulling itself up, or on, by its own bootstraps.)

If there is no disk, the Boot program puts on the screen an image of a disk with a question mark, in effect asking you to insert a disk.

Once a disk is in the disk drive, the program instructs the disk-controller circuitry to send the proper electronic signals to the disk drive to move the disk-drive head to the disk's outer edge and begin transferring information from the disk into RAM. First, the System file containing the RAM portion of the operating system is read from the disk. Mac then reads in the Finder from disk and creates the Finder display.

To find out what program and data files are stored on the disk, you select the disk image by clicking it with the mouse; you then choose Open from the File menu. The Finder creates a window showing the file icons and names.

You move the mouse so that the pointer is over the MacWrite icon. The Event Manager (in ROM) detects the mouse position. You double-click on the icon. The Event Manager tells the Finder about the clicks. The Finder checks the pointer location and concludes that you want to open the MacWrite file.

The Finder checks the disk directory for the location of the MacWrite file and passes the file location to the disk controller, which starts turning the disk and moves the disk-drive head over the beginning of the file.

As the disk-drive head reads the MacWrite file, the disk controller puts the information on the bus. From the bus, the information passes into RAM, in space allocated by a special ROM program called the Heap Manager.

Once in memory, MacWrite begins changing the screen. It replaces the Finder menu bar with the MacWrite menu bar, showing the MacWrite selections.

Almost simultaneously, the Window Manager (in ROM) puts a window on the screen, complete with scroll bars and title.

The Font Manager (in ROM), which has been busy creating the text on the screen, checks over the System file to see which fonts it contains. The Font Manager then passes the number and available sizes of each font on to the Menu Manager (in ROM), which sets up the Fonts menu.

As you can see from this incomplete outline, even something as simple as starting a program requires an enormous number of steps. That the procedure works at all is amazing; that it works so well is a tribute to thousands of engineers and programmers who, during the last 50 years, have made computers possible.

In the next several chapters we'll take a detailed look at Macintosh components.

Chapter 13 *The Video Screen*

Mac's screen is a cathode-ray tube (CRT) like an ordinary television screen, but with much higher resolution and a much sharper image. The image is made up of 175,104 dots (512 horizontally and 342 vertically), called picture elements, or pixels.

MAPPING THE SCREEN

All the information needed to generate the screen image is stored in a special part of random access memory called video RAM. This section of RAM uses 22 kilobytes (175,104 bits divided by 8), a significant portion of the 128-kilobyte total available RAM.

Each pixel corresponds, or is "mapped," to a bit in video RAM; in computer jargon, the screen is bit-mapped. To generate the screen image, Macintosh software takes the display information stored in video RAM and computes which of the pixels should be lit up and which should not.

Drawing bit-mapped images calls for a lot of computing. Every time you change anything on the screen, the computer must recompute each pixel of the changed object (it usually doesn't recompute stationary items). On earlier microcomputers, computing each pixel took so long that most models didn't try to bit-map and, as a result, couldn't

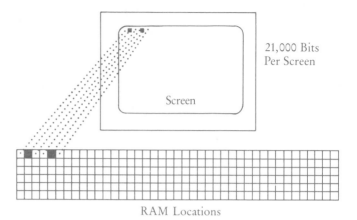

21,000 Bits
Per Screen

Screen

RAM Locations

*Bit-mapped screen: Each dot on the
screen corresponds to a bit in memory.*

draw high-quality graphics or show different typefaces on
the screen. To show that a character would be boldfaced
when sent to a printer, programs resorted to additional
characters. Instead of **BOLD** you got ^BBOLD^B
or some other confusing text cluttering up the screen.

The Macintosh overcomes the speed problems of the
old micros with fast hardware and special software. Its
central processing unit, manipulating 32 bits at a time,
works much faster than older 8- or 16-bit designs.

CREATING THE SCREEN IMAGE

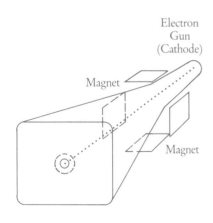

Electron
Gun
(Cathode)

Magnet

Magnet

Electrons strike phosphor, creating light.

Once all the screen bits have been computed, a video
controller circuit creates a video signal suitable for the
screen. The video signal controls a beam of electrons, turning it on or off. The beam, pointed toward the inner side of
the screen, passes between electromagnets that direct the
electrons' path. When the beam is on, the electrons strike
a phosphor coating on the CRT face, and light is produced
for that particular pixel. (Historically, electron beams were
called "cathode rays," after the device, a cathode, that produced them.)

The images you see are thus made of pixels that are
either on or off. The Macintosh has no true grays, although
objects may be made to look gray by turning off alternate
pixels.

164

The letter C shown as normal and dimmed

To keep an image constant on the screen, the electron beam sweeps across it repeatedly. Macintosh's circuitry refreshes the screen image more than 60 times each second, frequent enough that your eye and brain see a continuous image. If you turn up the screen brightness, however, or look at the screen out of the corner of your eye, you may see a slight flicker because human peripheral vision is especially sensitive to movement.

The Macintosh has a nonstandard video signal; it displays lines 50 percent faster than standard video systems and, unlike ordinary televisions which generate images by drawing every other line 60 times a second, the Macintosh draws *every* line 60 times a second (in jargon, the Macintosh produces a non-interlaced image). These differences mean that you cannot record or broadcast the Macintosh video signal directly with ordinary television equipment, to make a videotape for training, for example. You can, under some circumstances, use other video equipment with Mac; for more information see Chapter 29.

LARGER SCREENS

The 9-inch Macintosh screen has a 4¾- by 7-inch (12 by 18 cm) image area—small by most standards. Use of larger screens with the Macintosh is only possible by opening the case and redirecting the video signal. Caution: only experienced technicians should attempt this; see Chapters 29 and 30 for more information.

If you must have a larger screen image, you could buy a Lisa instead. Lisa uses a 12-inch CRT, with a 6¼- by 8¼-inch (16 by 21.5 cm) image area. Lisa's own software displays 364 by 720 pixels. If you run Macintosh software on the Lisa, some programs will give you a smaller Macintosh-style screen within the larger Lisa frame; others will let you use the full Lisa screen.

Another quirk: Macintosh pixels are the same size vertically and horizontally; ten dots in each direction measure the same distance. Lisa pixels are oblong—50 percent taller than wide. Consequently, software that draws a perfect circle on the Macintosh will put an ellipse on Lisa. The difference renders the Lisa unusable with programs such as MacPaint. Some structured graphics programs will adjust their display to look correct on a Lisa. Although the screen image may look different, the printer output will be the same for both computers.

COLOR SCREENS

Mac will not generate color video images. A color CRT with Macintosh resolution can cost as much as the computer and still not produce images as sharp as the built-in black-and-white screen.

A few companies have produced high-quality, color CRT display systems that can work with any microcomputer. From the computer's standpoint, the display acts as an output device, just like a printer or a plotter. To drive the display, you must find suitable software or write your own program.

Some color displays have large memories and sophisticated internal processing; some models display nearly 700 by 500 pixels and boast a palette of 16 million colors. Prices range from $2500 to $6000.

Unfortunately, these special displays do not work interactively the way the Macintosh does with its own graphics; you can't use a mouse with these screens. As the market grows, however, display companies will develop special software designed to work with the Macintosh.

Some software already built into the Macintosh ROM can handle color; these features aren't designed for CRTs but work with color printers and plotters.

SCREEN ACCESSORIES

Some people find that looking at a computer screen for a long period strains their eyes. Many companies have produced screen accessories that attempt to alleviate this problem.

Green and Amber Screens

Some companies claim special "ergonomic" advantages because of a green or amber screen, supposedly more restful for the eyes. There is actually little evidence one way or the other; Macintosh uses black characters on a white background to correspond with black ink on white paper.

Some self-appointed experts have called for regulations to require that a screen be green or amber—an unjustified step. They might just as well insist that all books be printed on green or yellow paper.

Green and amber filters designed to fit over Mac's screen will undoubtedly become available. If you don't mind the fuzzier image through the filter and are convinced that the results are more restful, you could try a color filter.

Anti-Glare Screens

Because Mac's screen surface is roughened slightly to reduce reflections, you don't need to set it up in a darkened room. Just look for a place out of direct sunlight; the brightness of the screen and the surrounding area should be about the same.

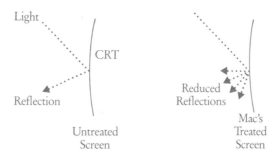

Still, you may not find a place for your Macintosh that avoids glare completely. If your room has a big picture window, it would be a shame to give up the view so you could stare at a computer screen. An accessory anti-glare screen may help, though some may darken too much. These screens come in three forms:

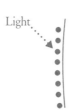

Mesh screens use closely woven, matte-black filaments to scatter room light from any direction. You will probably need to turn up the brightness to use a mesh screen, and the image will be a little less sharp. Clean dust from the mesh by blowing on it.

Venetian blind screens use many tiny parallel, horizontal strips embedded in a plastic sheet to control

167

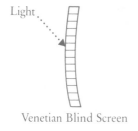

Venetian Blind Screen

light reflection. If you have strong lights directly over your Macintosh, these screens may solve your glare problem. The strips force you to view the screen from a narrow vertical angle, but brightness is not reduced much; sharpness suffers a little. Clean the screen with any mild window cleaner.

Optically coated screens use anti-reflection coatings of the type found on camera lenses and other optical surfaces. The flat glass does not degrade the image.

The less-expensive interference coatings work best with a darkening filter, which cuts screen brightness. Circular polarizing filters do not reduce image brightness as much but cost considerably more. Clean these screens with lens cleaners only.

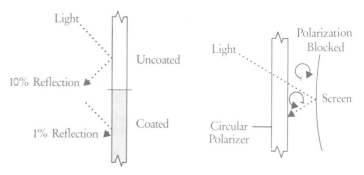

TAKING CARE OF THE SCREEN

Aside from occasional cleaning with a household glass cleaner, the Macintosh screen should require little maintenance.

One problem may develop if you leave the screen illuminated for weeks or months without actively working with it. When an electron beam strikes a screen area continuously, the phosphor there eventually wears. Stationary images left for long periods may thus "burn in," leaving a faint shadow. (You can see this wear on airport television screens that show flight schedules 24 hours a day.) To reduce phosphor wear, you should turn down the brightness control whenever you will not be looking at the screen for a long time.

Chapter *The* 14 *Keyboard*

ike any typewriter, the Macintosh keyboard has the standard QWERTY layout, named for the first row of letters. A typewriter usually has 84 or 88 characters, including the capital letters; like most computers, your Macintosh adds the symbols < > | \ ˜ and ˆ on the keyboard for a total of 94. Computer keyboards differ from typewriter keyboards in other ways as well.

UNIQUE KEYBOARD FEATURES

Some small typewriter keyboards have no number 1, and typists learn to use the lowercase letter l instead. If you do this, you'll have to break the habit; a computer needs to distinguish between a 1 and an l. Similarly, you can't type a capital O instead of a zero.

Shift and Caps Lock

Most typewriters have comma and period keys that produce the same symbol whether shifted or unshifted. Computer keyboards, including Mac's, only produce a comma and period if unshifted; you get < and > if you also press the Shift key.

The Caps Lock key isn't quite like the Shift Lock key on a typewriter. On Mac, the Caps Lock key only generates capital letters; you won't get !@# for 123 with only the Caps Lock engaged. For those symbols, you must always press the Shift key.

Command and Option

¡ ™ £ ¢ ∞ § ¶ • ª º – ≠
œ Σ ´ ® † ¥ ¨ ^ø π “ ‘ «
å ß ∂ ƒ © ◊ △ ⬚ ¬ … æ
Ω ≈ ç √ ∫ ~µ ≤ ≥ ÷

Edit	
Undo	⌘Z
Cut	⌘H
Copy	⌘C
Paste	⌘U

The Macintosh keyboard also has two special shift keys, Command (⌘) and Option, which work like the Control and Alternate keys on other computers: You hold down one of the keys while pressing another key to get special functions.

Although usage may vary with the software, you generally use the Option key to get special characters for a foreign language or a graphics symbol and the Command key as a shortcut to some menu commands. Some pull-down menu commands have a ⌘ symbol and a letter; holding down the Command key while pressing the letter produces that command immediately—just as if you had used the mouse to open and pull down the menu and choose an item. For common commands, you may find the Command key faster than using the mouse; the choice is yours.

When communicating with other computers, you may need to generate control characters. Control characters perform such functions as ringing the other computer's bell to wake up the operator (Control-g) or telling another computer when to start a new page (Control-l). To generate these characters on Mac, the communications program linking your Macintosh with other computers will probably make the Command key the equivalent of a control key; to produce a Control-c, for example, you will type Command-c.

Macintosh software doesn't normally need the Escape key common on other computers. If you're hooked up to another computer and need to generate the Escape character, your communications program will tell you how to send it (probably Command-[; on conventional computers, Escape is simply a Control-[).

Enter

Pressing the Enter key usually marks the end of an entry made from the keyboard, as when you fill in a blank in a dialog box. To give software developers flexibility, Apple has not rigidly defined the Enter key; its function varies from program to program. In some, the Enter key acts like the Return key except that the pointer moves in a predefined way after Return but not after Enter. In Multiplan, for example, a selected cell moves down one step if you press Return, but remains in place if you press Enter.

KEYBOARD ADJUSTMENT

You can adjust some aspects of the keyboard by choosing Control Panel from the Apple menu:

- You can set the rate at which the keys repeat when held down.

- You can also set the delay before the keys repeat.

 Click to set keyboard repeat rate.
Click to set delay time before key begins repeating.

PALM RESTS

The Macintosh keyboard is a little taller than other computer keyboards, particularly European ones. If you need support for your hands, almost any thin support will do, or you can make one out of wood. Commercial palm rests will also undoubtedly appear.

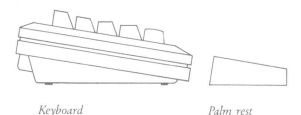

Keyboard   *Palm rest*

THE DVORAK KEYBOARD

The standard QWERTY layout used on the Macintosh keyboard was developed by Christopher Scholes in 1873 to slow typists down. The layout, which separated often-used letters from one another, prevented typists from getting ahead of the typebar mechanism in the first Remington typewriter. The QWERTY layout is thus the oldest component of modern computers.

With this century's emphasis on production-line efficiency, many alternative layouts have been proposed to improve speed and accuracy. August Dvorak devised the best-known alternative. He analyzed letter frequencies and letter-pair frequencies in English and placed the most often-used letters so they would be pressed by the most powerful fingers using the least motion. He even analyzed number frequencies, laying down the number row as 7531902468. This rearrangement proved too much even for Dvorak enthusiasts, who have mostly restored the 1234567890 order.

Although perhaps not optimal, the Dvorak layout is clearly superior to QWERTY. Speed improves some 5 to 25 percent with about half the errors made with QWERTY. The world's typing speed record (186 words per minute) was set on a Dvorak keyboard.

Experiment with Dvorak if you're curious; Dvorak layout programs will appear for Mac, but you must change all the caps on the keys, obliterating the standard arrangement. Since even Dvorak advocates claim only a few thousand Dvorak keyboards in existence, however, choosing Dvorak means choosing isolation.

Dvorak is probably a lost cause. The QWERTY keyboard is like irregular verbs: Everyone hates them but no one can change them.

THE NUMERIC KEYPAD

The optional numeric keypad adds a calculator-like keypad, handy if you work with many numbers; it plugs in between the normal keyboard and the system unit. Macintosh programs don't normally require the 16 additional keys, but the Macintosh can distinguish between a number

pressed on the main keyboard and the same number pressed on the keypad. Accessory programs may take advantage of this ability to let you reprogram keypad keys to generate specific characters or commands; the key-pad would then work like the function keys of other computers.

Four cursor keys on the keypad move the cursor, or pointer, on the screen. Although moving the mouse usually moves the cursor faster than pressing keys, very short moves—a character or two—can be done more quickly with cursor keys. Not all software, however, lets you use these keys.

TAKING CARE OF THE KEYBOARD

The keyboard and keypad will need little, if any, special care. The most common threat to both is spilled coffee. Many companies have a sensible rule against placing coffee or other drinks on any table occupied by a computer.

You might buy or make a cover to keep dust off. Although many commercial covers will become available, you can make a perfectly good one from coated rip-stop nylon, sold by outdoor/sporting goods stores.

Chapter *The* 15 *Mouse*

When using any computer, you are pointing at the screen much of the time—choosing a menu item, marking text when word processing, aiming rockets in a game, or drawing. Because pointing is so fundamental to computer operation, designers have developed many different ways to do it.

The debate over which pointing devices are best is far from over, so I'll digress a little here to discuss the major techniques before covering the Macintosh pointing device: the mouse.

CURSOR KEYS

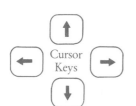

The cursor, or pointer, marks your position on the screen, and older computers have generally provided cursor keys for moving it around.

By far the most common pointing device, cursor keys work well for small movements—a character or two at a time—but they are awkward for longer ones; you have to bang away at the keys repeatedly or wait for an automatically repeating key to move the cursor where you want it. To shorten the wait, some programs have set up additional keys to move the cursor a word or a page at a time, but you still can't move between two distant points without many steps.

Clumsy for text, cursor keys are hopeless for drawing, where you must sometimes move just a pixel or two.

TOUCH SCREENS

Touch screens boast the most natural operation of all; you point at something by actually touching it on the screen. Different touch screens use different electronic techniques to locate your finger.

Touch screens are rare because they don't really work well. They have a place in computer systems that must be simple enough for a passer-by to operate, as in a store display, but for most uses they present intractable problems. A finger is too big to select a character on the screen, much less a pixel; few people will put their fingers in a pencil sharpener first. And while actually pointing at something, you can't see it because your finger is in the way. Moreover, fingerprints soil the screen. These problems are bad enough when word processing, but they are untenable for drawing, when you must have precise pixel-by-pixel control.

OK, say some companies, we'll simply offset the cursor so it will always be half an inch above your finger. Now you may be able to see the cursor, but you must still hold your hand up to the screen while jockeying the cursor around—or while you are thinking—a tiring proposition.

LIGHT PENS

A light pen is a pen-shaped device containing a light receptor that is activated when you press the pen against the screen. The receptor detects the electron beam from the CRT as it moves across the screen (see Chapter 13), and a timing circuit uses the beam to locate the pen. Most light pens won't work in the black areas of the screen.

Light pens share many of the same problems as touch screens, including arm fatigue; imagine holding a pen up to a vertical screen while composing your next sentence. Moreover, you must pick up and put down the light pen each time you need it.

176

Light pens come in several forms and work well for some applications, particularly computer-aided design. A light pen-like device might also be used with future computers with flat screens that fold down near the desk top.

JOYSTICKS AND TRACKBALLS

The joysticks and trackballs used with arcade games work well for moving laser guns to shoot at attacking monsters, but don't have the rapid, precise control essential to normal computer operation. No computer uses a joystick or trackball for professional work.

TOUCH PADS AND DIGITIZER PADS

Touch pads and digitizer pads offer many advantages for graphics work; many models will undoubtedly be adapted to the Macintosh.

Touch pads, operated by a finger, share the resolution problems of touch screens. They also suffer from "skid patches" left by finger grease; movement is often erratic and fine control difficult.

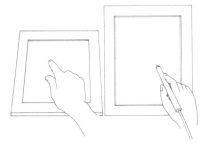

Digitizer pads, which use a stylus, offer excellent resolution and a natural drawing action. A pad works as an absolute-position device, much like a piece of paper; mice, we will see, only register relative positions. A pad could be programmed to operate as a relative-position device as well.

But present digitizer pads are expensive, and you must continually pick up and put down the stylus—a nuisance.

THE MOUSE

The most satisfactory general-purpose pointing device remains the mouse. Many studies have shown its superiority, but people are often skeptical until they try one.

Learning to use a mouse takes virtually no time, and once you have worked with it, you will appreciate its rapid, natural operation. You don't have to look at a mouse while operating it, and it stays in place when you let go; your arm generally rests comfortably on the desk. If you run out of desk space in the middle of a movement, you simply pick the mouse up (the pointer stays where you left it on the screen) and use the same space again to continue your movement.

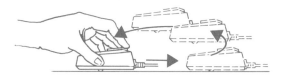

Moving a mouse over the same desk space

Disadvantages of the Mouse

A mouse is not ideal for every application. When using a word processor, for example, moving very short distances on screen means moving your hand away from the keyboard to the mouse, making a movement, and moving your hand back again. Such small motions are simpler with cursor keys. (The main Macintosh keyboard does not have cursor keys, but the accessory numeric keypad does.) Some word-processing software will probably use both the mouse and specially defined Command keys, and possibly the numeric keypad as well.

The mouse is not ideal for drawing either, because you can't use your fingers as effectively as with a pen. Skill does come with practice, though; Chapter 26 offers several tips for drawing with a mouse.

A mouse requires extra desk space, which may be hard to come by in a crowded office—but then, five years ago you probably didn't have space for a computer either. Because the Macintosh itself is so small, the total area required isn't much more than that needed for other computers without a mouse.

How the Mouse Works

Mac uses a mechanical/optical mouse; the roller on the bottom is mechanically coupled to two rotating vanes that interrupt beams from light-emitting diodes that light up phototransistors. The two vanes track vertical and horizontal motions. The vertical and horizontal orientations are defined by the mouse, not by your point of view. If you hold the mouse at an angle and move it straight back ("vertically"), the pointer will move at a corresponding angle.

A mouse registers relative movement; the controller electronics can tell how far the mouse has moved and in which direction, but not the mouse's absolute location.

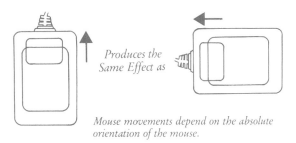

Produces the Same Effect as

Mouse movements depend on the absolute orientation of the mouse.

Taking Care of the Mouse

The roller can get clogged with debris picked up while rolling over a dirty surface. If your mouse falls ill, turn it over and undo the ball retainer ring. Clean the ball, brush and blow out the ball chamber, then reassemble the mouse.

Chapter 16 Disk Drives and Disks

Computers use disk drives and disks for long-term information storage. A disk drive records and plays back digital information much as a cassette recorder records and plays back speech or music, but instead of recording on tape, the disk drive records on a thin plastic disk. Disk drives may have one or two recording heads, usually called read/write heads. Single-sided drives have one head; double-sided drives have two, positioned opposite each other.

The disk itself, a circle of plastic coated with a magnetic surface, rotates inside a semi-rigid envelope. Disks are reusable; old information can be replaced by new information, and the same disk can be erased and recorded many times.

MACINTOSH DRIVES AND DISKS

The first Macintoshes have single-sided disk drives that can store 400 kilobytes (about 400,000 characters) of information on one side of each disk. Later, double-sided drives will store 800 KB on each disk, 400 KB on each side. Because they double the storage capacity of each disk, double-sided drives will be far more desirable than single-sided ones, even if they cost more. (Apple isn't responsible

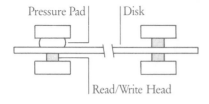

Single-sided disk drive uses a pressure pad opposite the read/write head (left); double-sided drives use two heads opposite each other (right).

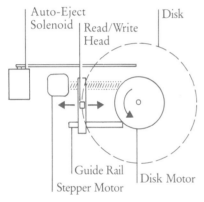

The disk-drive mechanism has two motors: one turns the disk, while a stepper motor moves the read/write head radially across the disk.

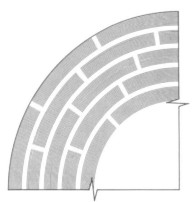

A Macintosh disk has 80 tracks on a side. The outmost 16 tracks have 12 sectors each; the next 16 tracks have 11 sectors, and so on, until the innermost 16 tracks have 8 sectors each.

for the delayed appearance; Japan's Sony, who makes the drives, didn't have the double-sided versions available when Mac was introduced.)

The Macintosh uses small 3½-inch microfloppy disks, also developed originally by Sony. These little disks are far more convenient and easier to handle than earlier, larger floppy disks.

When you insert a microfloppy into the Macintosh disk drive, a lever opens the disk's spring-loaded metal dustcover, exposing the magnetic surface; the drive's magnetic read/write head presses down on the disk surface while a pressure pad on the other side holds the disk against the head. (In a double-sided drive, the two heads press on opposite sides of the disk.) A motor then moves the head radially across the disk, while another motor turns the disk at 390 to 605 revolutions per minute.

Each read/write head records information as magnetic changes in 80 closed, concentric circles, or tracks (a total of 160 tracks with double-sided disk drives). Disks thus resemble phonograph records more than cassette tapes, although a record has only one continuous groove.

The larger-diameter outside tracks are longer than the inside ones and can therefore hold more information. To take advantage of this, Mac's disk-controller circuitry turns the disk slower when the drive head is at the outer edge and faster at the inner edge, so the drive head writes more information on the outer tracks than on the inner ones. The changes in motor speed produce the different tones you hear as the drive operates. (Because they operate at a constant rotational speed, most disk drives for other computers store less information on each disk.)

Each radial track of a Macintosh disk consists of several sectors; the outermost 16 tracks have 12 sectors each, the next 16 tracks have 11 sectors each, and so on to the innermost 16 tracks, which have 8 sectors each. Each sector contains 512 bytes of information.

Initializing Disks

When you buy disks to store your data, they are blank. Before using them, the disk drive must initialize, or format, each disk by laying down magnetic markers for each track and each sector. If you are reusing a disk, initializing erases any information previously stored on that disk. You need initialize a disk only once.

If you put in a brand new disk, or a disk that was used on another type of computer, a utility program in the System file puts a dialog box on the screen to ask if you want to initialize the disk. If you click the Initialize button, the drive goes ahead and initializes the disk; if you don't wish to initialize the disk—for example, if you realize you have put in the wrong disk by mistake—you must click the Eject button.

Write-Protection

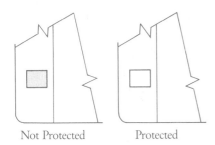

Not Protected   Protected

If the small square is blocked, you can write on the disk. If the square is open, the disk is write-protected; you cannot write on it.

A common danger when working with any magnetic storage medium is writing over (erasing) important information on a disk. A small plastic insert in each microfloppy disk lets you guard against this: If you set the insert so you cannot see it from above, the disk drive cannot write on the disk. When practical, you should set your original disks so they can't be written on and make working copies for daily use; you can't do this with some copy-protected programs, since you may have to use the original disk as the working disk. (Some programs require you to write on the program disk as you use them.)

THE DISK DIRECTORY

How does the Macintosh operating system know where on your disk to find a specific file of information? Several tracks store the disk's directory, an index to its files. The directory, along with a hidden Desktop file, holds the information you see in the Macintosh Finder—each file name and its icon; the operating system uses the directory to find the file on the disk.

When you select a file to work with, the operating system first goes to the disk directory, locates the file name, and notes which tracks the file is stored on. It then moves the disk-drive head to those tracks and begins reading the file into RAM.

When you finish your work and wish to save it, or write it on the disk, the Macintosh first adds a directory entry, finds tracks available for storage (these tracks won't neccessarily be in sequence), and then moves to each track in turn to record the information.

If you've run out of space on the disk, an alert box appears on the screen. In most cases (depending on the software you're using), you can switch the disk for another one with more storage space.

Speeding Up Disk Operation

Simply because it's mechanical, a disk drive operates more slowly than electronic RAM. In addition, a disk drive may perform many steps to read or write a file, moving back and forth between the directory tracks and the data tracks, which may be scattered about the disk.

To speed up operation, the Macintosh keeps some disk-directory information in RAM, in an area called the disk buffer. Some programs write changes from the disk buffer to the disk, either immediately or at regular intervals (this is called "flushing" the disk buffer), but other programs may not take time to do this. That's why you can't simply remove a disk from the Macintosh, but must use the Finder to eject it; the latest directory information is automatically written on the disk right before ejection. (On other computers, you can easily remove your disk at any time, including the wrong time.)

The speed improvement comes with some risk: A power failure will erase the directory information in the disk buffer. No computer is immune to power outages. Your best defense is to make frequent back-up copies of files and disks, or you can use uninterruptible power supplies, discussed in Chapter 21.

Sending a File to the Trash

When you want to erase a file, drag the File icon over the Trash icon so that the Trash icon reverses color, and then release the mouse button. The operating system responds by changing a single character in that file's directory entry to serve as a flag. The flag says, "Ignore this entry"; the file itself remains on the disk. The operating system only erases files when there isn't enough disk space for a new file or when you choose Empty Trash from the Special menu.

If you make a mistake in sending a file to the trash, you can thus recover it easily, but best do it soon: Open the trash (double-click the Trash icon) and drag the icon of the file you want to recover back to the disk window. The operating system changes the flag character back.

OTHER FLOPPY DISKS

Floppy disks come in several sizes. The original 8-inch floppies are now mainly used on larger office computers. The 5¼-inch "minifloppy" is the disk most commonly used with microcomputers. Both the 5¼- and 8-inch sizes have flexible plastic jackets with openings that expose the disk's fragile magnetic surface. Both require careful handling; a single fingerprint on the exposed surface or warping the jacket can destroy the disk.

Three microfloppy designs: Dysan, Hitachi/Maxell, Sony.

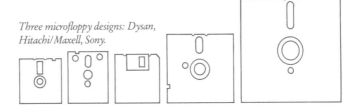

The exposed magnetic surface on older floppy disks is vulnerable to damage.

There are two other "microfloppy" formats. The 3¼-inch Tabor format is simply a scaled-down version of the 5¼-inch design and suffers from all the same handling problems. The 3-inch Hitachi/Maxell disks have a semi-rigid plastic envelope like Mac's 3½-inch disks, but store less information. Don't confuse them with disks for the Macintosh.

Several companies sell Sony-style microfloppy disks. You can buy and use Hewlett-Packard, Sony, and other brands as well as Apple microfloppy disks in your Macintosh. Some other 3½-inch microfloppies have a slightly different dustcover, but work fine on Mac anyway. If the cover of one of these earlier disks latches open, press with your thumb and forefinger on the arrow in the upper left corner labeled "pinch." Some of these microfloppies don't have as convenient a write-protect tab; you have to break off a plastic piece and reinsert it. Unlike older 5¼- and 8-inch floppies, you can write on the label with a ballpoint pen without damaging the disk.

MACINTOSH DISK COMPATIBILITY

Although the disk-drive mechanism in a Macintosh may look the same as in other microcomputer models, it differs from other 3½-inch microfloppy drives both in electrical and mechanical design. You won't be able to use other 3½-inch disk drives with a Macintosh. Lisa 2s use the same disk drives.

Because of the disk drive differences, the Macintosh and Lisa store information on their disks in a unique way, different from Hewlett-Packard, Sony, and others. Macintosh cannot read microfloppy disks written by other computers, and they cannot read Macintosh disks. A Macintosh cannot read the 5¼-inch disks used by an earlier Lisa model, but it can read disks from a Lisa 2 running Macintosh software. Data stored by Lisa's own software require conversion before a Mac can use the information.

The Macintosh disk-controller circuit board is essentially the same as in the Apple II and III. The same type of copy-protection mechanisms used on those models can work with the Macintosh as well. The Macintosh itself does not contain any special copy-protection hardware. Adapting a 5¼-inch disk drive to the controller will be difficult or impossible; not all the same electrical connections are supplied.

TAKING CARE OF DISKS

Although you should treat all disks with reasonable care, the microfloppy's semi-rigid plastic case and the spring-loaded metal dustcover mean that ordinary handling will cause no damage; you can't put a fingerprint on the magnetic surface unless you go to the trouble of holding the spring-loaded cover open. Since a determined assault can ruin even microfloppies, however, keep them away from small children and pets. And even with the cover, disks will not survive coffee spills and direct hits with cigarette ashes.

If you use a rubber band around your microfloppies, wrap it horizontally. Otherwise the band can get caught in the cover, opening it and exposing the magnetic surface.

When shipping a disk, wrap it in a plastic bag; the cover and the edges of the case are not sealed, so dust can sneak through. If you use a sturdy shipping envelope, further reinforcement is unnecessary. Always make a back-up disk before shipping.

The right way and wrong way to use rubber bands

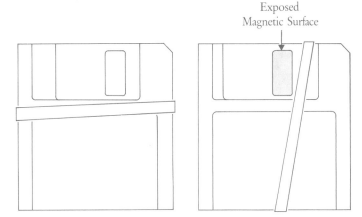

Exposed
Magnetic Surface

SHOULD YOU BUY A SECOND DISK DRIVE?

In a word, yes. Although you can get some work done with just the one built-in, single-sided drive, the 400-KB limitation will be a considerable nuisance. After storing essential system files and application programs, a single-sided disk won't have much space left for your data. A second disk drive solves this problem neatly.

With a single drive, if you want to duplicate a disk, you will need to swap the original disk and the copy many times. The Macintosh must first read part of the original disk into memory and write that information onto the copy disk. Then it must go back and read another portion, copy it, and so on. Because of RAM limitations, Mac can't read the entire 400-KB disk at one time.

So even if money is tight, think seriously about getting a second disk drive. If you use the Macintosh for business, consider the second drive essential.

You can mix single- and double-sided drives with one Macintosh, but if you do, you will have to keep track of each disk's format. A single-sided drive can't read a double-sided disk; you can't just turn the disk over to read both sides. A double-sided drive, on the other hand, can read a single-sided disk.

You can add just one additional microfloppy disk drive to the Macintosh, for a total of two. If you need more storage, such as for an accounting system or data base, you can attach a Winchester disk drive through a serial port (see Chapter 17 for more about ports).

Winchester Drives and Disks

Winchester drives also record information magnetically and store it in concentric circles on disks. But the disks are not made of thin, flexible plastic; instead, Winchester drives use a rigid metal platter coated with magnetic material and polished to a mirror-smooth finish. Whenever the power is on, the platter spins continuously in a chamber of filtered air. Most Winchester disks are permanently fixed in the drive.

These features mean that Winchester drives and disks are made to much higher precision than floppies and can store much more information in a small space. A micro-Winchester drive, which fits into the same space as Mac's microfloppy drive, can store 5 or 10 megabytes, compared to a microfloppy's 400 or 800 kilobytes. Other Winchester drives, which are physically only a little larger, can store up to 140 megabtyes and more. Winchesters are also much faster than floppy disk drives.

Of course, with all these advantages, Winchester drives cost much more than floppy drives—about four to ten times as much—but when you consider the cost per character of information stored, Winchesters are much cheaper than floppies.

With the Macintosh, you must connect a Winchester drive through a serial port. Although it will still work faster than the microfloppy disk drives, speed limitations in the port itself will prevent you from taking full advantage of the Winchester's inherent speed. (These Macintosh limitations are a function of its cost; a design with extra features for running Winchesters at full speed would cost much more. Lisa 2s could take greater advantage of a Winchester's speed, but then they cost a lot more, too.)

Winchester disk drives don't have to be attached directly to the serial port; they can be attached to AppleBus instead. Several Macintoshes could share such drives. For more information, see Chapter 30. Davong offers hard-disk systems for Macintosh using their Multi-Link™ network, a version of Datapoint's ARCNET™ network. Corvus has a hard-disk system that will connect to its Omninet network.

Tecmar has a Winchester drive for Macintosh that uses the SyQuest removable hard disk. This system offers performance similar to conventional fixed-disk Winchester drives, but with far more flexible packaging. Its disadvantage is the total amount of storage; a current SyQuest cartridge holds about 5 megabytes, whereas conventional Winchesters hold 10 or more megabytes. But for more storage, you can just change the $100 disk cartridge.

Chapter 17 Input/Output Ports

Ports are electrical pathways that carry information in and out of the computer; they are often called I/O, or input/output, ports. You attach all accessories to the computer through its ports.

Ports serve many purposes, handling everything from low-speed communications with a teletype machine to high-speed communications with a video screen. On the Macintosh, the available ports operate from low to medium speed.

Ports can be classified in several ways; one fundamental way distinguishes parallel from serial ports. Parallel ports transmit and receive all eight bits in a byte simultaneously on eight separate wires. Serial ports send and receive the eight bits in sequence on a single wire. Parallel ports generally work faster than serial ports, but the speed difference doesn't matter for many uses. A printer, for example, works so much slower than a computer that a serial connection works fine. For electrical reasons, serial signals can be carried over much longer wires than parallel signals.

The Macintosh has the following I/O ports:

- Two serial ports. In normal use, one is for a printer, the other for a modem.

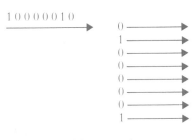

Serial links on left use a single wire; parallel links on right use eight wires. (Both links use an additional ground wire; for immunity to electric noise, the Macintosh serial port can use two signal wires plus a ground.)

- A disk-drive port.

- A mouse port.

- A keyboard port.

- An audio-output port.

THE SERIAL PORTS

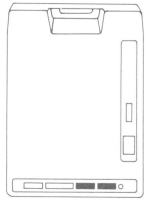

Serial ports

The Macintosh serial ports follow the RS-422 protocol, an enhanced form of the older, more common RS-232C protocol. A port's protocol is a set of rules specifying the timing, wiring, and voltage that a computer and its accessories must follow for communication to take place.

The RS-422's improvements allow higher-speed communications and longer connecting wires between devices. RS-232C connections are generally limited to 19,200 bits per second (2.4 KB per second) while Mac's RS-422 can run routinely at 230,000 bits per second (29 KB per second), and as fast as 920,000 bits per second with special techniques. RS-422 has much better immunity to electrical noise and can run over much longer cables.

The Macintosh serial ports will handle most RS-232C devices as well as RS-422 devices. Although RS-232C uses higher voltages than RS-422, the Macintosh serial ports will not be damaged. (Such compatibility with RS-232C voltages is not generally true of RS-422 devices, however; use caution when intermixing devices.) The nine-pin serial-port connector does not follow the RS-449 connector standard; for wiring information, see Chapter 30.

In many cases, an RS-232C device can be connected with nothing more than a suitable cable; the ImageWriter, for example, is an RS-232C device. Some devices, such as elaborate modems, use more complex connection and control schemes than the Macintosh port can support; you will either need to reconfigure the device or get a possibly expensive electronic interface.

Most ordinary RS-232C devices sold for microcomputers should work, if supporting software is available and you can figure out how to set the hardware and software. Unless you have considerable skill and great patience, don't try to attach an accessory device to your Macintosh that you have not already seen working properly on another Macintosh. In particular, try not to be the first on the block with some new accessory; it's safer to wait for someone else to solve the set-up problems.

The RS-422 ports are bidirectional—information can travel both to and from the computer. You can connect two Macintoshes together directly with a cable through their serial ports. The serial port also serves for communications through the AppleBus (see Chapter 30).

The Disk-Drive Port

The disk-drive port is also bidirectional and operates at 62.5 KB per second. It's designed to support just one additional microfloppy disk drive and is not designed for other applications.

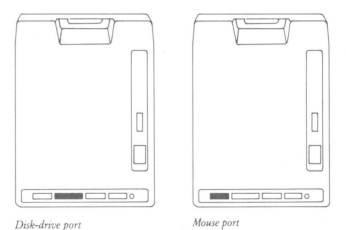

Disk-drive port   *Mouse port*

The Mouse Port

The mouse port is only suitable for attaching your mouse and other pointing devices. Digitizer pads and touch pads could be adapted to use this port if they are designed to emulate a mouse.

193

The Keyboard Port

The keyboard port is a slow, general-purpose bidirectional serial port, able to support at least eight devices. The optional numeric keypad also plugs into the same port. Musical keyboards, data-entry pads that accept handwritten entries, and other equipment that transmits data slowly can be connected through this port.

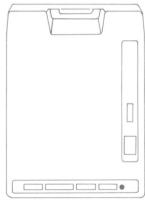

Keyboard port   *Audio-output port*

The Audio-Output Port

The audio-output port sends audio information outward only. The port is normally connected to a small 3-inch, built-in speaker. You can set the speaker volume by choosing Control Panel from the Apple menu. Set at minimum, the speaker should be inaudible. The change affects only the specific system disk; if you wish to silence the speaker at all times, insert a dummy plug without any connections into the audio-output port.

The audio-output port lets you connect the Macintosh sound output to a hifi system or tape recorder. The plug is a standard ⅛-inch phone plug. The signal is at speaker levels (maximum 1 volt, peak-to-peak) and should work satisfactorily through a high-level input on a hifi. Don't plug it into a magnetic phono cartridge input; you will overload most hifi amplifiers and get loud but distorted sound. If you want to record the sounds, connect the port to a tape recorder's high-level or auxiliary inputs.

The audio-output port plug (Radio Shack #274-286). To silence the speaker, don't make any connections to the plug; merely insert the plug.

Mac's sound generator can produce frequencies from below audibility to 11 kHz with four simultaneous voices. Although the generator uses digital techniques, it is in no way comparable in quality to digital audio recordings of music. Compact disc laser players, for example, use 16-bit digital-to-analog conversion, while the Macintosh generator uses 8-bit conversion. The generator is, however, flexible enough to synthesize speech.

Speech output

Speech output on the Macintosh requires only speech software; no additional hardware is needed. The speech output uses the audio port and operates as an input/output device, just like the printer or modem.

The speech software, written by Mark Barton and Joseph Katz, comes in two parts: The first part translates ASCII text into phonemes, a phonetic representation of the words. The second part, the synthesizer, takes the phonemes as input and generates the actual codes that are turned into sound. The technique used is formant synthesis, not linear predictive coding, the other common speech synthesis technology. In the preliminary versions, the ASCII-to-phoneme program is about 7 KB long and includes a small list of specially pronounced words; the synthesizer proper is about 15 KB long.

The sound generator can synthesize as fast as it speaks. Speed and pitch can be regulated independently.

To aid pitch and inflection, the synthesizer works on a sentence at a time. Punctuation is handled with simple rules: At a comma, the voice will pause slightly with a rising inflection; at a question mark, a longer rise; at a period or dash, a relatively long pause. The voice will pronounce acronyms with a vowel but spell out those without a vowel. Decimals are read as "point."

Since English has ill-defined pronunciation rules with many exceptions, more elaborate pre-processing may be needed to improve the speech quality. Such processing can define the inflection and timing of the speech. Users will be able to write programs that pre-process but will not be able to modify the synthesizer program directly.

The first speech software available for the Macintosh will synthesize a male voice; a female version may follow (female voices are slightly harder to do, because of the higher pitch). English will be the first language available. Only languages with well-defined text-to-phoneme and phoneme-to-sound properties can be synthesized effectively. Swedish and Japanese are clear candidates; other languages may be farther off.

A second speech synthesis program, Smoothtalker, is available from First Byte, Inc., Long Beach, CA.

Chapter *Printers*
18

For any computer, a printer is nearly essential. If you haven't bought one already, you probably will soon—unless you work in an office with multiple Macintoshes; since no one will be printing all the time, several units might share a single printer.

THE APPLE IMAGEWRITER

Initially, Apple is supplying only one (optional) printer for the Macintosh: the low-cost ImageWriter, built by Tokyo Electric to take advantage of Mac's special features. It can print all of the Macintosh fonts (typefaces) and graphics, as well as a screen dump—an exact replica of the screen.

With the ImageWriter, printing from your Macintosh is easy; just follow the steps described in the manuals. The ImageWriter is the simplest, most worry-free way of getting a paper copy of the work you've done.

The ImageWriter handles paper clumsily. For form-feed paper (discussed later), the paper is pushed rather than pulled under the platen. In addition, the clear plastic paper guide can get in the way of single sheets and the first sheet of form-fed paper, especially heavier-weight paper. The result is compressed print at the top of the page. Remove the paper guide to prevent this problem.

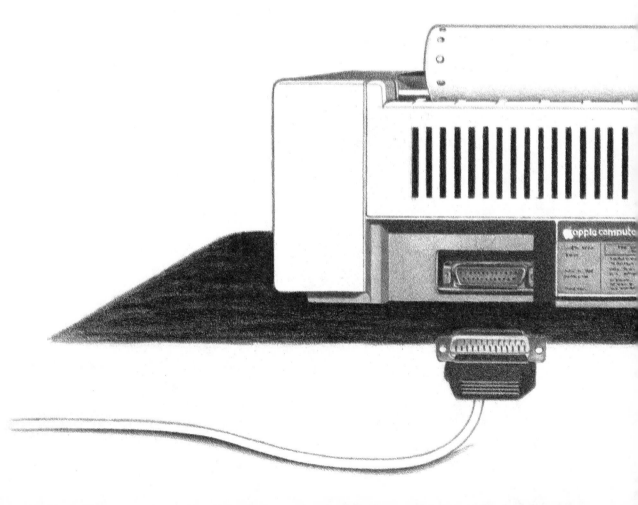

If you need to connect several Macintosh computers to a single printer, you can install a switch box between the printer port of each Macintosh and the printer.

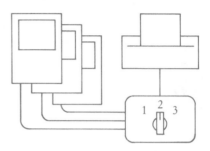

A switch box lets a single printer serve several computers.

The ImageWriter is a dot-matrix printer; the printer forms characters out of little dots. The printhead contains nine wires that dart in and out, pressing the inked ribbon against the paper as the head travels across it. Because the wires actually strike the paper through the ribbon, a dot-matrix printer is called an impact printer.

As with all low-cost printers, the printed images usually look a little less crisp than the screen display; printing lacks the contrast and uniformity of the screen. Also, the printed output fades as the ribbon wears out.

The ImageWriter prints in three modes: draft, standard, and high-resolution. The modes available depend on the application software.

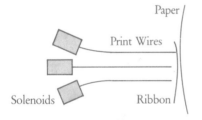

In an impact dot-matrix printer, solenoids drive tiny print wires against ribbon and paper.

Draft Mode

Draft mode is the fastest of the three, but also the lowest quality. Use this mode when you want quick results and don't care how the page looks. Draft mode only works for printing text and numbers, not graphics. Although

```
The ImageWriter   printer  operating   in draft
mode.   For  a typical  two  page  memo,    the
true  speed   is about  50  characters   per
second.
```

Apple quotes a speed of 120 characters per second (cps),.
the true speed, including paper handling for a two-page
memo, is about 50 cps.

Standard Mode

At 72 dots per inch (dpi), standard printing gives
about the same resolution as the Mac screen (80 dpi),
so we get on paper whatever we see on the screen.

Standard and high-resolution modes use proportional
spacing, varying the letter width so a capital M takes up
more space than a capital I, a w more space than an l;
numerals all have the same width so columns of numbers
will line up properly. Nearly all software will print without
complications in standard mode. For a two-page memo,
the true speed is 28 cps.

The ImageWriter printer operating in
Standard mode. For a typical two page
memo, the true speed is about 28
characters per second.

When printing in standard mode, the software uses
the same typeface data file to generate both the screen display and the printed page.

High-Resolution Mode

At 144 by 160 dpi, high-resolution mode offers twice
the resolution of standard printing. To achieve this, the
printer prints twice as many dots horizontally and makes
two passes over the paper for every line. On the second
pass, the paper is rolled up the height of half a dot. For a
two-page memo, the true speed is 11 cps.

The ImageWriter printer operating in
High-resolution mode. For a typical
two page memo, the true speed is about
11 characters per second.

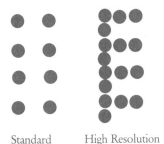

Standard   High Resolution

High-resolution printing uses twice as many dots per inch.

We cannot see on the screen what high-resolution printing will look like; the software puts in the additional dots when printing on paper. One way software creates high-resolution printed text is to shrink a double-size character to the size we need, using 24-point font data to create a 12-point printed character, for example.

Some graphics programs may not use high-resolution printing because they cannot interpolate, or fill in, the additional dots. If the program treats the image strictly as a set of dots, as MacPaint does, it has no way of knowing where to fill in additional dots for high resolution. For example, MacPaint does not know that a series of individual dots drawn in a row is a straight line, so it cannot tell if in high-resolution mode the dots should be discrete or a continuous line.

MacDraw, on the other hand, stores well-defined picture attributes. A straight line is always stored as a line of a particular length, orientation, and position. The letter A is stored according to its size, typeface, and location. The program, knowing the object's shape, can easily add dots in the proper places for high-resolution printing. Whenever we move an image, it is recreated from its attributes, not from a simple dot pattern.

Business graphics programs that produce bar charts or other unambiguous images also store picture attributes and can print at a higher resolution than the screen.

OTHER PRINTERS

You might wish to hook up a printer other than the ImageWriter for four reasons:

- Better print quality.
- Different features.
- Using a printer you already have.
- Lower cost.

Against these possible advantages, you must weigh some potential problems:

- Apple does not presently support any other printer models.

- Few printers will have all the ImageWriter features.

- Connecting a foreign printer may require special skills and experience.

- You may need extra-cost hardware accessories.

Beyond the hardware problems, each software package you use must also work with the printer; programs may have to be modified to work properly. If a program cannot be modified to work fully with a specific printer, you may get only text without typeface changes or graphics, or you may get nothing at all. Program modifications, when available, may cost money, though the charge is usually modest.

Virtually all software companies promise that their programs work with the ImageWriter, but they can't guarantee performance for printers with which they have no experience. Similarly, the printer companies won't know about every software product you might use, so there is no one to hold responsible if your programs don't work with your printer.

Letter-Quality Printers

The ImageWriter's high-resolution mode is fairly good, but doesn't reach the letter-quality standard of daisy-wheel printers and good electric typewriters; no dot-matrix printer does.

For business, you may need a true letter-quality printer. Such printers use a daisy wheel (or its close cousin, a thimble) embossed with molded letters. A print hammer strikes a petal, pressing it against the ribbon and paper and printing an entire character at once. In the most sophisticated daisy-wheel printers, the hammer strikes the letter M harder than it strikes a period, making the overall impression even. As with typewriters, print sharpness and resolution depend on the precision of each molded character. Since daisy-wheel printers generally use carbon ribbons that are discarded after one use, ribbon condition matters less than for dot-matrix printers.

But although daisy-wheel printers produce good-looking type, they have many disadvantages.

- They are slow, typically printing 8 to 40 characters per second (cps); dot-matrix printers generally operate at 50 to 200 cps.

- They are noisy, usually worse than dot-matrix printers, though lacking the high-pitched whine of a dot-matrix unit.

- They are limited to one typeface at a time. We can change typefaces by changing the daisy wheel but that slows printing considerably.

• Type size is limited by the size of the daisy wheel itself, so we can only get print sizes available on normal typewriters.

abc def ghi jkl

Daisy wheel print DAISY WHEEL PRINT
This is a sample of 15 pitch type.
ABCDEFGHIJKLMNOPQRSTUVWXYZ

mno pqr

Daisy wheel print DAISY WHEEL PRINT
This is a sample of 12 pitch type.
ABCDEFGHIJKLMNOPQRSTUVWXYZ

stu

Daisy wheel print DAISY WHEEL PRINT
This is a sample of 10 pitch type.
ABCDEFGHIJKLMNOPQRSTUVWXYZ

wxy

Print sizes available on a daisy-wheel printer and an ImageWriter.

Most important, daisy-wheel printers are only good for characters; they cannot effectively print graphics. Some daisy-wheel printers use the period to build up graphics images, in effect imitating a dot-matrix printer, but the process is slow, and the period petal on the daisy wheel wears out quickly.

Business users will probably need two printers, a dot-matrix model for graphics and a daisy-wheel model for letter-quality printing. Assimilation Process offers a driver for popular daisy-wheel printers.

Printing with an electronic typewriter

If you have an electronic typewriter, you might want to use it as a printer. You could use an ImageWriter for everyday printing and graphics, reserving the electronic typewriter for the occasional business letter. But there are drawbacks.

Like any daisy-wheel printer, the typewriter will print in only one font, without graphics. Typewriters print very slowly. If you regularly print documents more than a page long, you will have to find printer-driver software that lets you pause for paper changes. Even if you have such a driver, you will probably find changing the paper a nuisance. A few electronic typewriters have an optional tractor feed—a mechanical feeder for continuous form-feed computer paper. Of course, you will also need a suitable serial hardware interface for the typewriter.

Printer Compatibility

Tokyo Electric builds not only the ImageWriter for Apple but also printers sold by many other companies; in some cases the units share the same printing mechanism even though the external cosmetics differ. However, the printers may also differ in their electronic circuits. All printers contain a small processor and a program stored on a ROM chip that converts incoming information into a dot pattern on paper. The ROM inside the ImageWriter differs from other current Tokyo Electric printers. Although Tokyo Electric developed the special ImageWriter ROM to Apple's specifications, Apple does not have exclusive rights to it; Tokyo Electric printers that work properly with the Macintosh may thus appear from non-Apple sources.

Other printer companies may install ROMs inside their printers that work like the ImageWriter's. If a company advertises a printer as "Macintosh compatible," check the printer carefully. Does compatible mean only that text will print but not graphics? Do the height and width of the dots match the Macintosh's exactly, or are the dots squeezed horizontally or vertically? In the computer industry, many claims of compatibility evaporate on close inspection.

Okidata makes a version of its Microline 92 printer that emulates the ImageWriter; Epson has a software driver for using its FX-80 printer with a Macintosh.

Connecting a Non-Macintosh Printer

The best way to connect a non-Macintosh printer is to find someone who has done it already and copy the technique exactly.

You can adapt the Macintosh itself by changing the printer-driver program (the file "ImageWriter" on System disks). Although Apple initially supplies a driver program only for the ImageWriter, many more printer drivers will be available from third-party software vendors.

WHAT TO LOOK FOR IN A PRINTER

There will soon be many printers available for the Macintosh; before you buy any printer, ask yourself these questions:

- Is it easy to thread in form-feed paper?

- How quickly can you change from form-feed paper to single sheets (like letterhead) and back again?

- How fast does the printer print? Manufacturers usually quote printing speed in characters per second, advertising the most optimistic measurement. Most specifications do not take into account the time to advance the paper by a line or to the next page. When these times are included, overall printing speed is much lower, particularly for low-cost printers that lack a true form feed (they can only advance a line at a time; better printers can move an entire page quickly).

- Do you need a sheet feeder for loading successive individual sheets, such as letterhead?

- Do you need a wide carriage? The ImageWriter has a 10-inch wide carriage. Printers with wider carriages will let you create larger images, although some software may not initially take advantage of such width. The MacWrite program does not let you create documents wider than the screen, for example, although other programs do. A wide-carriage version of the ImageWriter will be available.

Cost

Here are approximate printer costs:

ImageWriter	$ 500
Conventional dot-matrix printers	$ 200 to $700
Fast dot-matrix printers	
Over 200 cps	$1000 and up
Electronic typewriters	$ 300 and up
Interfaces	$ 100 and up
Daisy-wheel printers	
15 cps	$ 500 to $700
35 cps	$1500 and up
Tractor feeds	$ 125 to $300
Sheet feeders	$ 235 to $1200

Ongoing Costs

Total printer costs include not only the purchase price but the cost of keeping the printer fed with ribbons and paper. Although paper costs the same for any printer, ribbon costs vary widely.

Printer ribbons

The carbon ribbons in daisy-wheel printers are the most expensive, often running about 3 cents per page. When considering a printer, find out if it uses standard ribbons available from many sources, or if the printer manufacturer treats you as a captive audience for over-priced ribbons.

Dot-matrix printers generally use cloth (nylon) ribbons. Unlike the fixed-length carbon ribbons, cloth ribbons form an endless loop inside the case. Ribbon longevity thus depends on your tolerance for slowly fading ink. Many users keep an older ribbon for routine printing and a nearly new ribbon for important jobs.

The ImageWriter ribbon is the same one used on the earlier Apple dot-matrix printer and some others, including the NEC 8023, C. Itoh 8510, and DEC LA50.

Depending on printer/ribbon design, you have several choices for replacing cloth ribbons:

- Buy a new one.

- Replace only the ribbon if the case can be opened and you don't mind messy fingers (in some printers, you can simply turn the ribbon over and print on another portion of the ribbon).

- Re-ink the ribbon using a kit advertised in computer hobby magazines.

One simple way to rejuvenate a fading cloth ribbon is to open the case and spray a little WD-40 or similar lubricant on the ribbon. Let the ribbon sit for a few minutes after spraying. The lubricant acts as a solvent, spreading more of the ink over the ribbon's surface. Eventually, though, the fabric itself will wear out, and you will have to replace the whole thing.

One last hint: Don't stockpile ribbons; because the ink dries out, just keep enough for a few months rather than a few years.

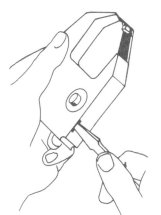

Open the ribbon case with a small screwdriver.

Paper

Form-feed paper

Form-feed computer paper has extra margins with holes that fit into a tractor feed; perforations let you tear off the edges for a clean finish. Form-feed paper comes in many styles and weights. For normal use, buy 20-pound, 9½- by 11-inch paper; tearing off the perforations will leave 8½- by 11-inch paper. In Europe and Japan you can set Mac's software for the slightly narrower and longer A4 size.

Removing the perforated margins of ordinary form-feed paper leaves the edges slightly ragged, but you can buy more expensive paper with much smaller perforations and much cleaner edges, suitable even for letterhead. Your dealer should be able to order special paper, as well as multipart forms for simultaneous printing of an original and several copies.

Mailing labels also come on form-feed stock. The labels are normally sized for six lines per inch. You will have to experiment with the ImageWriter; its spacing varies with font size.

Printer Stands

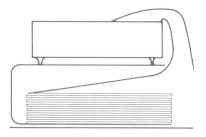

A printer stand makes it easy to use a printer on a table.

A printer stand can simplify operations by keeping form-feed paper from becoming tangled on the floor. If you have the space, build or buy a stand with space below the printer for a large box of paper. If space is limited, simple stands will fit on a table top. In all cases, check that paper leaving the printer doesn't interfere with paper feeding in.

Printer Sound Hoods

The ImageWriter is relatively quiet, but all impact printers—dot-matrix and daisy-wheel—make too much noise for anyone to work nearby; you can't carry on a telephone conversation in the same room. A sound

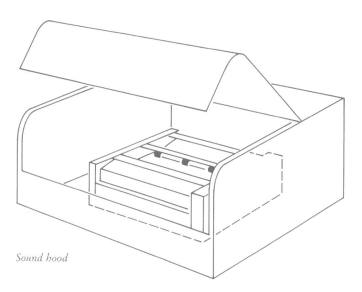

Sound hood

hood—a large, bulky box with a sound-absorbing lining—can make life with a printer much more peaceful. Prices run from $100 to $500.

If you use a hood, make sure that the printer has adequate ventilation, and check paper handling with the hood on; many hoods make getting at the paper very difficult.

Ink-jet and laser printers (see Chapter 24) are inherently quiet and do not need hoods.

PLOTTERS

Instead of printing dots, plotters draw lines by moving a pen directly on paper. Ballpoint, felt-tip, and liquid-ink pens produce a more even, continuous line than most dot-matrix printers, and many plotters offer a choice of pen colors. With suitable inks, a pen can write on transparent sheets for overhead projectors.

But plotters generate characters slowly and can't shade or fill in regions as well as dot-matrix printers can. As dot-matrix resolution has improved, plotters have lost ground, more and more becoming tools for specialists.

Chapter *Modems*
19

M any Mac owners will need a modem. Modems convert a computer's digital signals into modulated audio tones that can travel on a telephone line. They also do the reverse, demodulating the audio tones from a distant computer and modem back into digital form for your Mac. ("Modem" is contracted from MOdulator/DEModulator.)

THE APPLE MODEMS

Apple markets both a 300- and a 1200-baud modem for Mac. For these and other 300- and 1200-baud modems, a baud is a transmission speed equivalent to one bit per second. Most microcomputer owners have used 300-baud modems, which transmit 25 to 30 characters per second (cps). Thirty cps is slow, taking a minute to fill a Mac screen with characters, or up to 12 minutes to fill it with graphics. Despite this slow operation, 300-baud modems have been popular among hobbyists because of price— from $50 to $300. Higher-speed modems use more expensive components built to closer tolerances; 1200-baud models cost from $300 to $900. Unless you are on a very tight budget, 1200-baud modems are worth the extra money. They operate four times as fast, transmitting 100 to 120 cps. Most 1200-baud modems, including the Apple model, will also operate at 300 baud.

Compatibility with Other Modems

Compatibility among the many modems and communications schemes available is an extremely complex subject; I discuss it in depth in Chapter 27. For now, I will simply say that the Apple modems use the same signaling frequencies as other microcomputer modems sold in North America, so different modem brands are compatible as long as they operate at the same baud rate.

A modem protocol specifies which audio frequencies will carry the information and other details. All 300-baud modems use the Bell 103 protocol; most modern 1200-baud modems, including the Apple Modem, use the Bell 212A protocol. Bell Laboratories originally set the standards and gave the protocols their names. Avoid other 1200-baud protocols, at least in North America.

In addition to setting the correct modem protocol, you must make sure several other layers of protocol are compatible. Chapter 9 gives you a simple guide to setting these protocols, and Chapter 27 covers protocol issues more comprehensively. The Apple modems only operate asynchronously; they do not support synchronous communications.

Modem/Software Compatibility

The Apple modems contain control circuitry able to dial phone numbers, check the phone line, and hang up. To take advantage of these features, your communications software must send suitable instructions to the modem. The Apple modem's instruction set is similar to, but not completely compatible with, the Hayes Smartmodem models, which are among the most popular in the microcomputer industry. The similarity will create considerable confusion; software for one model may not work with the other. (This compatibility problem affects only the commands between the software and the modem, not modem-to-modem compatibility.)

Well-designed communications software includes installation procedures for different types of modems. If you buy a non-Apple modem, make sure that it will work with your software; as always, be wary of compatibility claims. Many companies claim that their modems work just like the Hayes, but they don't. Now companies may claim their modems work just like the Apple units.

CONNECTING THE MODEM

Whenever possible, the modem should connect directly to the telephone line through a modular jack. If your phone connection at the wall uses a four-pronged plug, buy a high-quality adapter plug; the cheap adapters aren't reliable.

Modems should not be connected to party lines. Another party picking up a telephone will disturb the computer link; in an emergency, another party cannot ask for the line.

Some telephone convenience features such as call waiting and forwarding that produce an audible sound may interfere with computer links. If the interference is rare, you may be able to live with it; otherwise you should disconnect these telephone features.

If you are traveling, you may not be able to connect your modem directly to the phone line. You will have to resort to an acoustic modem with cups, a small microphone and speaker that fit over a standard telephone receiver. Acoustic modems are less reliable because of noise and other problems. Always use a direct-connect modem when possible.

Acoustic cups fit over a standard telephone receiver.

USING MODEMS

The efficiency of modem communications varies with phone-line quality. Modem connections using local calls generally work satisfactorily, but long-distance calls frequently run into problems because of noisy lines. You may find that some long-distance services, such as AT&T, MCI, and Sprint, have noisier lines than others. The line quality can also vary with the time of day; during peak periods the lines will have more cross-talk (leakage from other conversations) than at nighttime. Also bear in mind that the lines of some cheaper long-distance services simply won't carry information at 1200 baud. If you have trouble at 1200 baud, try another line or switch to 300 baud and try again. In some cases, the local phone company can check your line for transmission quality.

Dialing

The Apple modem and most other modern modems now include automatic dialing and answering, so you can dial the telephone number from the keyboard (or use numbers stored on disk) and the receiving modem can automatically answer the call. Take care to turn off your modem's auto-answering feature unless incoming calls on the line are exclusively from computers; otherwise a human caller will be greeted with an irritating, high-pitched tone.

The Apple modem can dial either tones or pulses; you select one or the other depending on whether you have touch-tone or rotary-dial service. If the dial tone does not stop when the modem starts dialing numbers, check if your telephone service can handle touch-tone dialing. If so, find a way to reverse the red and green wires of the phone line.

Long-distance charges and billing

Whenever possible, you should make modem connections to other computers purely electronically: an auto-dial modem should call an auto-answer modem. In some cases, you may need to start the link through a human operator. A typical case might be:

- Dial the phone number manually through an operator.

- When the operator answers, arrange for a collect or credit-card call.

- Wait for the connection to be completed.

- If the call is collect, the other party must accept the charges.

- Arrange with the other party to switch to data mode.

- Switch together to data mode.

But you don't always have to deal with a human operator for a credit-card or an alternative long-distance service call. The exact procedure varies by area, but generally you do one of the following:

Credit-card call (touch-tone dialing services only; not available in all areas):

- Dial 0 and the complete long-distance number.

- After two or three rings, you hear an acknowledgment tone.

- When the tone sounds, dial your credit-card number. (If you wait, the special tone stops and a human operator comes on the line.)

Alternative long-distance service call:

- Dial a local access number.

- After two or three rings, you hear an acknowledgment tone.

- Dial your account number.

- Dial the complete long-distance number.

To perform the entire dialing procedure with an auto-dialing modem, you need to time the delay between completion of dialing and the start of the acknowledgment tone. For the Apple modems, insert commas into the dialing string for each two-second delay required.

For example, if you are dialing from inside a company through a private branch exchange, the dialing string 9,02135551234,,,1222-5551111 will cause the modem to:

- Dial 9, and wait two seconds, allowing time to receive an outside dial tone (the Apple modem does not detect dial tones).

- Dial 0-213-555-1234, indicating to the phone company that you are making a long-distance call with assistance—but you will not actually use operator assistance.

- Wait six seconds, long enough for the call to clear the phone company's exchange, ring the operator twice, and get an acknowledgment tone.

- Dial 1222-555-1111, the credit-card (calling-card) number during the acknowledgment tone. The operator will not come on line if the card number is dialed at this time.

For the exact sequence, consult the modem and communications-software manuals. You can change between pulse and tone dialing as required.

Making Connection

If you initiate the call, your modem will operate on the originate frequencies and the receiving modem on the answer frequencies. The two frequencies let each party send information simultaneously without interference.

The Apple modems contain an internal speaker so you can hear the connection until it switches over to data communications. With two 1200-baud auto-answer modems, this is the exact sequence:

- Your modem dials the other modem.

- The other modem answers the line with a 300-baud answer tone.

- Your modem responds with a 1200-baud phase-modulated originate tone.

- The other modem answers with a 1200-baud answer tone.

- Your modem switches to data mode and disconnects its speaker.

If the remote modem is a 300-baud unit, it will not respond to your modem's 1200-baud originate tone and so your modem switches to 300 baud.

If a human answers the phone, you should pick up an ordinary telephone and hang up the modem electronically.

Given the frequent problems with getting communications to work, you will probably find having a second phone line handy. With it, you can talk to the person operating the other computer while setting the parameters. Once you have established a link, store all the parameters. The connection should be easy next time, unless the line conditions have changed.

Chapter 20 Macintosh Software Issues

his chapter discusses several different software topics. If you have used other microcomputers or already have some experience with the Macintosh, you should find this grab-bag of topics useful. The topics include:

- The User Interface, which compares Mac's operational style with that of earlier designs.

- Other Operating Systems, which discusses the advantages and disadvantages of running other operating systems on a Macintosh.

- Choosing Software, which offers general guidelines on how to buy software that best meets your needs.

- Exchanging Information Between Programs, which explores what you can and cannot do when transferring information.

THE USER INTERFACE

At any given time while operating a microcomputer, you make choices—to open a file, close a file, insert or delete text, and so forth. Software designers face two key problems:

- How does the computer show you what choices are available?

- How do you indicate your selection?

Software designers have developed several types of interface as solutions to these problems. Solutions for Mac differ from solutions for other microcomputers because many essential software components are built in as an integral part of the computer. To understand the implications of this design difference, we'll first consider more conventional microcomputers.

Conventional Interfaces

Conventional interfaces are all based only on text because many computers cannot handle graphics well.

Command lines

With a command-line interface, the screen shows a prompt, such as A> or $, indicating that the program is ready to accept a command. There is no other information; you must know what to type next, and you must type it precisely.

Command lines are the easiest interfaces to program and the hardest to learn, but they offer great flexibility since the program can recognize any keyboard entry. Examples of command-line interfaces include CP/M-80, MS-DOS, and Microsoft BASIC.

Menu initials

With a menu-initial interface, you are presented with a menu of single-letter abbreviations for possible choices.

```
B C D E F G I M
```

Given a display such as B C D E F G I M, you must know which letter represents your choice. Often your choice results in the display of a second-level menu with more letters prompting a further choice. Still fairly cryptic, menu initials are nevertheless a little easier than command lines. Examples of menu-initial interfaces include VisiCalc™ and SuperCalc®.

Menu words

With a menu-word interface, instead of initials, you are given a list of words representing the possible choices.

```
Load Run Numerical Format Help
Copy GoTo Reset Quit
```

Again, selecting an item may take you to a second-level menu with more words prompting a further choice. Less cryptic than menu initials, menu words take more space on the screen. Examples of menu-word interfaces include non-Macintosh Multiplan, Lotus 1-2-3™, and VisiOn™.

Menus

With menu-driven interfaces, you are presented with a complete menu from which to make your selection. The menu takes up the full screen; with each choice a new menu appears until the selection process is complete.

```
Open a New Document
Load an Old Document
Merge another Document
Copy a File
Delete a File
Disk Directory
```

Menu-driven interfaces are good for the novice, since there is enough space for full instructions, but exasperating for experts because of slow operation. Examples of menu-driven interfaces include Wang word processors and Peachtree Software® Accounting.

A New Solution: The Visual Interface

Beginning in the 1960s, computer research groups began looking for ways to get around the user-interface logjam, setting as key requirements ease of use, consistency, and familiarity. XEROX's Palo Alto Research Center

(PARC) developed the mouse/icon/pull-down menu interface that is the most successful yet. The interface can provide many choices without interfering with ongoing work. You select a menu category from a menu bar, and "pull-down" the menu with a mouse. (Or the menu bar runs along the screen bottom and "pops-up.") The work area is obscured only while making the menu selection. Apple built the PARC interface into its Lisa and Macintosh.

The Impact on Programs

Apple encourages software developers to use the new visual interface; all the first Macintosh programs do. If the momentum continues, later software developers will feel much pressure to follow suit. Programmers who try to use a different interface will find their product hard to sell, for it won't be what Macintosh users expect.

Programs that were originally designed for other microcomputers will be available for the Macintosh in two forms: conventional interface and visual interface.

Conventional interface versions

Some companies will adapt their programs to run on the Macintosh as they do on other microcomputers. Avoid these programs unless they meet a specific need; even then you should probably replace the program when a Mac-style equivalent appears.

Visual interface versions

Other software companies will rewrite their programs taking advantage of the visual interface. You will use Mac's interface, but the programs will still retain their unique features and capabilities. In many cases the Mac version will use the same file format as versions for other computers so that it can exchange information with the other versions running on a conventional microcomputer. Chapter 28 discusses information exchange further.

Software for the Mac doesn't have to use the Mac interface; a programmer can write an entirely different interface or, more likely, add new elements to the present one. Some advanced software will probably do this.

Is Mac's visual interface the optimum one? No one really knows; the next ten years should see much more development of interfaces than the last thirty. Although the exact direction is unknown, future interfaces will clearly use graphics and will generally be more like Mac's than the command-line interfaces common in other computers.

Onward to specific software topics.

OTHER OPERATING SYSTEMS

As with any major new computer design, the Macintosh will at first suffer from a shortage of software until developers finish the programs they are in the process of writing. Until the software flood begins, Macintosh owners might look longingly at the many programs available for other computers and other operating systems.

Can you run another operating system on a Macintosh? Possibly...

With a few exceptions, other common microcomputer operating systems cannot run directly on Mac. Most operating systems were designed for other CPU chips and are incompatible because each chip type uses a different set of instructions. For example, the operating systems for the Apple II, IIe, and III run on the 6502 chip; TRSDOS® and CP/M-80 run on the Z80 chip; and MS-DOS and CP/M-86 run on the 8088, 8086, and 80186 chips.

Many microcomputers besides Macintosh use the Motorola 68000 chip. The other models use operating systems that generally require a different arrangement of hardware than Mac's. Apple's Lisa has a 68000 chip, but the Lisa operating system requires much more memory than the Macintosh has. Lisa 2 can, however, use Mac's operating system and most software.

While most operating systems cannot run on Mac, a few could possibly be adapted, though their advantages may not be great enough to tempt the average user away from the Macintosh's own operating system.

UNIX

The UNIX™ operating system, developed by Bell Laboratories for minicomputers, has been the most widely discussed operating system for sophisticated microcomputers. Versions of UNIX can run on microcomputers with 68000 CPUs; however, they require a minimum of 256 KB RAM and over a megabyte of disk storage, more than the first Mac model has. Future Macintosh models with more memory and hard-disk drives might use UNIX or a derivative, such as Microsoft® XENIX™. (Suitably configured Lisas can run UNIX/XENIX already.)

UNIX uses a command-line interface, even more cryptic than the average. Programmers enjoy special features in UNIX that make their lives easier, but successful application programs in UNIX will have to hide the command-line interface with a more modern one. Some parts of the Macintosh interface could be adapted to operate with UNIX.

CP/M-68K

CP/M-68K™ from Digital Research, Inc., a version of CP/M designed to run on the Motorola 68000 chip, could run on Mac, although it would offer few advantages. It is a traditional, cryptic command-line operating system. Even if CP/M-68K does run on the Mac, few CP/M-based programs will work; these programs are mostly written for CP/M-80 (and a few for CP/M-86™), a different and incompatible version of CP/M.

UCSD p-System

The UCSD p-System® also could run on the Macintosh. Softech Microsystems, which sells the p-System, has a version that works on 68000-based computers. A Macintosh has adequate memory to run p-System programs, but since these programs generally use older design concepts, Mac owners have little incentive to adopt the UCSD p-System.

Emulation: CP/M-80

Some of the operating systems used on micros with 8-bit CPU chips could conceivably run on a Macintosh if its 68000 chip were programmed to behave like (emulate) an 8-bit CPU chip. The most likely candidate for such emulation is the Z80 CPU with the CP/M-80 operating system. Although emulation works, performance is very poor—much slower than the original 8-bit chip.

Hardware Accessories: CP/M-80 and MS-DOS

Still another possibility would let Mac owners run a different operating system through add-on hardware. Products of this type for the Apple II include the Softcard™ (for CP/M-80) and the Rana module (for MS-DOS). These hardware additions contain a new microprocessor chip and associated circuitry—in effect another microcomputer. The Apple II operates as a terminal, supplying the keyboard and video display for the new microprocessor.

Hardware accessories such as these could let Mac run either CP/M-80 or MS-DOS software. Software is no longer being developed for CP/M-80, but the MS-DOS software base is large and growing, and includes many of the best new programs. Lisa 2 will run MS-DOS programs with an accessory. However, many MS-DOS programs have been developed specifically for use on the IBM PC; because of differences in the keyboard, screen, and other hardware, Lisa 2 and the Rana module for the Apple II are not compatible with IBM PC software, although some of the simplest programs for the PC may work.

The MS-DOS compatibility problems will ease as Microsoft® Windows and other hardware-independent systems become popular. With Windows, software independent of the specific computer model can be designed; the operating system translates the screen graphics from the program to match the actual hardware. Windows, like other MS-DOS products, requires an Intel® 8088, 8086, or related CPU chip, so you will need a hardware accessory like the Rana module on your Macintosh.

227

The cost of products like the Rana module is high enough that you may prefer to buy a separate MS-DOS computer, perhaps one of the cheaper IBM PC imitations. Then, with suitable communications software, you can transfer information back and forth between computers, using each micro for those tasks it does best. Be warned, though, that using Mac software and MS-DOS at the same time, whether through a Mac add-on or a separate computer, will magnify the fundamental differences between the two interface types.

In summary, don't bother with other operating systems or hardware accessories that can add a new microprocessor unless you have no alternative. Remember that conventional operating systems all use old-fashioned interfaces.

CHOOSING SOFTWARE

For all the important computer uses, there will be many competing software packages. For each software type, most packages will include the essential features. So how do you choose among them?

The choice may depend less on specific features than on how well the program meshes with your other work. Software selection between competing packages rests on such issues as personal preference, an analysis of your needs, and, increasingly important, compatibility among programs.

Past Experience

What have you used in the past? What are you familiar with? Even though the learning time for a new program on the Macintosh is short compared to other computers, if you are satisfied with a company's products, you should try them first for a new program.

Growth

Will the software grow with your needs? For example, can you increase the complexity of your models in a spreadsheet program? Can you incorporate information produced by other users in your spreadsheet?

If a program cannot expand with your changing needs, it may be a dead end; you may have to start over with a new program. A well-designed, complex program will let you use its simpler features without fuss; you can start using the more sophisticated features when you need them.

Style

Do you like the way the program works? Many programs try to anticipate your next step. This works well on some programs; on others, it gets in your way. You will develop your own ideas of how a program should work. Companies that develop their own software try to give each of their products the same "feel." Companies that simply sell software developed by others generally don't try to maintain as strong a relationship between programs.

Complexity

How complex is the program? Will you need all the features? If you never need to use the sophisticated interrelationships of a relational data base, you may not find one worth the investment in time and money; a much simpler and quicker file manager may do everything you need. Be careful, though; it may be better to err on the side of more power rather than less.

Generally, the more complex the program, the harder it is to learn and use. All complex programs contain features that you will rarely need and may not remember how to use on the rare occasions when you need them. However, some complex, rarely used commands can be duplicated with a simpler program by going through several steps. This might take longer, but if you are fluent with each of those steps, you will have less trouble than trying to remember every nook and cranny of a complex program.

Manuals

Is the program's manual well written and effectively organized? Does it use the same wording for operations as

Apple's manuals or this book? Apple provides a writing style guide, so anyone who writes about Macintosh software should use the same terms, such as *choosing* a menu item and *selecting* some text.

Support

Can the dealer you bought the software from adequately help you if you have a problem? Can a friend or business associate help out?

Compatibility

Will this program work with your other software? Can it transfer files to and from your other programs and other computers? With some programs you may need to do further work before the information is ready to use.

Although software selection has traditionally rested more on personal preference than any other criterion, more and more decisions will depend on compatibility. Software integration is a key concept that will take computers to a new level of productivity, and programs will increasingly be judged by their ability to exchange information with other programs and other computers. The next section discusses this issue in greater detail; see Chapter 28 for a guide to moving information from other computers to a Macintosh.

HOW MACINTOSH PROGRAMS EXCHANGE INFORMATION

Macintosh programs can exchange information in four fundamental ways:

- Through the Clipboard and Scrapbook.

- With a screen dump.

- By reading data files.

- Through special links between two programs.

The Clipboard and Scrapbook

Whenever you put something in the Clipboard (stored in RAM usually) or the Scrapbook (stored on disk), the information is saved in up to three forms:

- As a data file, using the format specific to the application.

- As an ASCII text file, without formatting.

- As a picture file, in the QuickDraw format used by most Macintosh graphics programs.

The originating program stores multiple formats because it cannot tell where the information is going; the safest strategy is to give the receiving program a choice. Not all programs or situations produce a Clipboard or Scrapbook in all three formats. In some cases involving large amounts of information, the program may give you a choice of how to store the Clipboard/Scrapbook.

The amount of memory available at times imposes limits on how much information you can put in the Clipboard. You may have to move the information in several blocks. The Scrapbook size is limited by available disk space.

When you paste something from the Clipboard or the Scrapbook, the receiving program checks the file formats and uses the most suitable file it can understand. Some programs may only understand their own Clipboard and you won't be able to paste in information from another program to them; a few programs might not be able to read any Clipboards at all.

As examples, a text file could be converted into a pictorial image of the text and merged into a graphics file, or a picture could be treated as a block and placed in a word-processing file to be printed along with the text. Because the files were created in such different ways, in most cases you won't be able to modify the picture file with the word processor or modify the text file with the graphics program. MacWrite can use MacPaint information pasted in from the Clipboard or Scrapbook, and vice versa. MacWrite can perform some simple changes to a MacPaint file included in text, such as moving or stretching it, but for any substantive changes, you have to go back to MacPaint.

Screen Dumps

If a program will not create a QuickDraw file for the Clipboard or Scrapbook, you can at all times save the program's screen image on disk (a screen dump) by typing Shift-Command 3. This operation creates a QuickDraw graphics file, called Screen0, on the disk. A second screen-dump file will be named Screen1, and so on.

You can look at, modify, and print the screen image with MacPaint. Within MacPaint, you can select the image and put part or all of it into the Clipboard. (You can print the whole screen dump by typing Shift-Command 4, or print just the top, or active, window with Caps Lock-Shift-Command 4.)

Reading Data Files

While nearly all programs should let you move some information with the Clipboard and Scrapbook, more complete information exchange requires that two programs be able to read the same data files.

Most Macintosh programs store files in a data format unique to the program. Data files come in many formats that have not been standardized, and no standard data format is likely. Some formats are shared by several different programs and some programs can generate multiple data-file formats.

Special data files include formatted text files, such as those created by MacWrite or Microsoft Word for storing text with formatting information—the typeface and size, margins, and tabs, for example. The two programs do not create compatible data files, but can exchange ASCII text files.

Other program types will create their own specialized data files. Each spreadsheet program will probably use its own unique format for the formulas and interrelations between the cells in a spreadsheet. Structured data programs, such as Microsoft Chart, store graphics in their own special format, again usually incompatible with other graphics programs, even if they incorporate some elements of QuickDraw.

Whether a program uses a particular file format is an important consideration in selecting Macintosh software. All the programs that you use regularly should be able to exchange suitable data. Data files can be transferred at several levels:

- Most desirable: Two programs can read each other's files directly.

- Next most desirable: Two programs use a common special file format, such as SYLK, that preserves all formulas and relationships.

- Better than nothing: Two programs use a common special file format that preserves current values, or all text-formatting information.

Common file formats only make sense for some classes of programs: A collection of accounting programs might read a common file format; a word processor and a graphics program are unlikely to share files. Unless specifically promised as an application-program feature, you should not expect any program to read another program's disk files.

Data Links for Information Transfer

Where complete file compatibility does not make sense, two programs might have special provisions to pass along specific information. For example, when you construct a spreadsheet with Multiplan, you can copy values you want plotted to the Clipboard. Then, with Microsoft Chart, you can paste these values into the graph data. Chart lets you choose whether you want to paste data just once, or whether you want to establish a link. With a link, you can change the Multiplan values and Chart will automatically look at the same spreadsheet locations for new values to plot.

Other programs designed to work together will appear as well, initially from the same software company. A successful program will attract other programs that can use its data.

Chapter 21 Problem-Solving

Your Macintosh will need only minimal maintenance and probably few, if any, repairs. If you encounter a problem that you suspect may be a hardware or software failure, try to reproduce the problem on another Macintosh. If you can reproduce the problem, it is either in the software or in the disk itself; try a different disk (not a copy of the suspect disk). If the problem persists, you probably have a software bug; if not, the first disk was probably faulty.

If you cannot reproduce the problem on another Macintosh, you may have a hardware problem. We're going to discuss some of the simplest and most common hardware problems; for more information about these and more serious problems, check your manuals and your dealer.

FAULTY CABLES

For any computer, the most failure-prone parts are the plugs and connectors. If you are having problems with any external component, try swapping cables first. Look at the plugs carefully. Are any pins bent? Some pins may be missing; this is normal, but compare with another unit if you have any doubt.

235

Before you swap cables, turn off the power to Mac and the accessory equipment. If you have problems when you are in the middle of an important piece of work, you may not want to turn off the power and thereby erase all the data you have in RAM. It is safe to unplug and check the cables to the mouse and the keyboard without turning off the power; it is best to turn off the power before unplugging anything connected to the serial port (some accessories may be damaged if you unplug them with the power on); and you should always turn off the power before unplugging an external disk drive.

GLITCHES

All computers are subject to glitches—minor problems that cause temporary setbacks but are not necessarily symptoms of disease. Often the best cure for a glitch is to turn off the computer and go away for a while; the problem may have disappeared by the time you start work again.

Static electricity can be an occasional problem. Many companies sell anti-static pads to put under your chair or to stand on, or pieces of metal you're supposed to touch before operating the computer. These products are effective only if grounded properly. They aren't usually necessary unless the air is so dry that you are personally uncomfortable and you set off sparks every time you touch a door knob.

Any computer will occasionally seize up so that you can't get anything to work. With Mac, this kind of glitch can be disconcerting because the mouse pointer may still work; it uses a separate portion of memory from the programs. Sometimes you won't be able to pin down the exact cause. If it is a software bug, the same thing should happen if you repeat each step exactly, but you won't always remember the steps exactly; something you did hours earlier could be the cause. Otherwise, it might be the power line or static electricity; or a bit of dust can make a disk temporarily unreadable. If the disk-drive head has gone on to read another part of the disk, it may be able to come back and read a track that was faulty minutes earlier.

Some problems simply have no explanation. You may sometimes run into a problem that does not repeat, and you will never know why it occurred. The semiconductor memory chips used in all computers are susceptible to errors resulting from bit changes induced by cosmic rays, though such errors are rare—much less than once per year. Rather than spending hours trying to figure out a problem that you cannot get Mac to repeat, accept that these things happen once in a while, even with the largest, most expensive computers.

If a particular program locks up frequently, install the INTERRUPT RESET buttons on the left grille; see the Macintosh manual. Press RESET to restart the computer. The switch is essential for programmers, since unfinished programs often behave badly and lock up the computer.

IF A DISK GETS STUCK

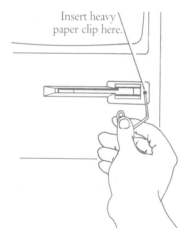

Insert heavy paper clip here.

Removing a disk using a heavy paper clip (if the power has failed)

If the computer seizes up and you can't get any response, there are three ways to remove your disk (all of them will erase RAM and may make the disk or parts of it unreadable):

- Press the reset button on the left side, if you've installed it. The computer will restart as if you had just turned it on.

- Turn off the power, press and hold down the mouse button, and turn the power back on. The disk drive will eject the disk.

- If the power has failed, you can remove the disk mechanically by inserting a heavy pin (a heavy paper clip bent open) into the small hole just to the right of the disk-drive slot.

POWER LINE PROBLEMS

Many companies sell power-line conditioners, costing $15 to $100, that eliminate short, sharp voltage pulses or the high-frequency interference that can induce errors in a computer. Whether you need a power-line conditioner depends on the quality of your power source and on what else is connected to it. If your Mac locks up or produces errors whenever an appliance is turned on elsewhere in the building, you should try a power-line conditioner.

If you have a choice, plug your Mac into an electrical circuit that is not used for any heavy equipment, such as air conditioners, refrigerators, power tools, or vacuum cleaners. The motors in these devices can generate a transient power-line spike that can occasionally be damaging. Vacuum cleaners are especially insidious, since they move around, unlike refrigerators. If you see a vacuum cleaner coming your way, save your file to disk, eject and restart the disk. Then continue working; you probably won't have a problem, but it's best not to take chances. Once you're sure a potential hazard creates no problems, you can ignore it.

Brown-Outs

A Macintosh is fairly resistant to brown-outs, or low-voltage periods. Although the announced specifications call for the Mac to operate on 105 to 130 volts, it actually runs satisfactorily with as little as 95 volts. If you need a little more margin, the international version has an even more tolerant power supply, specified for 90 to 130 volts in the low range, switchable to 180 to 260 volts in the high range. This version will actually run on 85 to 135 volts (low) and 170 to 270 volts (high). The power-line frequency doesn't matter; the specifications call for 47 to 64 Hz, but the power supply will actually run on anything from 30 Hz to 20 kHz. The leakage current increases with higher power-line frequencies; make sure your computer is properly grounded. The built-in clock/calendar uses its own quartz oscillator and does not depend on the power-line frequency.

Severe Electrical Storms

In case of a severe storm, unplug the computer and disconnect the modem from the telephone line.

Power Failures

Power failures are another threat. Whenever the power fails, everything in Mac's RAM disappears, and any open file remaining on disk may be lost as well. There are several steps you can take to combat this threat; three involve the purchase of more accessories, and the fourth involves the development of cautious work habits.

Uninterruptible power supplies

You can buy an uninterruptible power supply (UPS). These external accessories consist of a battery, an inverter (which converts the DC power from the battery to AC), and a fast power switch. If the main power fails, the unit quickly switches to the battery. The switching is so fast that the computer does not notice the change.

The battery usually stores sufficient power for 15 to 20 minutes' work, enough for you to close all your files and turn off the machine gracefully. Some UPS units have much larger batteries. For Mac, the UPS must be capable of supplying 75 watts of power. A UPS normally includes power-line conditioning as well.

Permanent battery operation

You can run off batteries (through an inverter) all the time. When you aren't using the computer, the battery is charged from an AC power supply or generator.

An inverter with a square-wave power output works satisfactorily. Battery operation may be wise if you are working in an area with exceptionally unreliable power or if you have no conventional power source. Because of battery maintenance problems, however, you probably shouldn't use a battery all the time unless you have to.

Recovering disk files

A few of the programs you buy may be designed to write the information in RAM to disk whenever you haven't entered anything from the keyboard for some time. Automatic disk writing is a powerful feature if the information written to disk can be recovered after a power failure. The recovery process itself may be a lengthy one, but any recovery is better than no recovery.

You can also buy a separate scavenger program that can save data by recovering it from disks that have not been properly closed. Scavenger programs are often hard to use, however, and cannot always recover a file. You will find it easier to save your information regularly than to rely on these programs.

Cautious work habits

One of the most undramatic and yet powerful ways to ward off the threat of power failures is to get in the habit of safeguarding your work. Two habits to get into:

Saving on disk frequently. You should save your work on a disk (from RAM) frequently. If there is a power failure, you will generally only lose whatever work you've done since the last save.

Warning: It is not enough to choose Save from the File menu in many programs, since the disk buffer is not always written to disk. Check the software manual to learn whether information is saved without ejecting the disk. The manual may not tell you; in this case, the only way to ensure that the file is properly closed and recorded on disk is to eject the disk; Mac closes files and writes the disk buffer before ejection. Then you can reinsert the disk.

Printing back-ups. For some types of work, a printed copy can act as a back-up. Although not ideal, since you will have to retype everything, at least this mechanical procedure is simpler than having to rethink everything.

MAINTENANCE

The Macintosh is not like an automobile that requires periodic tune-ups to stay in shape. The following are some tips on maintenance.

Routine Cleaning

If you don't use a dustcover, dust will eventually build up inside Mac. Modest amounts of dust won't affect the computer.

With or without a dustcover, Mac's exterior will

probably need occasional cleaning. Dust with a damp cloth; use sparing amounts of a mild, non-abrasive household cleaner if necessary, but take care not to get anything dripping wet.

Clean the screen with a glass cleaner; again, avoid drips. Clean out the mouse ball chamber when necessary by removing the retaining ring and blowing out the lint and dust.

There is little agreement about cleaning disk-drive heads. Many heavy users of microcomputers have never cleaned their disk-drive heads in years of use and have had no problems. Others claim that regular cleaning is essential. If you aren't having any problems, don't bother cleaning the heads. Certainly you should not have to clean them more than once a year under normal conditions.

Long-Term Maintenance

With long-term use, the Macintosh's mechanical parts may require service and alignment. The disk drives and the printer may need such work after several years; the rest of the computer should never require service unless a part fails.

Mac's internal design makes it very difficult for casual tinkerers to repair. Hobbyists should note that few of the integrated circuits are mounted in sockets; all or nearly all of them are soldered in. The boards have four-layer circuits; the chance of damage is very high when unsoldering components with an ordinary soldering iron.

Chapter 22 *Getting Help*

Almost every computer user needs help at one time or another. Whether you're trying to find out what you did to make that valuable data file disappear or how to connect some esoteric accessory, there are resources that may help you.

MANUALS

Your first source of information should be the manuals that come with Mac, or with the hardware or software that's giving you the problem. Apple's manuals are the best in the microcomputer business and bear careful reading. The manuals supplied for non-Apple products may possibly be as innovative as the computer's manual, but more likely they will be as hard to use and follow as they usually are. No manual can ever answer all questions.

Good manuals are so rare that a case can be made for selecting software on the basis of the manual's quality alone. Generally, a company that puts the effort into a good manual is also a company that cares about its customers.

HOTLINES

The best established microcomputer companies maintain hotlines staffed by trained people who are able to answer technical questions. Many companies do not have a hotline and insist that you direct queries to the dealer; they will accept technical questions only from dealers. Your questions will often be misunderstood in the process. Hotlines usually work out better for the user. Where possible, buy only products supported with a hotline.

Hotlines are expensive to staff and maintain; if you use one, you do have some responsibilities. You should have made a reasonable effort to find the answer to your question in the manual, and you should expect information only about the products produced by the company you are calling. If you are calling because a program failed ("crashed"), be specific about exactly what happened, any error messages you might have seen, and any action you might have taken that could have caused the problem. If you are using any nonstandard component—hardware or software—note that as well.

For some products, the company may charge for hotline access; such charges may be fair. See whether competing products have such charges and compare carefully.

COMPUTER STORES

Of course, you can always go back to your dealer; however, dealer competence varies very widely. Some dealers are helpful far beyond the call of duty; others are unable to answer even the simplest, most straightforward questions. Generally, salespeople should be able to answer simple queries and check the operation of your unit against others. Beyond that, it's hard to tell you what to expect.

Growing numbers of computer stores are part of rapidly expanding chains, and the shortage of competent sales staff is acute; too many salespeople are thrust out onto the floor with minimal training. As a practical matter, no dealer can really afford to provide comprehensive support for all software and accessories the store might carry. It's too expensive, and personnel able to answer more sophisticated questions are too valuable to leave exposed to ordinary customers. Furthermore, such personnel can probably find higher-paying jobs elsewhere in the microcomputer industry.

If possible, ask your friends where they bought their Mac, accessories, or software, and whether they are satisfied with dealer support. If your friends are pleased, then you should buy from that dealer also. Avoid dealers with a poor reputation for service, even if the price is a little lower. Computers are complex enough that most people will need help from their dealer at some time.

If you find a good dealership, cherish it and recommend that your friends buy there. If you have major problems with a dealer, tell your friends also. Remember, however, that one incident doesn't mean a dealer is bad; fairness applies here as elsewhere.

As with any other fast-growing industry, the microcomputer industry has attracted fly-by-night operators. Check with the local Better Business Bureau or consumer groups if you have doubts about a dealer. Always be cautious if you are asked to pay in advance for any item not immediately available. A small cash deposit may be reasonable for an unusual item, but you should never have to put a deposit on anything a store regularly carries.

MAIL-ORDER COMPANIES

Computer magazines are full of ads from mail-order houses, generally promising quick service at low prices. They can be a good deal, or they can be a disaster. Many mail-order companies accept your order, charge your credit card, and do nothing for as long as possible. The honorable ones ship your order when promised and submit the charge only when they ship. It's hard to tell the two apart; word-of-mouth helps, but a company's quality may change over time.

Most mail-order houses offer little or no support for the products they sell. Once you've bought something, they don't want to hear from you until you place another order. By eliminating support, they can sell for less than normal dealers.

There are a few good mail-order houses that offer excellent support by telephone—much better, in fact, than most dealers. If you find one, you're lucky. Tell your friends (but don't be surprised if the quality of support withers as the company grows).

Whatever you do, don't use the resources of a local dealer for information and then place the order with a mail-order house. It isn't fair, and discourages the competent stores who deserve a return from their efforts. A dealer offering useful information will also provide useful service after the sale.

PUBLICATIONS

Magazines and newsletters are starting quickly for Mac. The quality of information in publications varies like everything else. The computer press has grown up so rapidly that desperate publishers have hired many naive writers and editors. The best magazines are staffed by experienced journalists and computer users; they will bring you the latest information and perhaps a little hype.

The weaker magazines can be identified by their style: articles consisting mostly of quotes from computer-store sales personnel—genial, uncritical, and uninformative. A few magazines have gone so far as to ban all criticism of products. Paradoxically, some of the worst magazines make the fewest errors because they offer so little information in the first place. The more information in a publication, the greater the chance of error.

The quality of computer books varies widely also. Books inevitably take longer to produce than magazines, so you shouldn't look to books for the latest information. Instead, the best books offer insight or provide a reference. They anticipate questions and problems, and if they don't always solve the problem, they can give you the tools you need to find your own solution.

There will be dozens of books on Mac, many quickly written and superficial. The introductory-level books are less useful for Mac than for other computers since they won't tell you much more than you'll find in Apple's excellent manuals.

The only author, besides myself, who had access to the Macintosh long before its introduction is Doug Clapp, a knowledgeable, engaging writer. His book, *Macintosh! Complete*, is published by Softalk Press, North Hollywood, Calif., 1984.

User groups

Throughout this chapter, I've stressed the value of word-of-mouth recommendations. You can greatly expand your circle of Macintosh-user acquaintances by joining a user group. User groups or clubs will form quickly for Mac, many of them outgrowths of earlier Apple-user groups. Macintosh magazines will probably carry lists of such groups so you can locate one in your area—or you and your friends can start your own.

A good user group is probably the best single source of information about computers. Club members run the gamut from rank beginners to computer engineers, and everyone shares information. If you can't get a direct answer to a question, you will probably find someone in the group with a similar problem, and together you can find the answer.

Often the most sophisticated users are "hackers," people who spend every spare moment bent over their computers delving into some obscure hardware or software feature or bug. Such enthusiasts are like hot-rodders —they may be a good source of information about repairing your carburetor, but their ideas of how to choose and use cars may have little in common with your needs. Yet the best hackers will understand the computer's innards far more thoroughly than any dealer and can be an invaluable information source.

If you are thinking about buying a Mac, you may get advice from owners of competing micros. Many people who spend several thousand dollars on a computer system develop an emotional attachment to their investment and lose all their objectivity. If you buy a Mac, you may fall prey to the same syndrome. Keep in mind that there is no perfect microcomputer; all designs are compromises. Most major current models do at least a passable job for average applications. Every computer, including yours (whatever model), will be obsolete some day.

ELECTRONIC BULLETIN BOARDS

Electronic bulletin boards can be another source of information. These bulletin boards are stored inside a computer and you gain access to them through telephone lines with a modem. The simpler ones run by user groups generally don't charge for the service; the more complex operate on the national electronic database services run by CompuServe, THE SOURCE, and others, and may cost $5 to $20 per hour to use. Bulletin boards can be effective for short, clearly defined questions as well as for tips on many subjects.

Electronic bulletin boards have generally been designed for hobbyists, and all of them, including the commercial services, work badly. The Macintosh offers the possibility of an elegant and simple interface between you and the messages, but development and acceptance of such an interface will take time.

Chapter 23   The Macintosh Versus the IBM PC

At the beginning of this book is a statement that the views expressed here are mine and mine alone. That statement applies as much to this chapter as to any other. I do not speak for Microsoft, Apple, or any other company.

Apple was the leading personal-computer maker when IBM introduced its PC in 1981. By the end of 1983, IBM had taken the lead, riding on a flood of software and attracting dozens of imitation PCs from other manufacturers. Probably no one, not even IBM, anticipated such success.

How does the Macintosh compare with the IBM PC? There isn't a simple answer, as the comparison that follows shows. Both are solid, well-made, effective microcomputers. Both are capable of performing the major tasks expected of current microcomputers. The choice between them rests more on philosophical differences than on any clear superiority of one over the other.

The comparison that follows pits the standard IBM PC against the standard Macintosh. The many independently produced accessories for the PC and possible Macintosh accessories are not included; most require some nonstandard configuration and generally lead to software problems.

DESIGN PHILOSOPHY

IBM PC: Conservative design with few risks; appeared 2½ years before the Macintosh.

Macintosh: The most radical departure in microcomputer design to date.

The IBM PC follows the long-established tradition of general-purpose computers: It is merely a hardware base upon which software developers must build application programs and an interface. Complex programs and a visual interface are possible, but only with great effort on the part of programmers and at the risk of incompatibility with other programs. The PC's hardware employs older, long-established design concepts.

With a later start, the Macintosh benefits from later technology, including microfloppy disk drives and a fully developed visual interface. Macintosh gives programmers a built-in interface and many tools to make their lives easier.

Future microcomputers will resemble the Macintosh more than the IBM PC in design philosophy.

CENTRAL PROCESSING CHIP

IBM PC: Intel 8088, an 8/16-bit chip running at 4.77 MHz.

Macintosh: Motorola 68000, a 16/32-bit chip running at 7.78 MHz.

The two computers are too different to permit direct speed comparisons. The IBM PC has a relatively slow microprocessor but more memory and, under some circumstances, faster access to disk drives. Mac has a faster microprocessor but limited memory and more complex programs, so its overall speed may not differ greatly from that of the PC. In many practical applications, disk-drive access times effectively limit the operational speed. (Many magazine articles will publish speed comparisons, but these tests usually measure only one or two functions mainly interesting to programmers and don't really address overall operational speed.)

As for the microprocessor chips themselves, the Motorola 68000 is inherently faster and more powerful.

RAM

IBM PC: Maximum memory 640 KB, although the average system has 256 KB or less.

Macintosh: Present memory 128 KB; 512 KB will be available in the near future.

Although the IBM PC can handle 640 KB, an 8088 microprocessor can only work with 64 KB of data at a time, making life awkward for programmers. If an application program needs less than 640 KB of RAM, the remaining RAM can be used for emulating a disk drive for very fast "electronic disk" operation. The PC's video RAM is separate from the main memory.

Mac's 128-KB memory limit is its most serious drawback. Fortunately, a future model will handle 512 KB. You will be able to fit present 128-KB Macintoshes with the larger memory. Expansion beyond 512 KB will require that Apple come up with a new design or switch to the Lisa architecture. Disk emulation with internal RAM is impractical for the Macintosh. The Macintosh's video RAM is part of main memory, leaving less memory for the application program, but its 64 KB ROM helps by doing some work ordinarily performed in RAM.

Why does the Macintosh have so little RAM? Because it was designed at a time when 128 KB looked like a lot—a time when IBM announced a version of its PC with only 16 KB RAM. Both companies have drastically underestimated the importance of large RAM. Contrary to conventional wisdom, more RAM makes operation easier for a novice user; an experienced user can deal more readily with limited memory.

INTERNAL EXPANSION

IBM PC: One or two expansion slots available.

Macintosh: No internal expansion.

IBM left many essential circuits off the PC's main computer board in an effort to compete in price with the Apple II. Of its nominal five expansion slots, three must be taken up by a disk-drive adapter, input/output ports, and a display adapter, leaving at most two slots.

Mac doesn't need to use expansion slots for essential operations, but offers no hardware flexibility.

FLOPPY-DISK TYPE AND STORAGE

IBM PC: 5¼-inch, double-sided floppy disks with 360 KB of storage per disk.

Macintosh: 3½-inch, single-sided microfloppy disks with 400 KB of storage per disk.

The simpler IBM PC operating system and application programs allow its 360-KB disks to go farther than the 400-KB Mac disks. But the 3½-inch microfloppy packaging used by Mac is smaller, more convenient, and more resistant to careless handling than the older-style 5¼-inch minifloppies used by the IBM PC.

For both computers, you should have two floppy disk drives. A future double-sided Macintosh disk drive will permit 800 KB of storage per disk for a total of 1.6 megabytes with two disk drives. Hard-disk drives storing 10 or more megabytes can be added to both computers.

SCREEN GRAPHICS

IBM PC: Low-resolution (640 by 200 pixels) color graphics.

Macintosh: Medium-resolution (512 by 342 pixels) monochrome graphics.

The IBM PC's most serious operational problem lies in its two displays. Both choices are bad; with the graphics display, text is barely legible, whereas the medium-resolution monochrome display shows text only, no graphics. IBM could solve these problems with a new higher-resolution graphics adapter, but such a board would need revised graphics software and would have some compatibility problems with current software.

Because of a fundamental design decision, Mac will not support a color display.

Some rough definitions: Low resolution is less than 500 by 300 pixels; medium resolution goes up to 800 by 500 pixels. High-resolution screens are too expensive for current microcomputers.

SPACE REQUIRED AND PORTABILITY

IBM PC: 456 square inches of desk space; awkward to carry.

Macintosh: 207 square inches plus space for the mouse; fairly easy to carry.

The IBM PC comes in three pieces and is fairly bulky; one person alone cannot carry a complete PC, and it will not fit in the cabin of a commercial airplane. If optional software for the PC needs a mouse, then the desk-space requirement increases.

Mac is among the smallest desktop microcomputers; it comes in four parts including two small ones (the mouse and second disk drive), so it needs a case, but one person can easily carry a complete system. Apple sells a soft case that lets you carry Mac, with minor difficulty, on board an airplane.

USER INTERFACE

IBM PC: None; interface determined by the software.

Macintosh: Visual interface with mouse and icons.

The IBM PC offers no interface except to provide hardware for a screen display and a keyboard. A programmer can write an interface like Mac's, complete with mouse and icons, although the present IBM PC hardware won't run it effectively because of low screen resolution and slow screen processing.

The Macintosh has a built-in visual interface; programmers would have to do considerable extra work to replace it, and the results would not be uniform with other Mac software.

SOFTWARE BASE

IBM PC: Large base of MS-DOS software.

Macintosh: Small but growing base in own operating system.

The large and growing software base, which appeared in quantity within 14 months of the PC's introduction, is the IBM PC's most important asset.

At its introduction, the Macintosh, like all new computer designs, suffered from a software shortage. However, as with the PC when it was announced, many software companies were in the process of developing programs.

Although Mac will undoubtedly enjoy widespread software support, it may never have quite as many programs available as the IBM PC. One reason is timing; Mac got off to a later start. The other reason is more subtle. Because the IBM PC does not come with an interface, programmers write their own, so each product displays a different idea of how a program should work. The differences among programs are obvious. In contrast, Apple strongly encourages programmers to use the Macintosh interface, so the differences between programs are less obvious. As a result, a company may be reluctant to produce the 20th Macintosh word processor.

Is this important? Is having 10 programs to choose from worse than having 60? In theory, perhaps, but not in practice; although there are over 50 word processors for the IBM PC, only about 10 have significant sales. Furthermore, since the Macintosh frees programmers from having to write the interface, they can concentrate on making the programs themselves more powerful and sophisticated. Such program development will wait for the 512-KB Macintosh and will be interesting to watch.

LEARNING TIME

IBM PC: 15 to 30 hours.

Macintosh: 2 to 4 hours.

The key Macintosh advantage is ease of use. However, as software for the PC becomes more sophisticated, the time required for proficiency on it will start to drop.

MANUFACTURING COMPLEXITY

IBM PC: Over 200 chips.

Macintosh: 45 chips.

The Macintosh is a far more efficiently designed microcomputer than the IBM PC. It's too soon to say how the two units will compare for reliability; as a new model, Mac's reliability is unproven. The IBM PC is a reliable computer.

AVAILABILITY OF INFORMATION

IBM PC: Excellent for hardware; fair to good for software.

Macintosh: Poor for hardware; good for software.

IBM has published technical specifications for its PC hardware and interfacing information for MS-DOS, allowing many companies to build machines that are close copies of the PC. The copies have made the PC an industry standard.

Apple is less generous with its information and has taken legal action against companies that made copies of the Apple II. Apple has made a much larger investment in the Macintosh than IBM made in its PC, so Apple is understandably reluctant to share the details.

Both companies supply enough information for software developers. IBM gives thorough documentation for its much simpler PC; Apple gives comprehensive documentation with explanations for the Macintosh interface.

USER MANUALS

IBM PC: Traditional manuals, competently written but
badly organized.

Macintosh: The best manuals in the microcomputer
business.

CORPORATE STABILITY

IBM: A corporate colossus with a foot in most doors;
widespread sales force in place for large computers.

Apple: A large company equipped mainly for retail sales.

Both companies are in the personal-computer market
for the long haul. Both have well-developed dealer and
service networks.

PRODUCT-LINE INTEGRATION

IBM: Smooth integration of operations across IBM's
broad product line isn't realistic.

Apple: Now has two product families: the earlier-
generation Apple II/Apple III family and the
Lisa/Macintosh family.

IBM products in a specific category should work
together, but often don't. Designed independently, most
IBM office-automation products have little in common.
For example, two IBM products with essentially the same
design concept, the Displaywriter and the PC, work
completely differently and don't even use the same character codes. Many companies offer products to let the PC
work as a terminal to the larger computers; IBM's own
versions are among the more awkward. IBM did maintain
fairly close compatibility between the PC and the PCjr. PC
models for the next few years will probably maintain
compatibility with most present software.

The two Apple families have little in common. In
the new family, Lisa and Macintosh share the same microprocessor chip and a common design philosophy; the
Lisa 2 can run Macintosh software. Although now sold

as Apple's 32-bit microcomputer family, they were not designed to be compatible; the decision to integrate the two was made after development, and many rough edges show. Future development of the Apple 32-bit family will probably build on the Macintosh more than the Lisa.

OTHER MICROCOMPUTERS

The IBM PC and the Macintosh/Lisa are taking the lion's share of attention, but there are many other computers. The IBM PC clones compete mostly on price or transportability; few work as well as the PC itself. The IBM PCjr is carefully designed (crippled, actually) not to compete with the PC; it will not work satisfactorily as a business or professional computer and therefore does not really compete with the Macintosh either.

Aside from the Macintosh/Lisa, most microcomputer designs using the Motorola 68000 have put its power to work in multi-user systems with old-fashioned interfaces, not in sophisticated single-user interfaces. None has attracted significant software support.

Some older 8-bit microcomputer designs still survive, but software development for them has essentially stopped; the only reason to consider them is price. The exception is the Apple IIe, which has received yet another face-lift, this time adding a mouse and windowing software that keep it an important contender for the home and hobbyist market.

Chapter 24 *Future Products*

Two important Macintosh developments already underway will greatly improve the computer's operation: memory increase to 512 KB, and double-sided, 800-KB disk drives.

Existing Macs will be able to handle the larger memory and disk drives; their ROM programs already include the necessary features, and most application programs will automatically take advantage of more memory. Once the 512-KB Mac is available, everyone, whether novice or expert, should get it. Owners of 128-KB Macs can upgrade to the 512-KB version by taking their machine to a dealer for a circuit-board replacement.

From a user's standpoint, the extra memory will make operation faster and more powerful, but the operating system will still be designed to manage only a single application program at a time. In the future, more powerful Macintosh models could run two or more programs concurrently, as the Lisa can now. You could have both a word processor and a graphics program in memory at the same time. The programs would automatically switch according to your needs, and file conversion between the programs could be performed automatically.

Double-sided disk drives will add more convenience; you won't have to swap disks as much. A single-drive system will be a practical tool rather than a frustrating exercise. Even when double-sided drives are available, most users should still have two disk drives; many routine operations are then much simpler and easier.

The remainder of this chapter discusses products that will probably appear for the Macintosh in the future.

INTERNAL EXPANSION

The Macintosh has no internal expansion slots or unused connectors; you cannot add internal accessory circuit boards or cards as you can to an Apple II or IBM PC to add more RAM or special features such as an internal modem. The only standard expansion within the Macintosh is the memory increase to 512 KB, done by swapping circuit boards, not by expansion.

Chapter 30 includes information about several possible nonstandard internal modifications. Such modifications can only be done by skilled, technically qualified personnel and will in any case void the warranty. The vast majority of Macintosh owners will not need such drastic changes.

EXTERNAL EXPANSION

An external expansion bus for accessory cards could be constructed to connect to the Macintosh through the input/output ports. This expansion would involve no modifications to the machine itself. An external bus system would operate much more slowly (about 29 to 62 KB of information transferred each second) than an internal bus (typically a megabyte per second or faster). Some accessories, such as more RAM and very high-speed Winchester disk interfaces, are not possible in an external device.

An external chassis could contain expansion slots, possibly using the Apple II or IBM PC bus, even though those buses were designed for different microprocessors. It's been done before: The 68000-based Corvus Concept microcomputer uses an Apple II expansion bus.

THE EXPANSION QUESTION

Why have expansion at all? Because some users need more or different features from the standard configuration. Modems, special input/output devices, electronic test equipment, environmental monitors, and many other items can be attached to a Macintosh. Some are described below. Most items are specialized and appeal to relatively few users.

Should Apple have included expansion slots in Mac? The decision rests largely on trading costs against what the typical user will need.

The arguments for internal expansion slots:

- Individual users have different needs. Internal expansion slots provide a more flexible computer design that adapts to the needs of more users. Accessory cards can, in principle, turn Mac into a completely different computer.

- New hardware not available or too expensive at the time Mac was designed cannot be used unless there is a way to add it on at a future date.

The arguments against internal expansion slots:

- A computer without internal expansion slots is simpler and cheaper to build.

- If the computer itself is sufficiently complete, most users will not need internal accessories and should not have to pay for expansion capability that they will not use.

- Accessory cards create cooling problems. Unlike many other microcomputers, Mac does not need a cooling fan, so it can operate quietly and unobtrusively on your desk.

- Software for other computers usually requires accessories, such as a graphics card or a disk drive, that only some users have. Because everyone who owns a Mac has the same configuration, software developers need not be concerned with many variations; the simplification makes the software easier for developers to support and in the long run this should reduce software costs.

If you know that you're going to need more capability than the Mac can provide, you could get a Lisa 2 instead. The lowest-priced Lisa 2 model offers 512 KB of memory and an internal expansion bus and can run most Mac software. Lisa 2s have some disadvantages for running Mac software, however. Mac images are squeezed on the Lisa 2 screen because of a design difference (see Chapter 13), and some Mac programs may not run on a Lisa.

External Accessories

More conventional external accessories will add other features to the Macintosh. The most common accessories —hard disks, modems, and printers—were discussed in earlier chapters. Many other accessories are certain to appear.

Input/output adapters

An accessory box will adapt Mac's serial ports to a Centronics parallel port; any device using the ports will require suitable software. Adding a parallel adapter gives Mac both common microcomputer interface types, serial and parallel.

Printer buffers

As mechanical devices, printers almost always print more slowly than a computer can generate characters or graphics; normally a computer has to wait until the printer is finished to get on with other tasks. A printer buffer is installed between the computer and the printer; its random access memory accepts the output from the computer at full speed, and feeds it to the printer at a slower speed. Meanwhile the computer can return to normal operation.

Some printers come with a built-in memory buffer, but these buffers are typically small—2 KB or so—compared to buffers you purchase separately, which typically have 64 KB. Tecmar has announced printer-buffer products for the Macintosh; many other companies will have such products also.

Power controllers

Power controllers working with BSR X-10 switches will let you turn appliances on and off with your computer. Computer-operated controllers make sense for industrial applications and for the handicapped; they are less useful for ordinary offices or households.

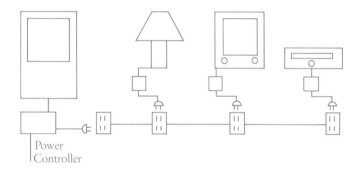

A computer-operated power controller can turn any standard electric device on and off.

Laboratory-instrument controllers

Laboratory-instrument controllers, many using the IEEE-488 interface, let you collect and analyze data from a wide variety of instruments.

Analog-to-digital converters

An A-to-D converter changes an analog voltage from any source (thermometers, machinery, fuel tank gauge, and so on) into a digital signal for a computer. A digital-to-analog (D-to-A) converter works in the opposite direction, turning a digital signal into an ordinary analog electronic circuit.

Telephone management systems

Telephone management systems dial numbers and track your telephone usage. These systems can be handy if you make many phone calls, but most people will find a conventional, stand-alone telephone dialer simpler to use. Who wants to dig out a disk and load a program just to dial a number? A sophisticated program can track calls and costs, however, and might make sense for some businesses.

Video accessories

Videodisc and videotape controllers provide all the functions of random-access tape and disc players. The video image goes to a standard television or monitor, not to the Mac screen, which continues to work in the normal way. Training software could use the Mac screen for text and high-resolution graphics while putting a normal, full-motion video image on a television screen. Other programs will use videodiscs for games; you use the Mac's screen for the computer interface, but watch video action on a separate television.

Sound accessories

Music keyboards and synthesizer attachments can use either Mac's sound generator or add special circuitry for more elaborate sounds while using Mac's microprocessor and disk storage. A piano-style keyboard attachment could be connected through the keyboard connector or via a serial port.

Electronic test equipment

A digital oscilloscope attachment will turn the Mac into an electronic tool to analyze waveforms. Using the computer, you will be able to store, compare, and analyze electronic signals. A logic analyzer will let you trace digital circuits. Signal generators will use the screen to display the waveforms; analyzers will display the distortion products. Eventually an entire electronic testing set will be centered around the Macintosh. These will mostly be tools for engineering.

COLOR SCREENS

Color screens present another future possibility. For effective operation, a hypothetical color Macintosh might add a graphics processor, since calculating three different colors simultaneously will begin to overload even a 68000 CPU. Based on present component prices, the cost of a color Mac would be about double that of the black-and-white version.

FUTURE PRINTERS

The future will bring many more printer choices. Provided you can get the necessary software support, you will be able to choose from the following printers.

New Dot-Matrix Printers

High-resolution dot-matrix printers will print from 200 to 300 dots per inch. Speeds have already reached 200 characters per second, and future units will run even faster. Print quality will edge ever closer to letter quality, yet will not quite match that of daisy-wheel printers. Color dot-matrix printers will continue to proliferate in the low-cost, low-quality market.

Ink-Jet Printers

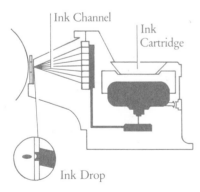

Ink-jet printer

Ink-jet printers squirt tiny drops of ink onto the paper. After early, mostly unsuccessful efforts to make ink-jet printers compete with daisy-wheel printers in quality, the trend has been toward low-cost, medium-quality, color ink-jet printers. Such printers are capable of better results than the impact dot-matrix color printers. Ink-jet printers are quiet and fairly fast in operation.

Thermal-Transfer Printers

Thermal-transfer printers press a plastic sheet coated with a color resin against the paper, and tiny heated pins melt the resin onto the paper. The resolution and print quality are generally better than ink-jet printers, but some people object to the glazed image. (Don't confuse thermal-transfer printers with the low-cost, low-quality thermal printers that use specially treated paper.)

Laser Printers

Laser printers use a laser beam to write an image, one dot at a time, on a photoconductive drum that operates in the same fashion as a xerographic photocopier. Laser printers create an entire page at a time and are quiet and fast; eight pages per minute is typical for the less expensive units, and the largest and most expensive can print two pages per second. The resolution is high, typically 240 to 300 dots per inch, with one model at 480 dpi. Because it prints so fast, a laser printer can be shared by many computers without making anyone wait.

A disadvantage is that because laser printers use photocopier technology, they put out originals that look like copies. Prices are also high; the cheapest units in 1984 cost about $10,000, although by 1985 laser printers for less than $4000 should be available.

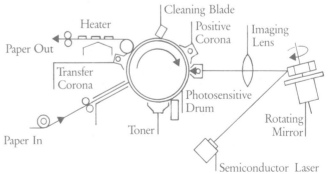

Laser printers use a rotating mirror to scan the beam across a photoconductor drum, writing the characters point-by-point.

Other Technologies

We may soon see wider use of other page-printer technologies. The Delphax printer, for example, uses a unique array of ion guns to squirt ions onto a photoconductive drum. The process resembles laser printing, but needs no moving parts to form the image.

Magnetic printers use an array of tiny magnetic heads to record a magnetic image on a magnetic belt. Toner particles, themselves containing magnets, adhere to the belt and are transferred to the paper. Unlike other page printers, the magnetic image remains on the belt until erased, so many copies can be made from one magnetic image.

FINDING OUT ABOUT NEW PRODUCTS

You will have no difficulty finding out about new products for Mac. The problem is going to be sorting out the good from the bad. The microcomputer industry will put out a deluge of announcements touting new Macintosh accessories and software. Claims and counterclaims will crowd the magazine advertisements.

Although we all have a healthy skepticism about advertising claims, we are often not skeptical enough about other forms of publicity. The "new products" sections of nearly all magazines are merely rewritten press releases, as are many apparent news stories about new products. The "news story" may even carry a fake dateline: "Sioux Falls, South Dakota—Gopher Software announced today..."; ten to one, Gopher Software will turn out to be the "reporter" behind the story.

Pre-Announcements

Many companies engage in pre-announcements, saying they will do something months—sometimes a year or more—in advance of the first delivery. They may want to preempt the field and discourage people from buying competing products; or they may simply be optimistic—even competent companies can run into last minute snags.

Magazines encourage pre-announcements by trying to be quickest with the latest news. For major products, a magazine may strike an implicit deal with the company, trading a splashly article or cover in exchange for early information. Few magazines publish corrections when the hot news turns out to be mostly hype.

Computer engineers tell many funny stories about last-minute crash projects to simulate a product for the press or investment analysts. The demonstration may have nothing to do with the product—usually it's a lot of fancy screen graphics—but it almost always convinces the gullible.

One semi-legitimate reason for pre-announcements is the result of a scheduling problem. Magazines typically plan articles and sell advertising space for each issue three to four months ahead of time. Many products will fail if they do not start selling successfully within a period as short as a few months of the date they are released; if sales are delayed, competing products will appear. So some companies start the announcement process months before the product itself is ready to make sure that the publicity will coincide with the product's release date.

The best companies take a more conservative approach, announcing products only when they are ready to ship. All other things being equal, these companies deserve more support than those that regularly jump the gun.

Problems with New Products

Should you always look for the latest and most glamorous product? I recommend that you resist the temptation, especially if you depend on Macintosh in your work. Instead, concentrate on products and companies that have an established reputation. Ask other people what their experience with a particular product has been. You might not always be the first with something new, but you won't be an unwitting guinea pig either. Far too many computer products appear in an unfinished form; some companies regard their first customers as the last step in the product-engineering process.

New software often does not work quite as well as the developer planned. Bugs, or errors, are common, particularly in early versions. Some bugs you can learn to live with, especially if they afflict only little-used features. A minor glitch may make a particular function awkward but not greatly detract from a program's larger benefits.

More serious are major bugs that affect the program's usefulness. A database program with a delete-record command that doesn't work, for example, can only lead to frustration and unpredictable results. Such major bugs aren't unusual; several best-selling programs for other computers have had such faults for years. Sometimes the seller will try to explain away the bug as an "undocumented feature."

The chance of bugs increases with program complexity. Often, very complex programs are never completely debugged; it becomes a question of how severe the bugs are and whether it is worth the effort to fix them. Frequently the bugs are fixed only in a new version that adds features—and new bugs. Nevertheless, the most highly developed programs should be bug-free for all practical applications.

MINIMIZING PROBLEMS WITH ACCESSORIES

Although you will generally have few interface problems if you use only Apple products or Apple-approved products, there are often good reasons not to use them. Other products may be cheaper or have more or better features, or you may simply have an accessory such as a modem already and not want to buy another.

One disadvantage of using other products is that your system then has components from several different vendors who may have no interest in helping you get their product working with those made by other companies. And Apple usually can't help you either; it cannot possibly keep track of all the products that work with Mac. As a result, you may find that a printer which offers many features with one particular program proves awkward or even impossible to use with another. If a program uses a copy-protected disk, you may not be able to move the program to a hard disk, so you won't be able to take full advantage of that expensive extra hardware.

Another disadvantage: When Apple updates Macintosh programs, such as the Finder or operating system, it will probably update everything in Mac's product line that is affected by the change. If you are using other products, there will probably be delays in getting updates for them, resulting in a period when things won't quite work together. The healthy independent companies will, however, update their products quickly.

How do you tell a healthy company from an unhealthy one? A long-term reputation helps. With the rapid growth of the microcomputer industry, many ill-planned business ventures have started up. Most of these will fold. In the early years of microcomputers, many successful companies, including Apple, started in the proverbial garage. Unfortunately, those days have now passed, as least for the development of major products. Few important hardware or software products can succeed now unless they are supported by millions of dollars in development, packaging, and promotion.

Buy with care from a company you have never heard of before; you many never hear from it again. Many smaller companies—and some bigger ones—will announce and ship a new product, only to discover problems and decide that the product is too difficult to redesign or support further. Customers who bought the product will be left holding the bag. These companies may have made an honest mistake, but if you've paid for the product, you will probably be stuck with it.

Chapter 25 *The Future of Microcomputers*

What does the future hold for microcomputers? This chapter looks at future hardware and software developments, not just for the Macintosh but for other microcomputers as well. Unless otherwise noted, the projections are for the late 1980s.

Although the computer industry, especially the microcomputer industry, is changing rapidly, the short-term future is fairly easy to predict. All the manufacturers use the same technologies; there are only a handful of important microprocessor chips and only a few ways to make a screen display. Everyone works with the same memory or disk-controller chips, and the same disk drives. Every hardware component that will be commercially available in the next four to five years already exists in some kind of prototype today.

The Macintosh represents today's state of the art, the best example of what can be achieved in a moderately priced computer. The entire Apple 32-bit product line, including the Macintosh, will mature as hardware accessories and software develop; Macintosh itself should survive for many years. Its brilliant internal engineering—combining striking economy of design and efficient use of parts—will keep the Macintosh cost-competitive longer than any other current microcomputer.

Within five years, successful computer companies will all offer a full family of models, from powerful desktop units to under-4-pound, battery-operated portables. All the models will work together, using as similar an interface as the specific hardware allows. With little effort, files will move back and forth between any member of the family; whenever you connect two computers, the operating system will automatically update files and make backups by checking the time and date of each file.

THE VISUAL INTERFACE

Because visual interfaces are so easy to use, many companies are developing them for other microcomputers. For the most part, these interfaces do not operate as well as that of the Macintosh or Lisa because the hardware on which they run was not designed or modified specifically for the interface.

The hardware for new computer models will increase screen resolution and speed up image processing. By 1985, many computers will operate with icons and mice; few important new products will be introduced with only the old-fashioned command-line interface. But many graphics-driven software products for the new machines will have been rushed to market and won't work well.

CENTRAL PROCESSING UNIT

The follow-on to Mac's 68000 processor, the 68020, is already appearing in prototype computers. The 68020 chip is a true 32-bit processor, featuring both a 32-bit bus and internal registers. It can address 4 gigabytes (4096 megabytes) of memory, and runs all present 68000 programs, including those written for Macintosh or Lisa.

Although this and other new processors will operate faster than those currently in use, software will become more complex; overall speed may not, therefore, appear to increase. If the new processor runs twice as fast but a complex new program does twice as much work, from a user's standpoint, there may be no speed increase.

MEMORY

Memory prices have been dropping at the rate of 4 percent per month for the last two decades, a trend that should continue for several more years. Memory costs make up a significant portion of total machine costs.

Macintosh already has provision for expansion to 512 KB total memory, and Lisa models can handle up to a megabyte. The next round of computers will handle even more; by the end of the decade, desktop computers with 10 to 50 megabytes of memory will be common. By present standards, this is a lot of memory—so much that the short-sighted claim that we will never need such power. Future software will use all of it, and advanced users will demand even more memory.

DISPLAY

The long-established CRT will remain supreme in desktop computers for the next five years. No other display technology has equaled its high-contrast, high-resolution features for a sufficiently low manufacturing cost. Only in portable computers will alternative flat-panel technologies dominate—and then only because size, weight, and power constraints are more important for portables than resolution or price.

CRT resolution will improve steadily. Mac's 80-dpi screen will give way to a 150- to 200-dpi black-and-white screen, about the resolution limit for low-cost CRT designs with present technology. More screens will display an entire 8½- by 11-inch page; some will display two pages, enough for effective window operations. High-resolution color screens are much harder to manufacture at reasonable cost than black-and-white, but color screens with Mac's present resolution will start appearing for microcomputers.

The higher the resolution, the longer it takes to compute the display's contents. Most present microcomputers, including Macintosh, use the main microprocessor to compute the display. Future micros will incorporate a special graphics processor to handle the display, freeing the main processor for other tasks.

MASS STORAGE

Although floppy disks will enjoy wide use for years to come, hard disks will soon become standard. Boasting storage capacities of 5 to 200 megabytes on either fixed disks or interchangeable disk cartridges, the hard disks themselves will give way to new storage forms with even more memory.

Optical discs should be widespread toward the end of the decade. Today, commercially available optical-disc systems can read only prerecorded discs, or they can write information permanently on the disc once and then read it back; they cannot erase information. But some laboratory prototypes of erasable optical discs have already been constructed. Erasable optical discs with a capacity of 2 to 10 gigabytes should be available for a few thousand dollars in a few years. Since one gigabyte can hold about 2000 books, entire libraries could reside on one disc.

NETWORKS

Today, all the computer products in an office or home can be tied together (via software and hardware) to share information and resources. Current networks are, however, awkward and hard to use. In the future, such networking will become much more prevalent as network software becomes easier to use. A user will not have to know where a particular file is located; the system will automatically find the most recent version.

Electronic mail, whether to the next office or another continent, will be embedded in computers as an operating-system function.

TELECOMMUNICATIONS

Many electronic telephone exchanges already in use can accommodate digital phone lines capable of transmitting 56 kilobits per second. These lines will, in the near future, be wired to most of our offices and homes, offering decent communication speed at last; a double-spaced, typewritten page will transfer in ⅓ second. Even the most complex Macintosh screen will transmit in three seconds;

most will take much less time. Conversion to high-speed phone lines will take time and a massive investment in optical-fiber links between exchanges. Many present local loops, from the local exchange to our telephones, can pass 56 kilobits a second.

Information services available by telephone will finally become easy to use. With higher transmission speeds and better graphics, these services will attract more people, in turn bringing the cost down low enough to attract even more people.

Everyone hopes that the advent of the new high-speed links will also help standardize communications protocols. Standardization is possible but unlikely. New software will at least insulate individual users from the protocol problems by automatically detecting which protocol is required and making any necessary adjustments.

GETTING INFORMATION INTO THE COMPUTER

In this decade, the keyboard, with help from a mouse, will remain the dominant method of entering information into a computer. Everyone wants a computer that will recognize human speech, but the problems are formidable.

With present technology, lower-cost units can recognize a limited vocabulary of isolated spoken words, but they are speaker-dependent—they must be "trained" to recognize individual speakers. Expensive systems can interpret limited connected (but not continuous) speech with a vocabulary up to 500 words.

A powerful system able to understand standard spoken business English will probably not be available until the 1990s. Such a system will require a sophisticated program to reduce the many ambiguities inherent in spoken English.

SOFTWARE

Although future software will still do present tasks, the ways in which the software does the work will change.

With more memory, computers will store more programs in RAM at the same time, as the larger Lisas do now. When we switch tasks, we won't have to wait for disk drives to store files and load new ones; the switching will be instantaneous.

New programs will remedy a major failing in present Macintosh and Lisa software by linking individual tasks. At present, once we move information from one program to another, the information is "dead." If we move numbers from a spreadsheet into a letter, for example, the software does not keep track of where the numbers came from; to update the numbers, we must first update the original spreadsheet, then move the numbers again to update the letter.

Future programs will not only move the numbers but will establish an active link among programs. If we change our spreadsheet, the numbers in the letter will automatically be changed also. Or we could change the numbers in the letter and the software will automatically update the spreadsheet. Of course, we will be able to override the link if we wish. Some programs, such as Microsoft's Multiplan and Chart, already have a limited linking function.

A second major software direction will be toward natural language—ordinary English. To retrieve information from a data base, we will no longer have to learn a rigid series of commands; we'll be able to type a question in plain English, and the software will analyze the syntax of our question (parse it) and figure out what information we want. Parsing is akin to grade-school sentence-diagramming exercises combined with a dictionary of meanings. With parsing, computers can for the first time be said to "understand" language.

Data bases with natural language input will be available as early as 1984, but that's just the beginning. The twin steps of parsing and linking open the way to a new era of software.

DATABASE MACHINES

All of us work by building upon old data. But computers need to work with organized data; people, in contrast, are usually disorganized. With today's computers, we spend an inordinate amount of time organizing our information so the computers can understand it.

Letters, for example, begin with an address and other information that is already stored in an address book or file. With present software, we must find the address or an old letter by explicitly searching for it. Future software will search automatically. The program will parse our input as we type. If we write the name John Doe, the program will immediately put John Doe's address and telephone number in a secondary window. If there is no John Doe, the program will offer the names with the closest spelling, in case we made an error.

If the name and address are new, the program will wait until we type in the new information. Regardless of where or how we type the address, the program will detect an address by scanning for "Ave.," state abbreviations, and so forth, and then look in nearby text for further address information. The information will be automatically organized into address format; we will have a chance to check it and then it will be added to the name-and-address data base.

If our letter begins "In response to your letter of last week...," the program will automatically go off, having figured out that last week means September 8 through 14, and check for letters from Doe. (All letters will arrive via electronic mail, of course.) If no such letter is found, the program will expand its search, looking further back in time. If we regularly underestimate the date, the program will automatically start looking earlier.

If we refer to a company name in the letter, all the information in our files about that company will be available instantly. The program will anticipate all common data needs, accepting natural-language guidance for less common requests. ("What is the telephone number of the hotel closest to the meeting?")

The software will be unstructured. We will not have to ask for a word processor or a data base when we start working; one large, seamless program will analyze and suitably organize our work. All program functions will always be available without arbitrary boundaries between them.

The software will analyze and adapt to our specific working habits. If we enter calendar dates in a specific way, the program will adopt the same format, while retaining the ability to read dates in any format from other sources. On-line dictionaries will always check spelling and offer corrections for our most common mistakes.

A CONCLUDING NOTE

Does this chapter sound too futuristic? It isn't (except perhaps the predictions about voice recognition). We already have, or will have within months, the hardware able to perform these marvelous functions. The software will take longer, so we'll probably be forced to wait until the end of the decade for truly powerful microcomputers.

Section

Special Macintosh Topics

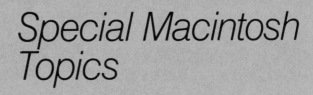

This section contains material for people with specialized needs or interests. Some of the material is highly technical, written for specialists and intended primarily for reference.

Chapter 26 *A Macintosh Medley*

When I finished writing this book, I found I had lots of useful bits of information left over; they didn't seem to fit logically anywhere. Believing that more information is better than less, I couldn't bring myself to simply leave them out; the result is two chapters, this one and Chapter 30, that should rightly be titled Miscellaneous One and Miscellaneous Two.

Chapter 30 is a compendium of technical tidbits that might interest experienced users; this chapter contains four unrelated topics that might be of general interest. They are:

- Graphic Arts with Macintosh—how to use MacPaint to create quality graphics.

- Fonts—using Macintosh typefaces for typesetting.

- Using Macintosh in Moving Vehicles—including motor vehicles, boats, and airplanes.

- Notes for the Handicapped—for those with hearing and vision impairments, those with motor-control limitations, and the one-handed.

GRAPHIC ARTS WITH MACINTOSH

Although MacPaint and MacDraw are very easy programs to use, creating quality images takes some skill, experience, and aesthetic sensitivity. This section gives tips on how to create graphics. The specific details given here apply only to MacPaint, but similar methods will apply to MacDraw. With practice you should be able to produce competent graphics using the techniques described; I cannot, however, be responsible for aesthetics...

Using Existing Artwork

The active area of MacPaint is 3⅜ inches high by 5½ inches wide (14.2 by 8.6 cm). The active area can be moved over an entire 8½- by 11-inch page, so an original page of artwork can be created in sections but printed out as a complete page.

For the best results, draw the image the correct size in MacPaint from the beginning. MacPaint lets you resize an object along the horizontal or vertical axis or both, but the resizing process may distort the image; the program will at times double the pixels to maintain the relative weight if you are making an object larger, and must delete dots if you reduce the size.

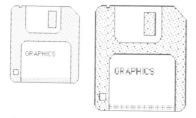

Stretching an image in MacPaint distorts some objects

If you want to work from existing artwork, you have five basic choices:

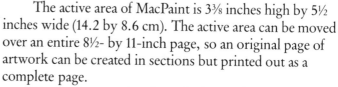

- Transferring the artwork to a transparent overlay that fits over the screen.

- Using a slide projector.

- Tracing the artwork with a mouse.

- Tracing the artwork with a digitizer pad.

- Using a television camera.

These techniques are discussed in detail in the following sections. For all the techniques involving tracing, you may not want to trace the entire line, but rather the end points of each line and other critical features. After tracing, you can add straight lines and curves using MacPaint's tools.

The overlay technique will not work satisfactorily with MacPaint on a Lisa because of Lisa's different aspect ratio. Tracing with a drafting machine and television input will work, but you have to get used to a squeezed image on the Lisa screen.

Making an overlay

To make an overlay, transfer the original image to a transparent sheet sized for the Macintosh screen. You can make the overlay by hand, or by photography or xerography.

To make an overlay by hand, use transparent acetate and a drawing pen with suitable ink. If you are lucky, the original artwork will have the right scale and you can simply trace it. If you need to change the size, use a pantograph. Then simply tape the acetate over the screen and use the mouse to trace the acetate image with the pointer. The eye-hand coordination needed will come with practice.

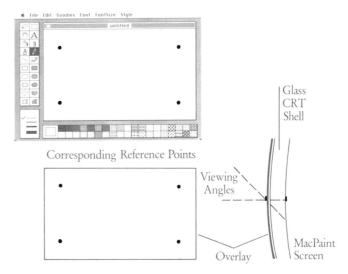

Corresponding Reference Points

Use reference points when tracing an overlay; otherwise your angle of view will introduce errors in position.

To make a photographic overlay, the Polaroid process is the quickest. Use black-and-white transparency film; for full size, you will need the 4- by 5-inch process, although the smaller 3¼- by 4¼-inch film size may cover enough area of the artwork for your needs. You can also make the overlay in several sections.

If you use a photographic enlarger to make the image, prepare a template with a mask for MacPaint's active area. You can print on large film sheets and process them in the same manner as photographic paper.

Xerographic overlays are the quickest, provided that you have a suitable copier. Copiers with continuous enlargement and reduction work best.

All the overlay-tracing techniques lead to parallax problems because of the glass CRT faceplate separating the overlay and the phosphor. While tracing, you must hold your head in the same position; to do this, mark three or four reference points initially around the overlay and check your head alignment against these points before tracing each line.

Using a slide projector

For quick-and-dirty results, you can project the artwork directly onto Mac's screen with a slide projector and use the mouse to trace the artwork with the pointer. This method has many drawbacks: The reflected projector lamp shines in your eyes as you work; the pointer is hard to see in the glare; and the image appears as a strong double image on both the screen's faceplate and on the phosphor layer. If you set up the projector for best geometric accuracy, it may get in your way. If you try this method, a filter to cut down the projector brightness may help.

Tracing the artwork with a mouse

A mouse isn't really designed for tracing objects. When you draw on paper, the pen is an absolute-position device; you put it down and pick it up at definite locations. The mouse registers relative motions—the distance and direction you have moved, not the place it started and stopped. If the rolling ball inside the mouse slips, you

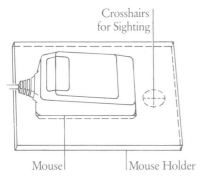

A Plexiglas holder for a mouse

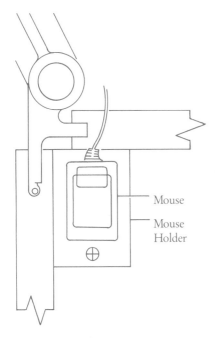

The mouse holder lets you use the mouse with a drafting machine, maintaining up/down, left/right orientation when tracing with the mouse.

merely move the mouse a little further while watching the pointer on the screen.

If you are careful and willing to touch up your work, however, the mouse will serve for tracing art. You will need to do a little construction. Get a 4- by 6-inch piece of Plexiglas®, and cut out an opening for the mouse. Leave clearance for the mouse cable. At one end of the Plexiglas, scribe cross-hairs on the underside.

When you trace with the mouse, you must maintain a strict up/down, left/right orientation, so it's best to use a drafting machine, which will maintain orientation over a drawing table. Tape the Plexiglas into the corner of the drafting machine; you can't simply put the mouse into the corner because the cable won't clear the rulers.

While tracing, you must drag the mouse, but pressing down on the mouse button is a nuisance when the mouse is attached to a drafting machine. You can add an external switch to duplicate the mouse button. (The mouse button connects pin 7 on the cable to ground, pin 1 or 3.) With a toggle switch, you simply turn the mouse on and off for each line, so you can concentrate on the tracing rather than on holding down the mouse button.

Again, you can use a pantograph to change the scale of your original artwork. The alternative is changing the mouse driver software—altering the "gearing" between the mouse ball and screen movement through software. These changes are relatively easy only for factor-of-two changes; other changes are more difficult.

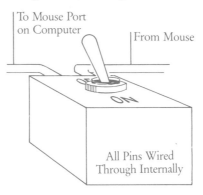

Accessory switch for mouse button; mouse button remains operational.

Tracing the artwork with a digitizer pad

A digitizer pad lets you draw or trace with a pen-shaped stylus, a more natural action than drawing with a mouse.

If you need to transfer a lot of artwork into Mac, you should buy a digitizer pad. Such pads are absolute-position devices, and the supporting software should let you use them as if you were drawing with a pen.

Digitizer pads use several different technologies and offer different features. Some designs are easier for casual drawing with a finger, others are designed for technical drawing.

Consider these questions before buying a digitizer pad:

- How are the mouse-button operations accomplished? By setting aside a special area of the pad to simulate the button? With separate buttons? Or with the mouse itself?

- Does the pad only operate as an absolute-position device? Can you switch it to relative motion?

- Can you use your finger to operate it? Can you use a pen? Does it require a special stylus? If it uses a stylus, do you see the results on paper as well as on screen?

- Can you trace through paper onto the pad?

- How reproducible is your work? Pressure-sensitive digitizer pads are difficult to manufacture uniformly. On other designs, it may be difficult to start and stop a line precisely, depending on how the pad is activated.

- Is the pad noisy? Some pads use a spark gap in the stylus and microphones to locate the stylus position through the sound delay. Some people object to the noise associated with this pad design.

- Can you control the scale factor—the ratio between distance moved on the pad and the distance moved on the screen?

Digitizer pads specifically designed to work with the Macintosh should be available from several vendors. The best and most expensive units will include their own microprocessors to change scaling. Many pads feature higher resolution than MacPaint needs; 200 dots per inch is routine and some can detect 1000 dots per inch.

Using a television camera

The quickest way to input artwork is with a television camera. Several companies will produce cameras designed to attach to the Macintosh through a serial port. The camera will incorporate a small processor and RAM; software will convert a bit-image into the QuickDraw graphics format that MacPaint and other graphics programs will be able to read.

The lower-cost cameras use a conventional television camera tube, such as a vidicon or saticon. These tubes work adequately, but suffer from slight geometric inaccuracy and deteriorate with age; the cost may be as low as a few hundred dollars. Solid-state television cameras, on the other hand, are immune to distortion and aging, but cost more. Select a model that lets you choose the threshold at which the camera sees a medium tone as black or white; set the threshold for the cleanest image.

Neither of these forms of television camera has sufficient resolution for the most exacting work; neither can achieve the resolution of Mac or Lisa over a full page. Still, the essential outlines of the artwork are digitized, and you can clean them up afterwards with software.

Because you don't need a perfect camera for this application, you can use industrial solid-state cameras that might have a few pixels missing or slightly uneven sensitivity.

For full resolution, only the high-quality imaging cameras designed for graphics will do. These cameras are expensive; the Datacopy 610™ costs $10,000. It uses a 1728-pixel linear array, moved over the image plane by a servo motor, and scans an image in 20 seconds. With the linear array, the camera can digitize an 8½- by 11-inch image at 200 dots per inch. You can set the threshold between black and white, or you can record 256 shades of gray. Placing a full-page image into bit-mapped memory would require 467 kilobytes (KB) and the screen resolution would have to be 1700 by 2200 pixels. All these requirements will restrict such cameras to specialists for some time, although prices will certainly drop. An imaging camera could interface to a hard-disk-equipped 512-KB Macintosh with suitable software. You would see a section of the image at a time.

Notes on MacPaint

In the present version of MacPaint for the 128-KB Macintosh, the active area where you create the screen image is held in RAM. The inactive area, which is out of sight (though you can see it with the Show Page command), is stored on disk.

Whenever you move the active area around the page with the small hand icon, the image in the old active area is stored on disk and the image in the new active area is moved from disk into RAM. To save disk space, MacPaint stores a compressed image, using two ROM routines, Packbits and Unpackbits.

If you want to work on an image larger than the active area, you must work in sections. If you are transferring existing artwork into the computer using one of the techniques described above, try to break the image into component sections so that each component can be created without moving the active area. Later, using the Show Page command, you can move the active area and align the components into a single image.

Matching up sections is easy if the complete image is rectangular; for irregular shapes you must use the lasso function. In some cases you may find it easier to duplicate part of the image and delete sections later.

With the 512-KB version of the Macintosh and a revised version of MacPaint, the entire page could be in memory at one time, making your work much faster and more convenient.

MacPaint versus MacDraw

MacPaint stores the picture as a bit-image, whereas MacDraw stores attributes. MacPaint stores a line as a group of independent pixels; MacDraw stores information placing a line of a particular length and thickness at a certain location with a certain orientation. MacPaint is easier to learn, but MacDraw can be more powerful for the skilled user. Individual components of MacDraw pictures can be changed without interfering with other objects that may overlay the component.

FONTS

The standard fonts supplied by Apple with MacPaint and MacWrite don't correspond exactly to any established fonts. Macintosh's 80-dots-per-inch screen doesn't permit a close match to a typeset font with the equivalent of over 1000 dpi. If you are creating text for typesetting, here are some roughly equivalent fonts along with ImageWriter samples:

New York:
Times New Roman (Monotype),
Garamond Condensed (ITC-
International Typeface Corp.)

abcdefghijklmnopqrstuvwxyz
ABCDEFGHIJKLMNOPQRSTUVWXYZ
1234567890.,;:`'&!?$
abcdefghijklmnopqrstuvwxyz
ABCDEFGHIJKLMNOPQRSTUVWXYZ
1234567890.,;:`'&!?$

Geneva:
Helvetica Light Condensed (Haas),
Antique Olive (Letraset)

abcdefghijklmnopqrstuvwxyz
ABCDEFGHIJKLMNOPQRSTUVWXYZ
1234567890.,;:`'&!?$
abcdefghijklmnopqrstuvwxyz
ABCDEFGHIJKLMNOPQRSTUVWXYZ
1234567890.,;:`'&!?$

Toronto:
Helserif (Mergenthaler),
Lubalin Graph Book (ITC)

abcdefghijklmnopqrstuvwxyz
ABCDEFGHIJKLMNOPQRSTUVWXYZ
1234567890.,;:`'&!?$
abcdefghijklmnopqrstuvwxyz
ABCDEFGHIJKLMNOPQRSTUVWXYZ
1234567890.,;:`'&!?$

Monaco:
Avant Garde Condensed (ITC),
Bauer Topic Bold (VGC-Visual Graphics
Corp.)

abcdefghijklmnopqrstuvwxyz
ABCDEFGHIJKLMNOPQRSTUVWXYZ
1234567890.,;:`'&!?$
abcdefghijklmnopqrstuvwxyz
ABCDEFGHIJKLMNOPQRSTUVWXYZ
1234567890.,;:`'&!?$

London:
London Text (Compugraphic),
Cloister Black (Mergenthaler)

abcdefghijklmnopqrstuvwxyz
ABCDEFGHIJKLMNOPQRSTUVWXYZ
1234567890.,;:□'&!?$
abcdefghijklmnopqrstuvwxyz
ABCDEFGHIJKLMNOPQRSTUVWXYZ
1234567890.,;:□'&!?$

Athens:
City Medium (Berthold),
Neo-Edelweiss (The Headliners
International, Inc.)

abcdefghijklmnopqrstuvwxyz
ABCDEFGHIJKLMNOPQRSTUVWXYZ
1234567890.,;:`'&!?$
abcdefghijklmnopqrstuvwxyz
ABCDEFGHIJKLMNOPQRSTUVWXYZ
1234567890.,;:`'&!?$

Venice:
Gavotte (Mergenthaler),
Zapf Chancery Medium Italic (ITC),
Book Jacket Italic (VGC)

abcdefghijklmnopqrstuvwxyz
ABCDEFGHIJKLMNOPQRSTUVWXYZ
1234567890.,;:`'&!?$
abcdefghijklmnopqrstuvwxyz
ABCDEFGHIJKLMNOPQRSTUVWXYZ
1234567890.,;:`'&!?$

292

Chicago:
Cruz Tempor Medium
(John Schaedler, Inc.),
Bessellen (VGC)

abcdefghijklmnopqrstuvwxyz
ABCDEFGHIJKLMNOPQRSTUVWXYZ
1234567890.,;:`'&!?$
abcdefghijklmnopqrstuvwxyz
ABCDEFGHIJKLMNOPQRSTUVWXYZ
1234567890.,;:`'&!?$

Seattle:
Helvetica Regular Condensed (VGC),
Machine (ITC)

abcdefghijklmnopqrstuvwxyz
ABCDEFGHIJKLMNOPQRSTUVWXYZ
1234567890.,;:`'&!?$
abcdefghijklmnopqrstuvwxyz
ABCDEFGHIJKLMNOPQRSTUVWXYZ
1234567890.,;:`'&!?$

Los Angeles:
Balloon (VGC),
Hand-lettered Script A-71 (VGC)

abcdefghijklmnopqrstuvwxyz
ABCDEFGHIJKLMNOPQRSTUVWXYZ
1234567890.,;:'&!?$
abcdefghijklmnopqrstuvwxyz
ABCDEFGHIJKLMNOPQRSTUVWXYZ
1234567890.,;:'&!?$

Cairo:
Dingbats

All these fonts, except for Monaco, are proportionally spaced. Monaco is a monospaced font, like a standard typewriter.

You may have already noticed that some Mac typefaces look better on the screen than others. Similarly, some printed typefaces will look better than others. The reason lies in the way the font data are stored. Because storing every dot of every font in every size takes up so much space, Mac stores every dot of some sizes and creates the other sizes by scaling them up or down. In the process, some scaling factors work less well than others. Scaling a 24-point original down to a 12-point copy, for example, generally works well, but scaling the size down to 18 point may leave rougher edges, since the scaling is no longer a simple matter of dropping every other dot.

The point sizes given in the style menus of many Macintosh programs are close to, but not quite the same as, the standard printer's point measurements. An American/British printer's point equals 0.013837 inch, or about 72 points to the inch. A European or Didot point equals 0.3759 millimeter or 68 points to the inch. The Macintosh screen fonts use 80 points to the inch, the ImageWriter 72 points.

Programs will be available that will let you design your own fonts, and independent companies will sell other font choices. Because of the limited screen resolution, many fonts will appear only in a large display typesize.

Please use the fonts with care. Don't make all your correspondence look like kidnappers' ransom notes; don't commit crimes against typography.

The only use for the San Francisco font is as an example of bad taste.

USING MACINTOSH IN MOVING VEHICLES

If you have a source of power and a small table, you can use Mac while traveling—in a boat, a large motor vehicle, or an executive airplane. The power supply should be 120 volts (North American version); the power frequency can be anywhere from 30 Hz to 20 kHz. A square-wave power supply of the kind

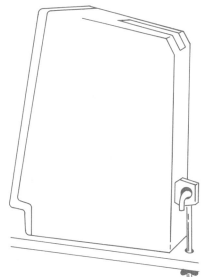

Fasten down the computer with the keyhole lock from Apple's security kit.

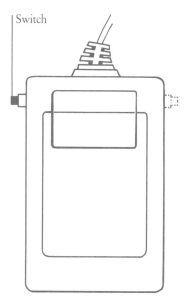

A switch on the mouse can activate motion detection. (The mouse button is not affected.) Switch should be momentary-contact, push-to-close, wired in series with pin 2 of the mouse cable.

produced by low-cost inverters from batteries poses no problems.

You may have a few problems if you run into heavy seas, rough roads, or turbulence that can upset the main computer unit or toss the mouse around. Since the main computer unit is a little top heavy, fasten the computer to the table. The keyboard can be held down with its security lock or you can simply tape it down.

The mouse might create problems if it rolls around while you are using the keyboard. However, since the mouse isn't active unless you push its button and the pointer never runs completely off the screen, you can probably live with a loose mouse.

If having a mouse on the loose bothers you, restrain it when not in use, or modify it so that it is active only while you are holding it. Add a small push-button switch to the side of the case (the left side if you're right-handed). The switch should be normally open (that is, you have to push to make a contact). Wire the switch in series with pin 2 in the mouse cable, the pin that carries the 5-volt supply for the LEDs in the mouse. When the switch is open it will extinguish the LEDs and the motion sensing. When you palm the mouse and press the switch, you will activate the LEDs and restore mouse operation.

Although the Macintosh is certified to be sufficiently free of electromagnetic radiation for home use (FCC type B), there are no certification procedures to qualify a device as safe to use on aircraft. For lack of space and power, this isn't an issue on commercial airliners, but you may want to use your Macintosh on a private aircraft. Consult with the companies that supply the avionics to see if they have advice or tests concerning possible interference from Mac. In any event, prudence suggests that you not use any device than might radiate interference during take off or landing procedures, or while flying near potentially hostile airspace.

The murky issue of using computers on board aircraft may take some time to resolve. For airliners, FAA regulations permit only hearing aids, heart pacemakers, tape recorders, and electric shavers. Even digital watches and calculators are not authorized, much less computers.

NOTES FOR THE HANDICAPPED ON USING MACINTOSH

This section offers a few suggestions of ways that the Macintosh can be adapted for use by people with certain physical handicaps. For more ideas and information about products for handicapped computer users, contact the organizations listed at the end of this section.

Mac for the Hearing-Impaired

If you are deaf or hard of hearing, you will generally have little difficulty using Mac. You can set the speaker volume to maximum with the Control Panel desk accessory. Other than for programs specifically designed to produce sound output, the speaker is used only for warning tones. These warnings are nearly always accompanied by a dialog box or an alert-box warning message. For a very simple visual indication of the tone, you can build a small circuit with a resistor and LED attached to the audio output port.

TTY/Baudot (or TDD) terminals are widely used by the hearing-impaired to communicate with typed characters. To use Mac as a TTY terminal, you will need a communications program and a 110-baud modem that can handle five-bit Baudot code. These items should be available from independent vendors.

There is no practical way to use Macintosh to decode closed-captioned television programs; the cost would be higher than the present decoders available for use with television sets.

Mac for the Vision-Impaired

Macintosh can be adapted more readily than other microcomputers to work for people with certain forms of visual impairment. People with acuity limitations will benefit from the variable type size used by word processors and some other programs. The font sizes offer the computer equivalent of large-type books; even larger sizes of type are also available. Not all programs offer flexible type sizes, however.

With MacWrite, use Font, FontSize, and Style
to select a typeface and size for comfortable reading.

The small type used to name each icon in the finder
may be a problem. However, since each icon stays in position unless you move it, you can keep track of positions
without reading the file names. Programs should be available that let you redesign the icons; use these programs to
make bolder icons if necessary. Similarly, a program could
create larger file names on screen.

The on-screen pointer for the mouse is limited to 16
by 16 pixels. Since the shape is under software control, the
pointer could be redesigned for greater legibility.

In some cases a larger screen will help. See Chapter
29 for information about adapting alternative display
screens to Mac.

The speech-synthesis feature will help the totally
blind. Since the speech synthesizer can read standard
ASCII text, the Macintosh could serve as a general-
purpose reading machine. The problem is Macintosh's
visual interface, which is less suitable for a totally blind
person than an old-fashioned command-line interface. If
your associates or relatives prefer a Macintosh for its ease of
use, however, you can still use the Macintosh as a reading
machine by circumventing the main problems.

The biggest problem is selecting files from the
keyboard; the standard interface will not do this, but
an accessory program could. Until such programs are
available, the disk and Finder must be set up so that icons
appear in fixed locations on the screen. Do this by resizing
the disk window to the full screen, then put the icons in a
specific order and choose Clean Up from the Special
menu. Eject the disk without closing the disk window.
Make a plastic template with notches marked off for the
mouse movement corresponding to the standard spacing
of icons within the Finder.

To use the disk, insert it and move the pointer to the
upper left corner of the screen by rolling a long distance up
and left. Then pick up the mouse and put it into the corner
of the template. To select an icon, run your thumb against
the template and feel for the notches while you move the
mouse.

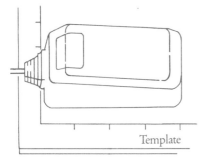

Template

*If you are blind, you can find
icons by first rolling the mouse to
the left and up; then by rolling the
mouse along the template and
counting the notches that mark
each icon's position.*

Use as many keyboard commands as possible during operation. You can eject a disk at most times, even when the Finder is not on the screen, by typing Command-Shift-1 (internal disk drive) or Command-Shift-2 (external disk drive).

Disk identification is another problem. The thin disk-drive slot doesn't leave enough space for attaching raised lettering or braille labels to disks. You can open the slot a little by filing on the upper edge; remove the front panel from the computer first.

Another way to identify disks is by cutting small notches along the edge. Use a knife rather than a file so plastic dust won't contaminate the disk; microfloppy disks are not sealed along the edge. Cut at a 45-degree angle instead of with a vertical cut; this gives you two more edges for coding.

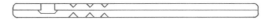

Identifying disks by touch:
Cut small notches at 45-degree
angles along the left and right
edges. Don't cut vertically, since
the edges are not sealed and
shavings might slip inside.

Mac for the One-Handed

The three keys that perform shift functions—Shift, Option, and Command—are used not only with the keyboard but also with the mouse. For one-handed operation, special software will let you toggle these keys, turning them on and off through a keyboard command. Since a software toggle may not show the status of each key, the switching could be done by a conventional on/off switch, wired in parallel to the key. There is space along the top of the keyboard to mount such switches.

Mac for Those with Motor-Control Limitations

If you have difficulty with fine motor control, the mouse may present problems. Sometimes the solution may be the same as for some graphic-arts problems: Change the

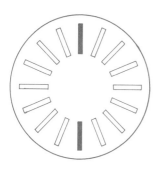

"gearing" of the mouse. Such changes are only easy for factor-of-two alterations. A permanent change can be made by opening the mouse and covering some of the slits in the optical vanes that interrupt light between two pairs of LEDs and phototransistors. The slits must be covered in opposing pairs. Doing this is a little tricky. Modified software could be designed to register only smooth mouse movements and ignore sudden or jerky motions.

Some users may find that moving the mouse button to a different part of the mouse or out of the mouse altogether makes it easier to operate. An alternate button can be installed between the mouse and the main computer unit, as explained in the section on tracing artwork with a mouse, above.

Sharing Good Ideas

If you have found a useful way for a handicapped person to use Mac or any other computer, publicize it. Write an article for a magazine or a letter to the editor. Put suggestions on electronic bulletin boards and pass them on to organizations for the handicapped.

Some clearing houses for information about computers and the handicapped are:

Association of Rehabilitation Programs in Data Processing
Physically Handicapped Training Center
University of Pennsylvania
4055 Chestnut Street, 3rd Fl/T7
Philadelphia, PA 19104

Electronic Industries Foundation/Project with Industry
2001 Eye Street N.W.
Washington, D.C. 20006

Project on the Handicapped in Science
American Association for the Advancement of Science
1776 Massachusetts Avenue, N.W.
Washington, D.C. 20036

The Trace Research and Development Center on
    Communications, Control, and Computer
    Access for Handicapped Individuals
University of Wisconsin
314 Waisman Center
1500 Highland Avenue
Madison, WI 53705

Chapter 27 Communications

Someday, fast and efficient communications between computers will give us instant access to each other, to the world's libraries, and to the latest political gossip. For now, communications are all too often merely frustrating.

Communications are difficult and complex and this chapter is necessarily complex as well, ranging far beyond the scope of most books about microcomputers. If your communications needs are straightforward, you may not need to read this chapter at all; instead read Chapter 9 to learn the essential steps for the most common types of communications. Read this chapter if you need more information about specific topics or want a broader understanding of the subject.

THE VARIETIES OF COMMUNICATIONS

When we use the Macintosh to communicate with other computers, we enter a chaotic world, for unfortunately, communications problems prevalent with other computers afflict Macintosh, too. And the situation is likely to get worse before it gets better; as products proliferate, many will be incompatible, making the murky waters of communications even murkier.

The answers to three key questions guide us through this difficult terrain:

With whom do you want to communicate?

- Another Macintosh or Lisa.

- Other microcomputers.

- Large computers.

- A dial-up data base (Dow-Jones, THE SOURCE, CompuServe, and others).

- Facsimile.

- Printers.

- Typesetting machines.

How will you communicate?

- Direct connection to another computer—
    Asynchronous link with or without error
        correction;
    Synchronous link, including error
        correction.

- Ordinary telephone lines—
    Asynchronous;
    Synchronous.

- Special leased or "dedicated" telephone lines—
    Asynchronous;
    Synchronous.

- Local area network (LAN) shared by many computers—
    Networks with only Macintoshes;
    Networks with other Apple computers;
    Networks with various brands of
        computer.

- Exchange disks.

- Printed text and optical character reader.

- Facsimile.

What do you want to communicate?

- Unformatted text.

- Word-processing files with formatting intact.

- Graphics—
  Using Apple's QuickDraw format;
  Using North American Presentation Level
  Protocol Syntax.

- Data files from spreadsheets or data bases—
  Text output only;
  Values or numbers only;
  Complete file with all formulas and rela-
  tionships intact.

- Programs—
  Source code in ASCII;
  Binary file in machine language.

Each of these areas could fill an entire book, and many of them have. This chapter examines the basis of communications by describing the level of protocol associated with each area, and then looks at some specific topics, such as using AppleBus and using a Macintosh as a terminal with a large computer.

THE BEGINNINGS OF CHAOS

Communications between Macs and Lisas may not be difficult, but problems begin when you try to use a Macintosh or a Lisa to communicate with other computers. The problems have nothing to do with the Macintosh or Apple specifically; the headaches belong to the whole computer industry. Occasionally you can get a transfer between computers to work quickly; more often it takes hours, occasionally even days, to establish a connection.

The problems lie in the profusion of protocols and hardware standards and non-standards that litter the microcomputer industry. Furthermore, the words that describe communications are often used ambiguously, adding to the confusion.

The ISO Protocol Layers

Considering how complex communications are in the world in general, the chaos in the computer world may not seem so surprising. In speech, for example, we follow protocols about who should speak first, forms of address (Mister, Ms., Sir, Madam), ways to keep others from talking ("...aah...," "you know"), and so forth. For most of us, these protocols are ingrained as part of our social training. Keeping the many levels of computer protocols straight, on the other hand, requires some concentration.

The International Standards Organization (ISO) has developed a model with seven protocol layers to describe communications among different computers. The following explanations of these layers include computer examples —which will be explained later—and analogous concepts from other forms of communication, principally the postal system. This list starts at the lowest hardware layers and works up to the highest software layers.

The physical layer. This layer comprises the mechanical, electrical, and functional arrangements necessary for a connection. Examples: RS-422, telephone lines. Analogies: Trucks, railroads, postal-delivery personnel.

The data-link layer. This electronic protocol is used to convey a unit of information from one node to another. A node is any device—a computer or printer, for example —capable of sending and/or receiving information. This layer includes flow control—who can send data and when—and some forms of error control. Examples: An asynchronous serial connection, a 1200-baud modem. Analogy: An envelope.

The network layer. This layer determines how information from the sender is routed to the correct receiver. This step is usually missing if only two devices are involved. Example: A token-passing network. Analogies: The address and the mail-sorting process.

The transport layer. These are the steps taken to ensure high-quality network service, including confirmation that the information has reached its destination and has been read without error. This layer is not always used; many computers simply send information out without knowing where it goes. Examples: The error-detection and correction features of many communications programs. Analogy: The sender requesting a return receipt from the post office or acknowledgment from the receiver.

The session layer. This is the procedure by which the two communicating computer devices coordinate action. Example: The sending computer requesting that the receiving computer open a file, accept information, and close the file; the user sitting at the receiving computer does not need to intervene. Analogy: The sender asking the receiver to perform an action they both understand.

The presentation layer. This protocol details all the formatting and code conversion necessary to make information from the sending computer intelligible to the receiving computer. Example: Supplying graphics information in a form that the receiving computer can display. Analogy: A lawyer sending a letter to a client explaining a court decision in plain English.

The application layer. This layer ensures that the information is sent in a form that can be used directly by an application program running on the receiving computer. Example: Moving a Multiplan file from an IBM PC to a Macintosh. Analogy: A lawyer sending a legal analysis of a court decision to another lawyer.

Many computer practices cut across several types of protocol, so things are not quite as tidy as this list implies. Nevertheless, we will use these concepts to guide us through the quagmire.

For your computer and another to communicate at all, you must agree on the physical and data-link protocol layers; for them to communicate smoothly, you must agree on the transport or session layers; and for integrated opera-tions, you must agree on the presentation or application layers. There is no shortage of protocols at each of the seven layers—and the problem is that they're all different.

THE PHYSICAL LAYER: CONNECTING THE HARDWARE

For the physical connection, the choices include:

Direct connection, using a simple set of wires tying two computers together via their serial ports. The wire is sometimes called a null-modem because it replaces a pair of modems. See Chapter 30 for a wiring diagram of Macintosh-to-Macintosh and Macintosh-to-other-computer null-modems.

Connection via a local area network (LAN), an electrical connection that links many computers and accessories, such as printers and high-capacity hard-disk drives. Unfortunately, two devices that can attach to the same network may not be able to talk to each other unless the upper-layer software protocols permit. The better networks accept a variety of computers; the restrictive ones accept only a single brand or model.

AppleBus is a simple, low-cost network; many other types of network will also support Macs and Lisas. Some can move data much faster than AppleBus, although the Macintosh will not be able to take full advantage of the speed because of hardware restrictions.

Connection via telephone lines. Two computers, each using a modem, can communicate through the phone lines. To accomplish this, both computers must be ready at the same time; one then calls the other. Depending on the software, an operator may not need to be at the answering computer, or even at the sending computer; everything can be run by a timer.

The telephone line may be:

- The same one we use for routine conversation; the quality of these voice-grade, dial-up switched lines varies greatly.

- Leased or dedicated lines with higher bandwidth and lower noise. Because these lines are tested for performance and sometimes have permanent electrical compensation added, they are also called conditioned lines.

- Via cellular radio from a moving car. This connection will need a robust error-detection and correction scheme.

- Air-to-ground and ship-to-shore radio links. These connections are too unreliable for any but the most determined users with the best error-correction protocols.

- Switched data lines that you can dial up much like present voice-grade lines. In the near future, these lines will handle 56 kilobits or 7 kilobytes per second.

Connection via a third computer. When connection between two computers proves too elusive or schedules don't match, then an indirect method may work. The first micro communicates information to a third computer; the second retrieves the information. All electronic mail services follow this scheme.

By using an intermediate computer for storage, the two micros don't have to be available at the same time. The third computer is usually a large one, often able to handle multiple protocols or at least a well-defined protocol. Getting a micro to communicate with such a large computer can be easier than getting two micros to talk directly with each other.

Radio transmission. On some frequencies, the FCC authorizes data communications by radio amateurs. The reliability varies tremendously with location, time, and frequency.

THE DATA-LINK LAYER: CODING THE SIGNAL

The form taken by the signal passing through the physical link depends on both hardware and software. The most common form is asynchronous ASCII communication: Each character is sent separately, preceded by a start bit and followed by one or two stop bits and possibly an error-detection bit. Because the receiver can always tell from the start and stop bits when a character is coming and when it is complete, the sending and receiving computers do not have to be locked to the same clock—they are asynchronous. They must, however, work at the same baud rate.

Putting in all the start and stop bits takes time. If the sending computer transmits not just a character at a time but a block of many characters (typically 256) at a time, the transmission rate improves considerably. To transmit a block, the sending computer must put timing information at the beginning of each one. The receiving computer uses the timing information to measure off each character in the block. Through the timing information, the two computers operate synchronously. If you use synchronous communications while typing, and you are a slow typist, there may be only one character in a block; the rest of the block simply marks time.

Synchronous communications is used mainly with mainframe computers and computer networks, such as AppleBus. We'll come back to synchronous communications later and concentrate now on the more common asynchronous form.

Asynchronous Communications

The quickest way to sort out data-link layer problems is to find someone else who has already used a Mac to communicate with another computer and do the same thing. If you're on your own, this section covers each step. It doesn't matter whether the other computer is large or small; the same principles apply.

First, you need communications software at each end. If possible, get software for each computer from the same company. Although the programs themselves may be different in order to run on different computers, they are more likely be compatible at several levels, sometimes as far as the session-layer protocol, provided that both programs are set up with the same parameters. If you can't get such software, then you must configure two different communications programs to use the same data-link protocol.

Some programs only send and receive with a special protocol operating at the transport-layer level. These will only work if the other machine is equipped for the same protocol.

The protocol may restrict the kinds of information you can send. Between different types of computers, the transmitted information is most often ASCII text. Although the strict definition of an ASCII code includes all possible 7-bit characters, when used in communications, an "ASCII file" normally means only printing characters: letters, numbers, and punctuation, plus tab, carriage return, line feed, and form feed. The remaining characters, including most control characters, are normally non-printing. Many communications programs transmit some control characters; Control-g is useful because it will ring a bell on most terminals (Command-g on the Macintosh Terminal program from Apple). Other control characters, such as the end-of-file marker, are usually removed before transmission.

Even if all you want to do is send an ASCII file, both machines must agree at the data-link level. The hardware determines some parameters, the software determines others; still other parameters can be set by either. The most important parameter is the baud rate.

Baud rate

Baud rate measures how fast information is sent. One baud is one change or modulation per second; at the common 300- and 1200-baud rates, one baud corresponds to one bit per second. (This isn't always true; several bits can be coded into a single modulation.) Depending on the exact data-link layer protocol, 300-baud transmission carries 25 to 30 characters per second, and 1200-baud carries 100 to 120 characters per second.

Although the baud rate can be continuously varied in some cases, the industry has settled on several standard speeds. If you use modems to communicate, they must operate at a common speed. For computers directly wired together, you can select the highest speed permitted by the equipment and the length of the wire; the longer the wire, the slower the speed. If in doubt, start at a slow speed and increase it until you encounter errors; then back off one speed step.

Low-speed modems

110 baud. Used by teletypes, Telex machines and other systems supporting older printers, and some radio applications. Also used for TTY communications by the hearing-impaired, with Baudot code instead of ASCII; you'll need a translation program and a 110-baud modem to connect to TTY devices.

300 baud. Most common with home microcomputers; most widely used speed. At 25 to 30 characters per second they are slow, taking a minute to fill a Mac screen with characters. Most people can read text at this speed comfortably (up to 300 words per minute).
The standard 300-baud protocol is Bell 103.

1200 baud. Most common in business and increasingly common with home computers. Transmission at 1200 baud is too fast for most people to read—a Mac screen fills in 15 seconds—but effective for scanning. If you're using a commercial database service, don't read everything while you are connected; save everything to disk and read it later; it's much cheaper.
The standard 1200-baud protocol is Bell 212A. The Racal Vadic protocol is still used, particularly by computing centers; most modems that use the Racal Vadic form can also use Bell 212A. Both protocols are full-duplex and work on ordinary phone lines. Avoid products that use Bell 202, a lower-cost, half-duplex protocol. (Full-duplex is simultaneous, two-way communications; half-duplex is one way at a time but the direction can be changed. Simplex is one way—and one direction—only.)

Medium-speed modems

2400 to 9600 baud. Normally used for synchronous communications. Prices climb quickly with speed, from about $2000 to $5000. Group 3 digital facsimile machines use 9600 baud modems with automatic switching to lower speeds for noisy phone lines.

Table 27-1 gives characteristics of all standard modem configurations. At 2400 baud and higher, modems must

Table 27-1. A summary of modem protocols

Bell Protocol	Speed (Baud)	Async/ Sync	Half/Full Duplex	Dial-up/ Leased Lines	2 or 4 Wire
103	300	A	F	D	2
202S (or C)	1200	A	H	D	2
202D (or T)	1200	A	H	L	2
212A	1200	A/S	F	D	2
201B	2400	S	H	L	2
201C	2400	S	F	L	4
208A	4800	S	F	L	4
208B	4800	S	H	D	2
			H	D	4
209A	9600	S	F	L	4

Note: The modem protocols outside North America are different. Neither European nor Japanese modems are compatible with the Bell protocols. If you need to communicate with a computer on another continent, you will need to get hold of compatible modems.

operate at half-duplex because they pass so much information down the line that they need the entire frequency bandwidth (3000 Hz on a voice-grade line). Systems that are half-duplex with a two-wire telephone line can often be turned into full-duplex with four wires or two telephone lines.

There is a 2400-baud, two-wire, full-duplex protocol in Europe. It is adaptive, adjusting both sending and receiving characteristics to the line condition while communicating. Such flexibility does not come cheaply, however.

High-speed modems

Over 9600 baud. Used for specialized applications. Some short-haul models can operate at a megabit per second. Special digital communications links may use microwave or television circuits. Few computer users work directly with this class of modem.

Other parameters

After setting matching baud rates, both sides must also agree on these other data-link layer parameters:

Character width or data bits. The number of bits in a character, either seven or eight.

Stop bits. Either one or two bits, signaling the end of a character.

Parity. Even, odd, or none. A single parity bit lets the systems determine if there is a one-bit error in the received signal. For even parity, the computer adds up all the bits in the character. If the sum is even, the parity bit is 0; if odd, the parity bit is 1. Either way, the final sum is always even. If a one-bit (or three-bit) error occurs, the sum will no longer be even. A two-bit error will not be detected since the sum remains even. Odd parity works the same way except the sum is always odd. Some systems specify Mark or Space, variations on no parity.

What the receiving system does upon encountering a parity error depends on the software. The parity bit is simply an error flag letting programs signal for retransmission—if the sending computer is set up to recognize the signal.

Duplex. At 300 and 1200 baud, most phone links are full-duplex—information can go both ways simultaneously. With a full-duplex link, the two computers use a different frequency band. So that both don't try to use the same band, one is set to the originate band, the other to answer. Which is which doesn't matter as long as both sides agree. With most modems and software, the calling party is set to originate.

With a half-duplex link, information travels only one way at any given time. The line can be reversed with signaling codes, but frequent reversing slows the transfer rate considerably. If the application calls mainly for one-way transfers, there is no speed penalty.

Echo. When you are communicating to a remote computer, how do you know that your characters are getting through? With full-duplex and echo, each character you send out is returned ("echoed") by the distant computer. Echoing is only practical with a full-duplex protocol (it takes too long in half-duplex), but not all computers operating full-duplex will echo.

If your echoed characters are occasionally garbled, the line is noisy. If the remote machine does not echo, your computer must generate the characters on your screen ("local echo"). If all your characters appear doubled, turn off local echo; if you don't see anything, turn on local echo (some software confuses duplex with echo).

For a second group of data-link layer parameters, communications will be more efficient if sender and receiver agree, but if the messages are sufficiently short or the receiver is willing to rework the received information later, complete agreement is not absolutely necessary. These parameters include the following:

Handshake. The sending machine sometimes transmits faster than the receiving machine can receive. Handshaking can overcome this problem. The receiving machine sends a signal (usually DC3 or XOFF, Control/- Command-s) to the sending machine, which then stops until it receives another signal (usually DC1 or XON, Control/Command-q). Handshakes help when the receiver must write the transmitted information to disk. Unfortunately, many senders do not recognize handshakes.

Line ends. Macintosh, in its internal files, uses a carriage return to indicate a move back to the left margin and a one-line paper advance. Some computers distinguish between a carriage return and a line feed and require both. Communications software for Mac should add line feeds to carriage returns if necessary and strip incoming line feeds when accompanied by a carriage return. If these steps aren't taken, you may see double line feeds in some cases, and the other party may see all your lines overwriting each other.

Filters and pauses. For some systems, you must remove certain characters or else you will see spurious characters on your screen. Some receiving computers require a short pause at the end of each line to allow them to process the line.

THE NETWORK LAYER:
ADDRESSING THE MESSAGE

This protocol layer generally affects only local area networks, specifying the addressing scheme. It is built into the network hardware and software; for example, it is part of the AppleBus software.

THE TRANSPORT LAYER:
ERROR-CORRECTION AND VERIFICATION PROTOCOLS

Protocols that send standard ASCII files in a continuous stream cannot send every possible bit combination because some codes must be reserved for marking the end of a file or signaling for the handshake.

Transport-layer protocols get around this difficulty by sending information in blocks of a fixed size (called protocol data units in ISO jargon). Since sending and receiving computers both know exactly how many bits will be in a block, all bit combinations are permissible. The longer the file, the more blocks it uses.

Files that can contain any combination of bits are called binary files, because they are just a sequence of binary bits. Programs that run directly on a computer are binary files, as are many types of data files.

For error detection and correction, the sending machine calculates an error-detection code from the data in the block and adds the code to the end of the block. The receiving machine takes each block, independently calculates the error code, and compares it with the code sent. If the codes don't match, the receiver requests the block again. Because of this additional information, the transfer rate is slower than sending straight ASCII without error correction. In some cases, the error detection is done at the data-link layer and the correction at the transport layer.

Transport-layer protocols with error correction are sometimes called protocol transfers or verification protocols.

Error correction is always handy but not always essential. English text survives occasional typos. For financial data or programs, on the other hand, any error—even a single bit—can be serious, so error detection is essential.

The computer industry has no standard transport-layer protocol; several dozen are in use, many for a specific brand of hardware or software. Most work in a primitive way. Before receiving information, the receiving machine must open a file and then let the sending machine know that it is ready to receive. The sender transmits the information, and the receiver closes the file.

The transport-layer protocol best-known among computer hobbyists has been the Xmodem protocol, used in several public-domain communications programs. Xmodem is effective but works only at the transport layer; it needs modification for more sophisticated use. The trend has moved toward more advanced session-layer protocols.

THE SESSION LAYER: COORDINATING ACTION

At the session layer, two computers can automatically take actions such as opening and closing files on command from one of them. Thus the transmission not only moves the contents of a file, but essentially the file folder itself, neatly labeled and ready for use.

Microcom is putting its Microcom Networking Protocol (MNP) on Macintosh. With MNP, the file type, icon, and other attributes are sent along with the file contents when transmitting between Macintoshes and Lisas. In a future version, the Microcom program will let one Macintosh user take over a remote Macintosh and operate it directly.

Microcom is licensing MNP to other companies. Since neither MNP nor any other protocol is likely to dominate communications completely, most equipment using MNP will remain compatible with ordinary data-link layer protocols. An MNP-equipped computer will query a remote computer to see if it can also handle MNP. If so, the communications will take place at the highest protocol level the two sides have in common.

Between identical or similar computers, MNP works in a special mode, transferring icons and other file attributes. Between different computers, the sending computer queries the receiving computer about what attributes it can use. The file name is transmitted, but the icon may be replaced with a file type, and the receiving computer then creates a directory entry. MNP also tries to use transport-layer error correction whenever possible; if the receiving machine is not equipped for error correction, MNP automatically falls back to data-link layer communications.

No single protocol will suffice for all possible communications; there will be many different session-layer protocols. The most intelligent communications software will select or detect the most appropriate protocol so the user need not fuss with the details.

THE PRESENTATION AND APPLICATION LAYERS: THE HIGHEST LEVELS

At the presentation level, the receiving computer can make use of the information in a standard form. Presentation-layer protocols range across many applications.

- Graphics protocols use a standard way to write on the screen. The North American Presentation Level Protocol Syntax specifies a coding system for screen graphics, used for videotext.

- A few data formats permit moving information between different programs and different computers.

At the presentation layer, software must still convert information before use, and a widely used protocol may not be able to take advantage of all the features of any specific computer.

At the application layer, the file is moved between two computers that can use the information directly. Until there are more standards, this level is achieved mainly when moving information between similar computers.

For specific information on moving files from another computer to the Macintosh, see the next chapter.

COPING WITH THE DATA FLOW: CONCENTRATORS AND MULTIPLEXERS

Macintosh and other graphics-driven microcomputers create and manipulate far more information than earlier microcomputers. Files include not just ASCII text, but typefaces, icons, graphs, and drawings as well. These large files gobble up time in transmission and run up the phone bill.

If you frequently send large quantities of information, you should consider several ways to increase the effective transmission rate.

Higher-speed modems. These modems may not operate reliably on noisy switched lines; if you go to leased lines, the telephone line charges go up to about $1.50 per mile per month.

Data concentrators. An English-language text file contains much redundant information. A trivial example is the letter Q, which is always followed by a U. If sender and receiver agree, the U can be deleted from the transmission, saving time; the receiver inserts a U after every received Q.

The widely used Huffman coding algorithm compresses English text to about half the original length. A complementary algorithm restores the original text. You can use the algorithms manually, or use software that automatically performs compression and expansion; such software usually provides error correction as well (transport-layer level). A 1200-baud line with compression functionally runs at twice the speed. The compression ratio depends on the information; the more powerful compression techniques work with a variety of data, not just English text.

Multiplexers. A MUX (multiplexer) takes the incoming data stream from two or more computers and puts them on a single telephone line. Often a MUX includes a built-in data concentrator. Both sides of a communications link must have matching MUXs. Prices range from $1200 up.

Combined MUX/concentrators. A combination MUX and concentrator can run two channels at effectively 2400 bits per second with a single 1200-baud synchronous modem. Concentrators and MUXs work at the transport layer.

COMMUNICATIONS BETWEEN MACINTOSHES AND LISAS

For simple communications between two Macs and/or Lisas, see Chapter 9.

The simplest way to connect three or more Macintoshes together is to use AppleBus, a low-cost communications link that can tie together up to 16 devices—different model Apple computers, shared hard disks, and printers. The shielded two-wire cable has a maximum length of 1000 feet. To connect more than 16 devices, several AppleBus configurations can be tied together, or a device on the AppleBus can act as a gateway to another type of network. Apple will supply software to run AppleBus that should make information transfer among computers and accessories simple.

The AppleBus connects through a serial port run at the maximum speed, 230 kilobits per second (29 KB per second). This performance should work effectively for moving files in a small assemblage of computers and accessories; it does not compete with the expensive networks that may offer transfer rates of several megabits per second.

For more information on the AppleBus, see Chapter 30.

COMMUNICATIONS WITH OTHER COMPUTERS

When two computers communicate, their relative size often affects terminology more than the technology.

Nearly all computers consist of a processing unit and a keyboard/display unit. A microcomputer contains a processor and a keyboard/display unit in the same package. A mainframe computer is a large machine with very fast processing, enormous capacity disk drives, and many megabytes of memory. Its processing unit fills big boxes installed inside air-conditioned rooms; its keyboard/display units, or terminals, may be scattered around the building. The traditional, or dumb, terminal does not contain any processing power and can operate only when connected to its large computer host.

To a large computer, Mac is just another dumb terminal. But since Mac has processing and storage capabilities, it can act as an intelligent terminal, manipulating information before sending it on to the mainframe and storing the mainframe's responses for later use. For example, you can use MacWrite to prepare text before sending it to the mainframe; you can also feed information from the mainframe into Multiplan for further analysis.

Terminals come in many forms, and suitable software will turn Mac into most of the popular types. The differences between terminal types involve many details, such as the code to erase a line on the screen. Although some terminal configurations truly offer special advantages, most came about because of arbitrary design decisions. Apple's MacTerminal program emulates the Digital Equipment Corporation VT52 and VT100 terminals. Other companies will probably write programs to emulate the DEC VT200 and Tektronix® graphics terminals, and many others.

With so many terminal types, some systems fall back on the simplest one: an electronic version of the old mechanical teletype. A teletype has minimal features—just the ability to print along a line and advance the paper. It won't even erase. In a rare display of nostalgia, many flashy terminals, including Mac, can emulate a teletype.

When you buy software for Mac to emulate a terminal, make sure it emulates an intelligent terminal rather than a dumb one. Look for several key features:

- Disk storage and recording. The program should let you create information with Mac software, store it to disk, and then transfer the disk file to the mainframe, as well as store returning information on disk.

- Ability to store communications parameters on disk so you can set them once and recall them.

- Ability to suspend communications without disconnecting from the remote computer. This way you can use a Macintosh program for some task and return to the other computer without having to reestablish a connection.

SYNCHRONOUS COMMUNICATIONS

Earlier in this chapter we saw that synchronous communications work by sending information a block at a time, with timing information so the receiving computer can extract the characters from the block. There are, naturally, several variants of synchronous communications. The various physical-layer protocols can be shared by most forms, but the data-link layer changes.

Microcomputers have generally used asynchronous communications because it's easier, and the performance penalties aren't too serious for small quantities of data. Synchronous links are mainly used by large computers. For best performance, a microcomputer connected to IBM and many other mainframes should use a synchronous link. The physical link between the mainframe and the micro may be a wire or a modem. Many modems made for microcomputer use, including the Apple 1200-baud modem, will not handle synchronous links.

The conversion from asynchronous to synchronous communications can be performed in several ways. Although Macintosh is normally asynchronous at its serial ports, the ports will accept external timing signals on pin 7 to clock data in and out to support common synchronous protocols. The Macintosh can therefore emulate the terminals that the mainframe software expects to see at the end of each cable. The AppleLine converter connects between Mac's serial port and a synchronous port on a mainframe to emulate the IBM 3278-4 terminal.

If several different Macs need to communicate only occasionally with the mainframe, a single AppleLine converter can be switched between them. Some non-Apple converters can connect to several microcomputers or terminals simultaneously, with software-selected switching. Or the mainframe may have several ports adapted to asynchronous operation.

Many large computers, particularly IBM models and copies of IBM models, don't use ASCII for coding characters. (Virtually all microcomputers, including the IBM PC, use ASCII.) Instead they use EBCDIC (Expanded Binary Coded Decimal Interchange Code); it's similar to ASCII and the conversion software simply looks up each incoming character in a table and sends out the translated code.

The supporting software for the AppleLine will perform ASCII to EBCDIC conversions.

System Network Architecture (SNA)

System Network Architecture (SNA) is IBM's umbrella architecture for its present communications offerings. The actual implementation is known as Synchronous Data Link Control (SDLC), a version of the international standard High-Level Data Link Control (HDLC).

The IBM computers that work with SNA include the 370, 308X, 4300, and 8800 series, as well as System 32, 34, 38, and Series/1.

The most widespread type of IBM synchronous terminal is the 3270 series, so most terminal emulators, including the AppleLine, emulate such terminals. Fewer microcomputer products emulate the less-common 3780 batch-communications devices, such as the 2780 terminal.

Help with a Mainframe Connection

Getting micro-mainframe links to work successfully is often an involved process, but in most cases, an organization big enough to have a mainframe is also big enough to have a data-processing department that can help you get started.

Chapter 28 Moving Information Between Computers

F or this discussion I assume that you've read Chapter 27 and now have two computers talking to each other at some level of protocol. What kind of information can you move and what can you do with it?

PROGRAMS

The actual machine-language file will only be understood by another computer of the same type, so there is no point in moving a program except to another Macintosh or a Lisa running Macintosh software. To move program files, use a transport-layer protocol.

Source code for programs—the original instructions in BASIC, Pascal, Logo, or other languages—can be transferred as an ASCII file (with Microsoft BASIC, you should save the program with SAVE "FILENAME",A). Depending on the program's origin, some adjustments may be necessary to run the program on Mac. And you will need the appropriate language interpreter or compiler to turn the source code into instructions for Mac.

TEXT FILES

Text files can be moved easily to Mac from another computer, but after transfer, the file may look a little odd;

in most cases the formatting information, such as location of page breaks, tabs, paragraph indentation, and so forth, will be lost. If formatting information is coded into the text, the codes should, if possible, be removed before transmission.

The files for some word-processing programs are so hard to work with that you should transfer a page image rather than the normal data file stored by the word processor. A page image is the disk equivalent of the printed page, complete with headers, footers, and page numbering. Most powerful word processors let you make a page image (with the command "print to disk" or something similar). Page images are not particularly easy to work with either, but at least they are free of embedded formatting commands. They do, however, have a carriage return at the end of every line. If you use Mac to do any work on the file, you will need to remove those carriage returns to restore word-wrapping.

Getting Rid of Carriage Returns

If your word-processing program permits, here is the quickest way to get rid of unwanted carriage returns: You want to preserve the carriage return at the ends of paragraphs, so search for all carriage returns followed by three spaces (or a tab or whatever you use for paragraph indents) and replace them with a # or some other rarely used character. Then replace every carriage return with a space or with nothing, depending on whether or not the word at the line end runs together with the word at the beginning of the next line. Finally, replace the # symbol with a carriage return and the paragraph indent. Although this procedure may mangle a few lines, it's a lot faster than deleting carriage returns one by one.

Eight-Bit Text Files

A few word-processing programs—WordStar®, for example—store their text using eight bits for each character instead of the more common seven bits; the extra bit must be stripped off before transferring the file. Do this on the original computer, before moving the file to Mac.

Many computer hobby magazines have published programs for stripping the eighth bit.

With all the complications, retyping short text files may be simpler than trying to establish communications to transfer them. For some computer enthusiasts, this suggestion is heresy; they would rather spend hours manipulating a file than ten minutes retyping.

Optical Character Readers

If transferring a text file from another computer proves impossible, you can use an optical character reader (OCR) to scan a printed page. Get a clean printout—with daisy-wheel printer and carbon ribbon—from the original computer. The OCR operator can tell you what restrictions apply to the typeface and page layout. The resulting printed page is the only way to automate input from electric and most electronic typewriters. Although some service bureaus offer a document-conversion service with OCRs, reliability and cost restrict OCR use to planned, high-volume jobs.

OCRs remain finicky, unreliable machines; they can only read originals, not photocopies, and they can't read dot-matrix printer output. Few, if any, OCRs can read an ImageWriter page.

Moving Macintosh Text Files

Moving a MacWrite or other Macintosh text-formatted file to an ordinary computer loses the typefaces and other formatting information, unless the receiving computer has the ability to use the information. Initially, only Apple Lisa 2s will be able to accept and use such information. In time, typesetting equipment and other sophisticated computers will preserve the formatting, taking advantage of the full MacWrite file.

Some specialty typesetting companies are planning to offer a service that takes Mac disks and produces finished, commercial-quality typesetting, complete with the fonts and sizes you selected with MacWrite, Microsoft Word or other word-processing programs.

OTHER NON-GRAPHICS FILES

Generally each spreadsheet, data base, or other program stores files in a unique way that other programs cannot read.

File-Interchange Formats

Although several file-interchange formats exist, none is widely supported. The most common is the DIF format created by Software Arts, the company that wrote Visi-Calc. DIF files work at the presentation-layer protocol level and contain printable data only; they do not store the formulas and relationships of VisiCalc or other programs. DIF has found its widest use in moving VisiCalc data to a graphing program.

The SYmbolic LinK (SYLK) format devised by Microsoft can store all formulas and relationships; several companies now use this format. SYLK is the only common microcomputer exchange format that runs functionally at the applications-layer protocol level. Because the format was designed for universal application, it is large and inefficient; it is best used only when transferring information, not for normal storage.

The Microsoft programs that can read and write SYLK files normally use a special optimized file, unique to each computer type. However, data files in SYLK can be moved to any other computer that has a program capable of reading SYLK files; all the functions remain intact—to the extent that the second program can take advantage of those functions.

Both DIF and SYLK can be transferred as ordinary ASCII files; they do not require special handling, although transport- and session-layer protocols will make transfers much easier.

ASCII FILES

Many programs can produce an ASCII file on disk that is equivalent to printed output so their information can be added to a word-processing document. These ASCII files usually lack formulas and relationships.

For programs that contain information in ordered, discrete blocks, such as cells in spreadsheets or records and files in data bases, the ASCII output can often be delimited with a comma or tab placed between each block. Without delimiting, the information is only useful for transferring to a word processor. With delimiting, the information can be placed, block by block, into another program.

Tab-Delimited Files

One way to create delimiters with a spreadsheet program is to add many spaces to each column—more than necessary for any cell. Then save an ASCII representation that includes the spaces; search and replace a block of spaces with a tab. This may be a multistep process, as you must then remove excess spaces and take care that empty cells are not inadvertently deleted.

You can write a program in BASIC or another language that reads the original file and converts it to another form or creates a tab-delimited file.

Multiplan for Mac can read tab-delimited data; each block is placed in a cell and each tab moves data into the following cell. A carriage return moves down to the first column of the next line.

Comma-Delimited Files

Comma-delimited data pose several problems. Commas are often used in large numbers (as in 1,000,000) and Europeans often use commas as decimal points. Because of this confusion, Multiplan on the Mac does not read comma-delimited data. If you need to use such a data file, you must convert the commas to tabs before moving the file.

If there are no commas in numbers or as decimals, then the switch is easy with a simple BASIC program, or it can be done on many word processors. Use the global search-and-replace function of the word processor, but first check to make sure it can replace with a tab, as some programs can only search and replace ordinary characters. If your program does not accept a tab as a valid character for replacement, try Control-i, the ASCII code for tab. You may need to change valid commas within fields to another character temporarily and restore them afterwards.

Unless you are moving a SYLK-format file, all this effort still leaves you with incomplete information, for the formulas and relationships have been lost in the transfer. Nevertheless, for a spreadsheet model, the headings and number entries are correct and reconstructing the entire model is simpler than starting from scratch.

If you don't need to change the Multiplan model, you can use the information for Microsoft's Chart program or use the Clipboard to move the information to MacPaint. You can then use Mac's powerful graphics to produce a presentation-quality report with far more flexibility than on the original computer.

Some specific cases

This section gives procedures for moving information from some specific programs running on the IBM PC to the Macintosh.

Some of the specific programs mentioned here will appear in Macintosh versions that can read files generated by their counterparts on other computers. If so, simple file transfers will be possible. Until then, here are some strategies for moving information stored by several popular programs to Multiplan on Mac. You must be reasonably fluent with these programs to make these steps work; if necessary, find someone who can help you the first time through. The principles described in this section apply to many different types of programs running on other computers.

The notation and instruction formats used here follow the style of each program's manual. In the following steps, all characters, including quotation marks, are literal; __ means a space.

Multiplan

Moving Multiplan files between the Macintosh and another type of computer is easy, once the communications problems have been solved. On the IBM PC, run Multi-plan and then follow these steps:

First use

Transfer Load filename then use the

Transfer Options command, and select the

Symbolic (SYLK) rather than normal mode. Finally,

Transfer Save the spreadsheet.

Use a communications program to move the new SYLK file. On the destination Macintosh, simply read it as a SYLK file (see below). No changes will be necessary and all functions and formulas will work.

Since Multiplan can consolidate data from several spreadsheets, you can thus prepare part of the data on one computer and move the file to another one.

VisiCalc

Save the VisiCalc file on disk, using the normal /SS command (not the /S#S command for DIF). Use the MS-DOS or PC-DOS version of Multiplan and then follow these steps.

First use

Transfer Option Other to set Multiplan to read a
    VisiCalc file, then

Transfer Load filename: to load the VisiCalc file into
    Multiplan. You need to save it in SYLK format
    with

Transfer Option Symbolic and save the file with

Transfer Save filename.

Now move the new file in SYLK to Mac; you can read it directly with Multiplan on the Mac. The formulas and relationships will be intact.

dBase II

Since dBase II is a database program and Multiplan is a spreadsheet, you won't be able to perform all the same functions, but Multiplan can use information from dBase II files as well as pass it on to Microsoft's Chart program.

On the originating computer, load dBase II, and type

```
.USE <filename>
.COPY TO <filename>.TXT DELIMITED WITH "
```

Instead of double quotes you can use any other unambiguous character. Empty logic fields will appear as a space, empty numeric fields as 0.0.

Modify <filename>.TXT with a word processor. Each field in the file will be separated by "," (quotes-comma-quotes). Search for and replace these characters with a tab. Records are separated with a carriage return and do not need modification. Then move <filename>.TXT to Mac and use it as a tab-delimited file (see below).

dBase II applications put any formulas and relationships among the contents of a data base in a dBase II program that cannot be transferred. If you need the formulas on Mac, you must enter them manually.

SuperCalc

The SuperCalc file format is shared by all three versions (SuperCalc, SuperCalc2, SuperCalc3) as well as by PeachCalc®.

Save the SuperCalc spreadsheet in the normal way, producing a file with .CAL extension. Load Sorcim's Super Data Interchange program and select from the menu:

SuperCalc files to Comma Separated Value file.

The new file will have the extension .CSV. Convert it into a tab-delimited file by searching for the commas and replacing them with tabs using a word processor. Since SuperCalc does not accept European-style decimals, there should be no ambiguous commas.

The formulas and relations in the SuperCalc model are lost during the transfer.

Lotus 1-2-3

The easiest way to convert a 1-2-3 file is to go via a third program. You can output the 1-2-3 file to a dBase II file, following Lotus's manual (the exact instructions depend on which version you have), then convert the dBase II file with the instructions above. Or you can create a DIF file, and then read the DIF file with Microsoft's MS-DOS Chart program. The Chart program can then output the information as a SYLK file; move this file to the Mac.

Without the help of a third program, you must figure out how to get 1-2-3 to produce a delimited file. This is a little complex, but the general steps are:

1. Insert a column containing && or some unique character pattern between each column on each line in the 1-2-3 model. You can automate this step with a keyboard macro program; find someone who is a whiz at 1-2-3 programming, since it's a little tricky.

2. Save the file to disk with:

   /Print File Options Unformatted.

3. With a word processor, remove all the multiple blanks—but not the single blanks that are valid information. Do this by replacing all double blanks with single blanks several times. This will eliminate all spurious blanks except for those before and after the &&.

4. Then successively replace

   __&&__
   __&&
   &&__
   && with tabs.

5. Now move the file to Mac and read it with Multiplan.

Again, the formulas and relationships are lost with the transfer.

Using a SYLK File

Once you have the SYLK file on a Macintosh disk, you can read it easily. Start an application program, such as Multiplan, that can read a SYLK file. Once the program is loaded, choose Open from the File menu. The SYLK file will appear in the list of available files; select it and click the Open button.

Using a Tab-Delimited File

When you have the tab-delimited file on a Macintosh disk, start a word-processing program and choose Open from the File menu; select the file. When the information is on screen, select it and choose Copy from the Edit menu, putting everything into the Clipboard. Then choose Quit from the File menu. Start Multiplan, and after it is loaded, choose Paste from the Edit menu. The Clipboard contents then go into the spreadsheet.

GETTING INFORMATION FROM A LARGE COMPUTER

All the problems of moving information from one microcomputer to another also apply to large computers. Mainframe computers are at their best handling large data bases and crunching huge arrays of numbers. Since large computers are always managed by data-processing specialists, the software they use appeals to the specialist rather than to the ordinary professional. Or, to put it another way, mainframe software is much harder to use than microcomputer software, especially Macintosh software.

Getting information out of a mainframe and into a micro isn't easy. In most cases, you must go through a normal session with the micro acting as a terminal to the mainframe data base and store all the results on disk in the micro. Then you must go through the information, and spend considerable time manipulating the data into a form suitable for a microcomputer program. The whole process is so tedious that most people don't bother to do it electronically; instead they print out the results and then type those results into the microcomputer, one by one. Finally, they can look at the results with a spreadsheet or graphing program.

A few microcomputer programs can now perform this transfer with less pain. These programs act as a buffer between you and the mainframe. You ask for information through a microcomputer interface; the program converts your requests into commands understood by the mainframe database manager. Information from the data base then passes through the microcomputer and appears in a spreadsheet, ready for your next step. In time, all important mainframe programs will have such microcomputer support; until then, there will be much wasted and repetitive work.

A similar problem applies to many data bases designed for access by microcomputers. All of the popular dial-up information services currently use awkward, obsolescent interfaces; they appeal only to determined computer hobbyists and specialists. The better ones will soon change to incorporate elements of natural language; the data base will understand simple English as well as cryptic commands. Software for the Macintosh will help as well. If you want the airline guide, for example, you should be able to point at it to make the communications program send the correct command to the data base. The lack of such programs is a puzzle, for they are fairly easy to write.

A SOFTWARE OPPORTUNITY

The problem of moving information between programs and computers is so complex that it creates an opportunity for independent programmers. Since lone programmers find competing in the major program categories increasingly difficult without major financial backing, they might consider writing conversion programs.

Chapter 29 Reproducing the Macintosh Screen

To share a Macintosh screen image with a small group of people, a simple printed output will usually do. For presentations to large groups and for publication, advertising, or training, the choices are more complex. This chapter discusses the main methods of reproducing the screen.

Much of this chapter is highly technical; for each section, I assume the reader has the technical background appropriate to the specific topic at hand. Essential terms are defined in the glossary, but this chapter is not a substitute for a technical handbook on photography or video.

Many readers will want to review just the sections on still photography. For the most part, you will get satisfactory results if you just follow as much of the advice as your equipment can handle. If you are a cinema buff, you might read the section on motion-picture photography to learn how the professionals do it. Similarly, video enthusiasts might be interested to see where the Macintosh fits into the flood of present and forthcoming video equipment.

The alternatives for reproducing the screen image are:

Print a screen image on paper (low to medium quality; cheap).

Photograph the screen directly:

- Still photography (medium quality; low cost [$250]; quick).

- Motion-picture photography (very low quality without special equipment; medium quality with expensive [over $10,000] special equipment).

Move Mac's video signal electronically; requires a modified Mac:

- Photograph the image with a CRT/camera combination (medium or better quality; moderate-cost [$2000 to $3000] equipment).

- Put image on photographic film with electron beam or laser imaging device (high quality; very rare, extremely expensive [over $40,000] equipment).

- Distribute video signal to special monitors and projection televisions (medium to high quality; moderate-cost [monitors $1500 to $2000, projection television about $6000] equipment).

Convert Mac's video signal to a conventional video signal; distribute via closed-circuit television, broadcast television, videotape, or videodisc:

- Point a TV camera at the Mac screen (very low quality; simple, low-cost [$2000] TV camera).

- Electronic standards conversion (low to medium quality; complex, extremely expensive [over $60,000] equipment, not yet built).

Print screen image to disk; create reproduction-grade image with typesetting equipment (high quality; expensive [$20,000 and up] equipment).

Although the choices are complex, you probably have only a few of the techniques readily at hand, effectively limiting your choices. If you need commercial photographs or a motion picture of the screen, a small group of professionals specialize in CRT images. Other options such as typesetting are provided by some service bureaus.

Many of the video techniques described here require that the video signal or some part of it be brought out of the Mac. To do this, you must have Mac modified, which will void the warranty. Since the Mac screen and video circuits were designed as an integral unit, there is no composite video signal anywhere inside Mac. Three separate lines carry the horizontal sync, vertical sync, and video image. To create a composite signal suitable for use with other electronic devices, you must add an adapter board. Such a board is neither complex nor expensive; Apple may someday produce a special version of Mac that has a built-in adapter with a video-output plug. If Apple doesn't, other companies will undoubtedly develop adapters. If your work requires video output, it may be best to use a Lisa, whose expansion bus permits video-output boards.

STILL PHOTOGRAPHY

You can either photograph the screen directly or photograph a printed screen image (a screen dump). Photographing the printed image is much easier, especially if you have a copy stand and macro lens. The results, however, lack the visual impact of the screen itself, and the tones are always uneven since no printer is ever perfectly aligned and no ribbon is free of irregularities or wear.

If you are using a Lisa with Macintosh software, one factor that may influence whether you photograph the screen or a screen dump is the acceptability of its squeezed screen image. If acceptable, all the techniques described here generally work for the Lisa, with some differences in detail because of screen size and refresh rate. If unacceptable, you should print the image (the screen dump will not be squeezed) or move it electronically. Lisa's own software should be free of these problems.

Photographing the Screen

The comments here apply to a 35-mm single-lens reflex camera, the most common high-quality camera type available.

Equipment

Mac's image size is 4¾ by 7 inches (12 by 18 cm), a 5:1 reproduction ratio for 35-mm film. Most normal lenses will not focus close enough for a full-screen shot; in most cases, extension tubes bring the camera in too close. Supplementary close-up lenses won't provide the sharpest results, but a +1 diopter lens with a 50-mm main lens will work.

A macro lens gives the best results. The Mac screen has a slight curvature, so straight lines may come out slightly curved with shorter-focal-length lenses. A 50- or 55-mm macro lens works satisfactorily; a 100-mm macro works even better. Macro zoom lens pictures won't be as sharp in the corners because of inherent design problems aggravated by the screen curvature.

Use a darkened room. If there is any stray light in the room, put a hood between the screen and camera; any closely woven, dark-colored cloth serves well.

Photographic novices should note that the Mac screen creates its own light; if your camera reads inadequate light, a flash will not help, and you cannot take a usable picture.

Settings

Adjust the screen to a high, yet comfortable brightness level. In order to duplicate the screen brightness, you can put a tiny dab of nail polish on the brightness control.

Mac refreshes the screen 60.15 times a second. A shutter speed faster than ¹⁄₆₀ second will show only part of the image. A ¹⁄₆₀-second shutter speed won't show the entire image either, because of the time required to open and close the shutter curtains. Slightly longer exposures will be uneven, as part of the image may be refreshed one more time than the rest of the image; the unevenness will partly depend on which direction your shutter travels.

To mark the screen brightness for photography, put a dab of nail polish on the brightness control.

338

An uneven refresh will be less of a problem if the overall image is overexposed a little. You should achieve passable results at a ⅛-second shutter speed, and better results with longer exposure. With a shutter speed of one second, the density variation is at most ¹⁄₆₀ of the overall exposure and will be invisible.

Note that different CRTs vary in their light decay characteristics, so experience gained with other computers or television sets may not apply to Macintosh.

With such slow shutter speeds, the camera must have a rigid support or tripod.

For exposure, take a through-the-lens reading on any mostly white image, then set two stops more exposure as a first trial; this will render the whites as white instead of a medium gray tone. Standard light meters may not be accurate because of a spectral sensitivity that is not matched to the screen's spectral balance. Light-meter readings may be off by as much as two f/stops.

For most macro lenses, the best f/stops will be f/8 or f/11. Smaller f/stops will be less sharp, while larger f/stops make focusing and depth of field more critical. Bracket exposures by half stops the first time, three stops total in each direction, and keep a record.

Film

If you are going to project the image, in most cases you will want a positive image (black letters on a white background as on the Mac screen), especially since some graphics and icons are hard to understand when shown in negative form. The exceptions may be cases where you must project in a partially lit room, where negative images can be easier to read.

Black-and-white positive films are rare; the only common high-contrast positive film, which is the best choice and also gives quick results, is Polagraph HC™ instant slide film for Polaroid's instant 35-mm Autoprocess system. The other two Polaroid instant slide films (the continuous-tone, black-and-white Polapan CT™ and the color Polachrome CS™) don't work as well.

If these films are unavailable or not suitable for some reason, you can check with graphic-arts facilities to see which processes they can handle. Most graphic-arts labs use a two-step process, printing negative-to-negative to get a positive. Kodak High Contrast copy film works well as the negative material; use it when you need reproduction-quality images for printing or reproduction. As with all high-contrast materials, the exposure latitude is small. For black-and-white film, no filters are needed.

If you don't have a convenient graphic-arts facility nearby, you can use color film with commercial processing. The exact color balance of CRTs depends on the phosphor coating that creates light. Macintosh uses a P-4 two-component phosphor with two emission peaks, at 460 nm and 560 nm. You can see the two components with a magnifying glass; some regions are a little more bluish than others. Because of a peaked emission, the color balance depends on exposure and emulsion choice. The concept of color temperature only applies to smooth emission curves, not the P-4 spectrum profile, but the rough equivalent color temperature is high, about 11,000 degrees Kelvin.

Color correction

Optimum correction of the Macintosh color balance will require some experiments with your exposure and film-emulsion preferences. As a starting point, use daylight color film and a color-correction filter. An 85C filter should yield neutral white tones; the more common 85 filter also works, yielding a warmer tone. You may need a CC (Color Correction) filter as well. If you must use tungsten-light color film, try to find the rare 86 filter or combine an 85B with an 81EF. Kodachrome emulsions have better contrast and sharpness than other color films, but fewer laboratories can process the film, so you may have to wait longer. If you want to experiment, you can create multiple exposure images on Mac with color filters.

Some photographers and art directors may question the need for color correction, arguing that if the screen is bluish, then it should look that way in print. Perhaps they think the blue confers a cool, high-tech feel. However, when we look directly at the Macintosh screen, it appears white, not blue. Our visual system adjusts the predominant illumination to white in the same way that we adjust to daylight or tungsten light.

Photographing the Screen as Part of a Larger Picture

If Mac's screen is only part of an overall picture, the bluish screen will mar the image. You can correct this by retouching or in the exposure. You have two strategies you can follow for the exposure:

- Single long exposure, if all elements are static and the overall light level can be balanced against the screen.

- Double exposure, once for the scene and once with a long exposure for just the screen. For the first exposure, black out the screen with photographic velvet; for the second, extinguish all other light sources and use a matte box if necessary to reduce spilled light from the screen.

To achieve color balance, you can:

- Filter the overall light to match the color balance of the Mac screen. If you have people in the scene, try an 80C or 80B gel over electronic flash units and a warming filter over the camera lens. Run tests if the results are critical; small errors can be corrected in the lab.

- Filter a double-exposed image separately, using the filters appropriate to the light source.

- Place a color gel over the screen. An 85 gel, available from motion-picture supply houses, may be roughly correct.

- The screen photograph can be taken at a different time and inserted as a photo composite. Achieving high-quality results with this method is difficult and expensive.

MOTION-PICTURE PHOTOGRAPHY

With ordinary cameras, motion-picture photography of CRTs will always show bars moving rapidly over the screen. If you have the resources, here's what to do to produce the best possible results.

Get a very stable, crystal-controlled, variable-speed motion-picture camera with external synchronization, reflex viewing and a 180-degree or larger shutter. For best results, the shutter should move vertically, from bottom to top (to match the direction Mac writes the image, from top to bottom—inverted for the camera lens).

Bring the 60.15-Hz vertical-sync signal out of the Macintosh (the signal is on a wire connecting the CPU board and the video/power-supply board) and divide it by two to 30.08 Hz; use the signal to control the camera's speed. The division won't be necessary with some units.

You'll need a phase control between the Mac and the camera, adjusted so that the image has the largest blackout when viewed through the reflex finder. Because Mac has a short vertical blanking interval—7.5 percent of the cycle—you may have some image loss, but if you split the difference between the top and bottom of the frame, the results are usually acceptable. A larger shutter opening will reduce or eliminate this problem.

For sync sound, simply operate normally; the Pilot-tone track on a Nagra or other recorder will record a 25 percent higher frequency that poses no problem for most resolving equipment.

After you have the film and sound track, you can transfer them to videotape: one frame of film to one frame (two fields) of video instead of the ordinary 24-frames-per-second film transfer. The slight speed shift downwards to the 59.94-Hz NTSC broadcast-standard field rate isn't important.

If the result will be used in a 24-frames-per-second motion picture, then you will have to convert speeds with a step printer, essentially dropping every sixth frame. Correct the sound frequencies with a Lexicon model 1200 pitch shifter. Step printing is expensive and may not work well, depending on the action.

The method just described generally works better than the classical technique for filming a television screen, which does have the virtue of producing a 24-frames-per-second film. This technique requires that you use a movie camera with a 144-degree shutter and external sync; slave the camera to Mac's vertical-sync signal.

The common practice of filming European television systems (50 Hz field rate) at 25 frames per second with a 180-degree shutter will not work with Mac.

Step-Frame Motion-Picture Photography

For the best results, script and budget permitting, shoot the motion picture with double exposure. On the first pass, black out Mac's screen and shoot the live action or other surrounding material. Then shoot the screen on the second pass with a step-frame motor control, exposing each frame as a still image with an exposure of ⅛ second or longer and filtration. Use computerized stepping motors for camera movements if necessary. Matching the action may require a traveling matte shot. You could create the matte with a program that generates a blank, white screen. For a clean matte with adjustable brightness, take an empty Macintosh case and replace the screen with a translucent white screen. Cut a mask that matches Mac's screen area and illuminate the screen with a floodlight; use a filter for a blue screen matte.

ELECTRONIC USE OF THE MAC VIDEO SIGNAL

If you have a video-output adapter on your Mac, you can use its video signal in many different ways. In all cases, the equipment receiving the signal must be capable of handling a 22.255-kHz horizontal sweep frequency, much higher than the standard 15.738 kHz used in North America and Japan or the 15.625 kHz used in Europe. The equipment should also have convenient controls to adjust vertical and horizontal size as well as linearity. Some of the ways you can use the signal electronically include:

Using a camera/CRT combination system to photograph screen images in a specially designed, light-tight box. Most current units cannot handle Mac's sweep frequency, but the Lang model 1014 ($2800) can.

Driving an electron beam recorder (EBR) with the video signal for the ultimate in real-time photographic imaging. An EBR essentially replaces the CRT phosphor with photographic film; the scanning electron beam strikes the film directly without any optics. The entire mechanism works in a vacuum chamber. EBRs are extremely expensive and used mainly for high-quality video-to-film transfers. Laser-beam recorders work similarly but their color capability isn't needed for ordinary Mac images.

These elaborate techniques don't really make much sense for a still image; the typesetting technique described later in this chapter works just as well or better and is much cheaper unless you need a very large number of images.

Driving an external monitor or series of monitors with Mac's video signal. The monitor quality must be high; the bandwidth of ordinary televisions is limited to 4.5 MHz (more typically less than 3 MHz) and good closed-circuit monitors have 5- to 10-MHz bandwidth. The Mac video signal needs a 20-MHz bandwidth monitor for best results.

Both Conrac and Electrohome have 25-inch monitors that work with Mac's sweep frequency at a cost of about $1500. The Electrohome model EDP 57 video projector can show Mac images.

A distribution system using Mac's video signal will work with ordinary video signals as well, but the monitor settings for sync and sizing will usually be different.

CONVERSION TO AN ORDINARY VIDEO SIGNAL

The simplest way to get an ordinary video signal out of Mac is to point a television camera at it. The results are poor, with a major loss of sharpness. Nevertheless, with a good camera, the results can be good enough for training and other less critical applications. For most people, this is the only way to get a videotape of the Mac screen.

Aside from the sharpness loss, the difference in framing rates between Mac and 60- or 59.94-Hz television produces a line or bar that runs slowly across the screen every few seconds. The line flutters more disturbingly on European 50-Hz television.

The only way to get rid of the bar is to slave the television system to Mac's vertical sync. In a studio, slave the studio sync line to the Mac and operate all equipment, including the videotape recorder, at 60.15 Hz.

As with other methods using two scanning processes, moire problems may emerge at some magnifications. (Since the Mac image is black and white, you can kill the color burst signal to reduce the quite separate NTSC moire problem.)

The best way to convert the video signal would be with a standards converter, similar to those used for converting European to American television and vice versa. The original image is stored in a large bank of random access memory (RAM) called a frame store or buffer. Unlike a CRT where the image begins to decay when the electron beam passes on, a frame store holds each part of the image until it is replaced by a new frame. Meanwhile the image is read out by a separate circuit operating at the rate of the converted signal, so the frame store acts as a buffer between the two video systems. No sync bars or other artifacts are visible.

The problem with standards converters is cost: upwards of $60,000. Since few personal-computer images are designed for viewing by large audiences, companies have had little incentive to build such converters for Mac or other computers with nonstandard video. (Computer-driven image synthesizers designed for television use create compatible signals that need no standards conversion.)

For conversion to videodisc, use one of the still-image techniques when possible; otherwise use a 60.15-Hz video system.

In the long run, higher-quality television distribution systems could preserve all of Mac's image quality. The high-definition television systems now proposed by several organizations can in some cases meet or even exceed Mac's requirements. Japan Broadcasting Corporation's experimental HDTV (High Definition Television) uses 1125 interlaced lines with a 20-MHz video bandwidth. To achieve such quality, HDTV has to replace every component of our present television systems, from cameras to recorders, transmitters to television sets. A less drastic proposal from CBS uses a dual-channel system that transmits two conventional 525-line images on two separate channels and combines them to double the resolution. This dual system will not produce the quality of the Japanese method and can't quite deal with Mac images satisfactorily.

If you need the best possible image, photographic or video, contact consultant John Monsour, 2062 Stanley Hills Drive, Hollywood, CA 90046.

TYPOGRAPHIC REPRODUCTION

For presentation-quality screens for manuals and other publications, save a screen dump on a disk (depress the Shift key, then press Command and the number 3 simultaneously) and send the disk to a typographic house equipped to turn the screen image into reproduction-quality art. George Lithograph, 650 2nd Street, San Francisco, CA 94107, Manhattan Graphics Corp., 163 Varick Street, New York, NY 10013, and ImageSet Corp., 1307 South Mary Avenue, Suite 209, Sunnyvale, CA 94087, can already do this, and others will follow.

The typographic route takes the disk information and feeds it to a high-resolution CRT/camera combination. This CRT reproduces the entire screen in small sections, displaying each section over the entire CRT screen; a lens reduces the image size to a small square of photographic film. After exposure, the CRT displays the next section of the image while a precision motor moves the next square of film into place.

Most major magazines use such typesetting equipment to create pages; the CRT may display just one character at a time, so an entire page can be built from hundreds of exposures. The effective resolution is high, at least 700 dots per inch and as much as 1500 dots per inch or more in some designs. When run through a typesetting machine, each pixel of the Mac screen is rendered as a tiny, perfect square.

A typesetting system can also take a Macintosh text document, complete with font information, and produce finished typeset pages.

Chapter 30 Technical Topics

T his chapter offers background information for people with some knowledge of computers; this information isn't essential to the average Macintosh user.

THE ORIGINAL PLAN...

The Macintosh project originally set out to produce a new visual-interface computer for under $1000. The initial concept used a 6502 microprocessor chip, just like the Apple II. This original plan proved impossible; the computer couldn't be produced for $1000, and the 6502 simply doesn't have the horsepower, since a good visual interface must handle complex screen graphics quickly. However, a simpler visual interface with a mouse is now running on the Apple IIe, which uses the 6502.

Apple's Lisa was under development at roughly the same time as the Macintosh. The two projects were run independently but shared some resources. For example, both computers use the same QuickDraw ROM program to generate screen graphics.

MEMORY

Of the 128-KB RAM on the Macintosh, the bit-mapping for the screen takes up about 22 KB, and the operating system and other overhead take up another 20 KB, leaving 86 KB for an application program.

Because the Macintosh cannot be expanded internally, the only way to add more memory without redesigning is to use denser memory chips. The initial Mac uses 64-kilobit (K) RAM chips. As 256-kilobit RAM chips become widely available at a reasonable cost, they will be installed in the Macintosh, quadrupling the total memory to 512 KB.

The 256-K chips are the same size as the 64-K chips, so there is no need to redesign the board. A data selector component, two resistors, and a capacitor must be changed as well. All the software and the ROM can handle 512-KB memory already.

Because the 64-K memory chips are soldered into the Macintosh circuit board, it is not practical to remove them. When the 512-KB boards are available, 128-KB boards can be exchanged and replaced. If Apple sells the conversion parts (the memory chips will be standard items), you could change the memory chips yourself if you have the tools and the skills. Unless you have a specialized integrated-circuit desoldering tool, you will probably find it easier to clip the old memory chips off and then unsolder the leads, sacrificing the old chips rather than risking damage through long heating to remove the chips intact.

The memory does not use parity checking.

What about more than 512-KB memory? Since the 68000 CPU can directly address 16 megabytes of memory (compared with one megabyte for the 8088 and 8086 and four megabytes for the 80286), there's plenty of room for expansion. The current memory addressing allocates 4 megabytes each to the RAM, ROM, Input/Output, and disk controller. Installing megabytes of memory calls for an essentially new Macintosh model. A new model would change the internal design with a different board layout.

VIDEO SCREEN

Video screen: 9-inch diagonal, black-and-white

Resolution: 512 by 342 dots, bit-mapped, non-interlaced

Image area: 4¾ by 7 inches (12 by 18 cm)

Phosphor: P4, medium-fast, dual component
Spectrum peaks at 460 nm, 560 nm.
CIE color coordinates: x = 0.27 y = 0.30
Equivalent color temperature: 11,000 degrees
Kelvin

Horizontal scanning frequency: 22.254545 kHz

Horizontal flyback time: 13 microseconds

Frame rate: 60.1474 Hz

Vertical blanking interval: 1.24 milliseconds, 7.5 percent
of duty cycle

Dot rate (frequency of generating dots on screen):
15.6672 MHz

Scanning time per pixel: 65 nanoseconds

If connected externally, required video amplifier
bandwidth: 20 MHz. (There is no internal video
amplifier.)

Screen operating speed: 60.15 Hz instead of 60 Hz.(60.15
Hz is the speed that falls out from dividing the master
clock frequency. The Macintosh uses only one clock,
aside from the little clock/calendar.)

THE KEYBOARD

The keyboard contains its own processor, an Intel
8021, programmed for Apple. The 58-key keyboard has
2-key rollover. The international version distinguishes
between the two Shift keys.

THE MOUSE

The mouse motion resolution is 90 positions per inch
(35.4 per centimeter).

DISK DRIVES

Until early 1983, Mac was going to use Apple's
"Twiggy" disk drive with the unusual four-opening disks.
These drives were used in the early production Lisas.

Apple cancelled the Twiggy project in favor of the Sony microfloppy drives. Because this change was made late in the development cycle, designers elected to retain Mac's plastic case; this is the reason for the extra space in the case, space that was to have been occupied by the Twiggy drive. Unfortunately there isn't quite enough space for two microfloppy drives. If future microfloppy drives come in a thinner housing, then a revised Mac case might accommodate two drives.

The change in disk drives led to another problem: storage capacity. The double-sided Twiggy drives store over 750 KB per disk. When Apple switched to microfloppies, only single-sided drives were available with 400-KB storage—not enough to do much work. Thus, the second disk drive is essential for nearly all Mac users. In time, double-sided microfloppy drives will ease the disk-capacity problem; each will then store 800 KB.

Mac is limited to two disk drives by the ROM and physical wiring.

The disk controller is a custom Apple design, not compatible with other disk controllers. The variable-speed controller is similar to the 5-inch disk controller in other Apple models. Mac contains no special components to support copy-protection schemes, although many schemes that were developed for the Apple II will work with Mac.

There are three different Sony-type microfloppy drives: the original Sony interface version, a 5¼-inch emulator version, and the Apple unit. Each type will come in single- and double-sided models. The Apple version has a variable-speed disk controller and an auto-eject mechanism; the other two types are not compatible with the Macintosh.

The boot blocks (blocks 0 and 1) are reserved on each disk. The directory is in block 2.

INPUT/OUTPUT PORTS

The RS-422 serial ports are specified to operate up to 230,400 bits per second. With external clocking, the ports can run up to 920,000 bits per second. The RS-422 interface uses balanced signal lines in pairs; the related RS-423 interface uses unbalanced lines.

Apple does not follow the RS-449 connector standard in its 9-pin RS-422 plug. (The standards for RS-422 and RS-423 specify the RS-449 connector standard, with a 37-pin D connector for primary circuits and a 9-pin D connector for secondary circuits.)

Wiring for the Macintosh RS-422 Ports

1 Cold ground

2 +5 volts

3 Cold ground

4 TXD + (transmitted data)

5 TXD −

6 Filtered +12 volts

7 Handshake for printer or carrier detect; also for external clock in synchronous communication

8 RXD + (received data)

9 RXD −

Although power is available on lines 2 and 6, any connecting devices should not depend on the power; the available current is small and the power is not guaranteed in future designs.

Wiring for a Null-Modem Cable, RS-422 to RS-422

Connector 1		Connector 2
1		1
2	No connection	
3		3
4		8
5		9
6	No connection	
7		7
8		4
9		5

Wiring for an Adapter Cable to RS-232C

9-Pin on Mac	RS-232C	RS-232C
	DTE	DCE
1	1	1
3	7	7
5	3	2
7	20*	*
9	2	3

The handshake line, marked with an asterisk, may require different handling depending on the devices. These two wiring schemes also serve as null-modem cables to an RS-232C port on another computer.

The balanced RS-422 interface is strapped to the unbalanced RS-232C form for the ImageWriter, or for RS-423 devices.

The Mouse Port

Any device connected to the mouse port must emulate a mouse. A digitizer pad could be made to emulate a mouse, generally with additional hardware. A touch screen could be adapted to Macintosh, although the common touch-screen technologies lack sufficient resolution for Mac. These pointing devices may need their own separate processor and memory to generate suitable signals for a Macintosh.

Wiring for the Mouse Connector

1 Cold ground

2 +5 volts, filtered

3 Cold ground

4 X-2

5 X-1

6 Not connected

354

7 Switch bar for mouse button. Pressing the button connects this line to ground

8 Y-2

9 Y-1

The X and Y connectors are the quadrature signals for the horizontal and vertical axes. If, for some reason, you want to reverse the mouse action, you can swap X-1 and X-2 or Y-1 and Y-2.

APPLEBUS

The AppleBus system will not appear until well into 1984. AppleBus uses a shielded, 78 ohm, twisted-pair cable, supporting 16 nodes over a total path length of 1000 feet (300 meters), terminated at both ends. A transformer isolates each device from the cable. Information travels in packets, or frames, similar to SDLC/HDLC communications.

The packets contain the address of the destination device in addition to data. So that only one device is sending a message at any given time, bus control is handled by a master device that polls the other devices ("slaves") periodically to determine if there is a message to be sent. A slave can send a message only after receiving permission from the master. The master keeps track of the activity of each slave and polls the active slaves more often than the inactive ones. The master device can be a server (such as an intelligent hard-disk drive, or a special device) or it can be a Macintosh or Lisa. Since being master takes some computing time that may detract from a computer's performance, mastership may pass from device to device.

If there is no activity for a period, the master stops polling and sends a "sleeping" message to the slaves, who then send a wakeup call instead of waiting for a polling signal.

SOUND GENERATION

The sound generator operates during the horizontal flyback time. The 68000 CPU processes sound-generating information when it is not busy with the screen—while the electron beam is traveling back ("flyback") from the right edge of the screen to the left edge. The flyback occurs at the horizontal sweep rate, or every 44.93 microseconds. All frequencies are built up out of multiples of this time. The highest possible frequency is twice this period, 89.96 microseconds, or 11.116 KHz (Nyquist limit).

From the programmer's point of view, there are three different sound synthesizers:

- The four-tone synthesizer for harmonic tones; 8-bit digital-to-analog conversion.

- The square-wave synthesizer for beeps and other effects.

- The free-form synthesizer for complex music and speech.

CLOCK/CALENDAR

The very low-power CMOS clock/calendar operates off the battery and contains its own small separate memory in a custom chip. Besides date and time, the memory has a few extra bytes; these could be used to store a computer configuration—possibly identifying the user as a novice or expert. An application program could query this information and take different strategies depending on the answer.

POWER SUPPLY

See Chapter 21 for information about voltage requirements.

The switching power supply produces +5, +12, and −12 volts. The clock and calendar run on a separate battery, an Eveready No. 523 or equivalent.

EXPANSION

If you are really determined, you can expand the present Mac internally without modifying the existing boards. By removing the 68000 CPU, installing a special circuit board into the CPU position and then replacing the

68000 into the new board, you can bring the 68000 bus off the main circuit board. Because of ventilation and power-supply restrictions, you'll need to mount any additional circuitry outside or add a fan inside. However you do it, you'll need considerable knowledge and skill. Any such modification will void the warranty.

Production Macintoshes have all chips, including the 68000 soldered in (the ROM might be in a socket). The main circuit board is a four-layer design; it's very hard to remove components without damaging the board. The best way to remove the 68000 might be to cut its leads, remove the chip and then each individual lead. The 68000 is destroyed in the process.

DIMENSIONS

Main unit: 9.7W × 10.9D × 13.5H inches
    (24.6W × 27.6D × 34.4H cm)
Keyboard: 13.2W × 5.8D × 2.6H inches
    (33.6W × 15D × 6.5H cm)
Mouse: 2.4W × 4.3D × 1.5H inches
    (6W × 10.9D × 3.7H cm)

WEIGHT

Main unit: 16.5 lbs (7.5 kg)
Keyboard: 2.5 lbs (1.2 kg)
Mouse: 0.4 lb (0.2 kg)

ENVIRONMENT

Operating temperature: 50 F to 104 F (10 C to 40 C)
Storage temperature: −40 F to 122 F (−40 C to 50 C)
Humidity: 5 percent to 90 percent relative humidity,
    non-condensing
Altitude: sea level to 15,000 feet (4500 m)

Glossary

Accessory card: Electronic circuitry printed on a hardware board (card) that adds features to a computer. The Macintosh does not take internal accessory cards.

Acoustic modem: In computer communications, a device that uses a small speaker and microphone to convert a computer's digital signals into sound and back again; allows transmission of information via telephone lines. Acoustic modems have special cups that fit snugly around the ear- and mouthpieces of a standard telephone handset.

Alert box: In Macintosh software, an urgent message on the screen, generally a warning. You must usually take some action before Macintosh allows you to proceed.

Analog-to-digital converter: An electronic circuit that changes continuous analog signals into discrete digital signals; abbreviated A/D. (See *digital-to-analog converter.*)

Application program: Software that does a particular task the user needs; word processors, spreadsheets, and graphics programs are applications. (See *utility program.*)

ASCII (text file): American Standard Code for Information Interchange; a standard scheme for coding characters as bits of data. Used by nearly all microcomputers and many large computers. (See *EBCDIC.*)

Asynchronous communications: A means of transmitting data that uses a special signal to indicate when each transmitted character starts and stops. The receiving computer therefore does not need precise timing information to read the data. (See *synchronous communications.*)

Audio-output port: In the Macintosh, the hardware and software connection that makes sound generation possible; connected either to the built-in speaker or to the ⅛-inch audio jack.

BASIC: Beginner's All-purpose Symbolic Instruction Code; the most common programming language for microcomputers. Although BASIC is relatively easy to learn, it is not especially flexible.

Baud, baud rate: In digital communications, one change in the transmitted signal per second. At low speeds (1200 baud or less), one baud corresponds to one bit per second.

Bit: Binary digit; the most fundamental unit of digital information; represents either an electronic on (1) or off (0). One character is usually eight bits (one byte).

Bit-mapped image: A computer display technique where a special section of random access memory (RAM) is set aside for the screen; one bit in RAM corresponds to one dot (pixel) on the screen. (If the screen has color or grays, each pixel actually takes more than one bit.)

Boot: A computer's start-up process; begins with special start-up information stored in ROM. The term comes from "pulling yourself up by your own bootstraps."

Brown-out: A period of low-voltage electrical power, usually caused by heavy demand or equipment problems at the electrical utility.

Buffer: A portion of memory that takes information from one device and feeds it to another; acts as a holding tank if the information from one device is coming in faster than it can be processed by the other.

Bug: A software problem. Named after a moth that caused the failure of an early (1945) digital computer at Harvard; evocative but inaccurate entomology: moths (and butterflies) are in the order Lepidoptera, whereas true bugs are in the order Hemiptera.

Byte: A sequence of eight bits; usually equivalent to one character of information.

Cathode-ray tube (CRT):   The screen used in nearly all televisions and most computers; an electron beam (the cathode ray) strikes a phosphor coating on the screen to produce light.

Central processing unit (CPU):   A computer's main information-processing circuit. In a microcomputer, the CPU is a single silicon chip called the micro-processor or CPU chip; on larger computers, the CPU may consist of many chips.

Character width: In Apple usage for its communications programs, the number of bits, generally seven or eight, in a transmitted character; usually described as the number of data bits.

Chip: A tiny electronic circuit combining many components built on a base of silicon.

Clicking: For the Macintosh mouse, pointing at an object and pressing and releasing the mouse button once.

Clipboard: A region of random access memory that stores information you Copy or Cut while working with a Macintosh application. Clipboard information can be Pasted into files created with the same application program or with different programs. Clipboard contents remain intact until you replace them or turn off the computer.

Comma-delimited files: A data file in which commas separate data elements.

Command key (⌘):   A special shift key to the left of the space bar, used to issue commands to Macintosh software; equivalent to the control key on other computers.

Command-line interface: An old-fashioned way to get information into and out of a computer; displays commands a line at a time on the screen.

Communications protocol: The specific details governing how information is sent between computers.

Compiler: A program that translates a high-level programming language (source code) into machine code that the computer understands; an entire program is generally compiled as a unit. (See *interpreter* and *source code.*)

Control character: Normally non-printing ASCII characters that control operations or perform other functions. Control characters code for breaks between pages of text, tabs, line feeds, and so on.

Copy-protected disk: A disk that cannot be copied, usually because it is in non-standard format.

CPU: See *central processing unit.*

CRT: See *cathode-ray tube.*

Cursor: The flashing marker indicating the current working location on a screen; called a pointer in Macintosh applications.

Cursor keys: A set of (usually) four keys found on many computers that can move the cursor in the four compass directions. The Macintosh keyboard has no cursor keys, although the accessory numeric keypad does.

Daisy wheel: The printing element in one type of letter-quality printer; the element resembles a daisy with embossed letters at the tips of plastic "petals."

Data: Any form of information; the raw material that you process with a program.

Data base: A structured file of information, such as an address book, organized for storage, retrieval, and updating.

Data bits: Bits that code a transmitted character in computer communications. Seven or eight data bits usually make up a character; Apple refers to this number as character width.

Data disk: A disk that contains only data, no programs or start-up information.

Desk accessory: One of several small programs in the Macintosh system file that can operate at the same time as an application program, including an alarm clock, note pad, calculator, and so on.

Desktop: The image on the Macintosh screen showing disk icons and disk windows; produced by the Finder.

Desktop file: A hidden data file created on all Macintosh disks by the Finder; contains housekeeping information the Finder uses to keep track of file folders, icons, etc.

Dialog box: In the Macintosh, a box on the screen asking for information that you must supply before the program can proceed.

Digital circuit: An electronic circuit that works with information coded in binary digits.

Digital-to-analog converter: An electronic circuit that converts discrete digital signals (bits) into continuous analog signals; abbreviated D/A. (See *analog-to-digital converter.*)

Digitizer pad: A computer accessory shaped somewhat like a pad of paper that registers the motion of a special stylus; used most often for graphics.

Direct-connect modem: In computer communications, a device that plugs directly into a telephone line and converts a computer's digital signals into sound frequencies and back again; allows transmission of information via telephone lines.

Directory: A file stored on disk that indexes the location of information on the disk.

Disk buffer: A special portion of random access memory that temporarily holds often-used information (for example, the directory) from the disk; since the information does not have to be constantly read to and from the disk, operations are speeded up.

Disk controller: An electronic circuit that converts information on the microcomputer bus to a signal used by the read/write heads in a disk drive.

Disk drive: An electro-mechanical device that records information on and plays it back from a magnetic disk.

Disk-drive port: In the Macintosh, a parallel port designed for connection to an external microfloppy disk drive.

Disk emulation: Using part of random access memory as an electronic disk drive; once set aside, this part of RAM emulates a normal disk drive but runs much faster. Not possible on the 128-KB Macintosh.

Dot-matrix printer: A printer that creates characters and graphics out of small dots.

Double-clicking: For the Macintosh mouse, pointing at an object and quickly pressing the mouse button twice.

Dragging: For the Macintosh mouse, pointing at an object, then moving the mouse (and object) to another screen location while pressing and holding down the mouse button.

Dvorak keyboard: A keyboard layout devised by August Dvorak to improve typing efficiency.

EBCDIC: Extended Binary Coded Decimal Interchange Code; a scheme for coding characters as bits of data. Mainly used by large computers. (See *ASCII.*)

Echo: In computer communications, the characters returned to the sender by the receiving computer. The echo mirrors the original transmission.

Electronic bulletin board, electronic mail: Two related forms of communication; the sender transmits a message to a central computer that stores the message until the recipient can retrieve it electronically.

Enter key: A special key on the Macintosh keyboard, most often used to complete a keyboard entry.

Ergonomics: Considering the human element in engineering design. A truly ergonomic computer—both hardware and software—would work smoothly with people, but the standards are ill-defined; whether a device is "ergonomic" is usually decided by the advertising department.

Expansion slot: A place inside the computer for adding accessory circuit cards; absent in the Macintosh.

Exponentiation: Raising a number (a) to a power (b); the number a is multiplied by itself b times. Two cubed is two times two times two, or two raised to the power of three.

Fat Mac: A Macintosh with 512 kilobytes of random access memory.

Field: In a database file, a unit of information; a collection of related fields constitutes a record. A name or zip code would be a field in a complete address record.

Finder: Macintosh software that manages files and disk directories.

Firmware: Programs embedded in a computer's circuitry; such programs cannot be changed as easily as a program on disk (software), but are not as fixed as the other electronic circuits (hardware). Read-only memory programs are often called firmware.

Formant synthesis: A common method of synthesizing speech, based on a small number of resonant or formant frequencies.

Frame store, frame buffer: In television technology, a memory buffer for video images.

Full-duplex transmission: In communications, simultaneous two-way transmission, as with a conventional voice telephone. (See *half-duplex transmission.*)

Gigabyte: 1024 megabytes; sometimes 1000 megabytes.

Half-duplex transmission: In communications, transmission between two points that can go in either direction, but only one way at a time, as in citizens-band radio.

Handshake: In computer communications, an electrical signal used by the receiving device to stop transmission from the sending device until the data can be processed. The handshake between printers and computers allows the printer to catch up with the characters coming from the computer.

Hardware: The physical components of a computer—electronic parts, wires, screws, cases, and so on.

High-level language: A programming language such as BASIC or Pascal that incorporates elements of English into its syntax.

I-beam pointer: The standard Macintosh text-editing cursor.

Icon: In the Macintosh, small graphic symbols that represent files or functions.

Impact printer: A printer that forms characters by physically striking an inked ribbon against paper.

Initializing (a disk): Placing address markers on new disks so the disk drive can locate information.

Ink-jet printer: A printer that forms characters or images by squirting tiny drops of ink onto paper.

Interface: The common boundary between two entities, such as user and computer, printer and computer.

Internal modem: A modem built into a computer; not possible with the Macintosh.

Interpreter: A program that translates a high-level programming language into machine-readable code; the translation is done line by line. (See *compiler.*)

Kilobyte (KB): 1024 bytes; the most common measure of computer file length or memory capacity. A typical double-spaced typewritten page is 1.5 KB.

Laser printer: A printer that forms images by scanning a laser beam across a photoconductive drum; after electrostatic development, the printer puts the image on paper with xerography.

Light pen: A computer pointing device shaped like a pen in which a light receptor senses the scanning beam across a CRT face. Not practical with the Macintosh.

Lisp: A high-level programming language used principally in artificial intelligence research. Lisp is the progenitor of the Logo programming language.

Logo: A high-level programming language derived from Lisp. Though simple functions are easy to learn, complex functions are fairly difficult.

Low-level language: A programming language (assembler) that is closely related to the intrinsic operation of a computer. Programs in assembler are fast and flexible, but also hard to read and write.

Macintosh, Charles: Scottish inventor (1766-1843) of waterproof rubberized fabric, used in mackintosh (with a "k") rain jackets.

Magnetic printer: A printer that uses an array of recording heads to create an image on a magnetic belt. Toner containing magnetic particles develops the image, which is then transferred to paper with xerographic techniques.

Mainframe: A large traditional computer shared by many users.

McIntosh, John: Discoverer and cultivator of the McIntosh apple in Ontario, 1796. His name was misspelled by Apple when the Macintosh project began.

Megabyte: 1024 kilobytes; sometimes 1000 kilobytes.

Menu bar: The line with available menus at the top of the Macintosh screen.

Menu-driven interface: A user-computer interface in which menu selections usually take up the entire screen.

Menu-initial interface: A user-computer interface in which single letters indicate available menu choices.

Menu-word interface: An user-computer interface in which single words arranged in a line or two on the screen indicate available choices.

Microcomputer: A small computer designed in both size and price to serve (mainly) a single user.

Microfloppy: A 3½-inch flexible disk within a semi-rigid plastic envelope; designed by Sony and used in the Macintosh.

Microprocessor: A single silicon chip containing thousands of electronic components, capable of manipulating information when operated in conjunction with accessory devices.

Millisecond: One-thousandth of a second.

Minifloppy: A 5¼-inch flexible computer disk, currently the most common in personal computers.

Modem: An electronic circuit that converts digital signals into sound frequencies and back again for transmission by telephone lines.

Moire pattern: Images created by the juxtaposition of two repetitive structures, for example, the pattern you see looking through two railings on a distant bridge.

Mouse: A palm-operated pointing device used with the Macintosh and other computers that registers movement; contains a signaling switch, the mouse button.

Nanosecond: One-billionth of a second, or 0.000000001 second.

Network: An electronic communications pathway linking multiple computers and accessories such as printers and large disk storage units. Any device can send a message to any other device on the network.

Null-modem: A simple wire connection for communicating between two computers.

Operating system: Essential software that acts as a traffic cop within a computer, directing information flow to and from different components.

Optical character reader (OCR):   A machine that scans a typed or printed document optically, turning the text into computer code.

Optical disc (with a "c"):   A recording and playback medium. To record, a laser beam makes tiny deformations on the surface of a reflective material; to play back, a laser beam plays across the same surface, and a photodetector measures the reflectance interrupted by the deformations. (Some optical disc systems use other techniques.)

Optical fiber: A long thin strand of glass that carries information as a modulated light beam; can handle far higher communication rates than ordinary wire connections.

Option key: A special shift key on the Macintosh; similar to the Alternate key on some other microcomputers. Pressing Option at the same time as a character key produces characters for foreign languages or symbols.

Overlays: A program fragment stored on disk until needed by the main program core. With some large programs, only the main portion fits into random access memory; the overlays are brought in as needed for specific tasks, each overlay replacing ones no longer in use.

Pantograph: A mechanical device with a series of rods and joints that can reproduce drawings at different scales.

Parity: An error-detection technique that adds up the number of bits in a character or other unit; the result is usually noted as an even or odd number. Both sending and receiving devices compute the parity independently; a mismatch signals an error.

Pascal: A high-level programming language favored by many educators.

Phoneme: A phonetic unit of language representing a single sound and used in speech synthesis.

Phosphor: Any material that emits visible light when struck by an electron beam; used in CRTs.

Pixel: A picture element, or single dot in an image.

Plotter: A mechanical drawing device in which a pen and/or paper move in both vertical and horizontal directions to create charts or other graphics.

Power-line conditioner: An electrical network that filters out very short anomalies in a power source.

Printer buffer: A memory buffer between a computer and a printer. The computer writes characters into the buffer at high speed and is then free for other tasks; the mechanical printer reads information out of the buffer more slowly.

Printer port: The hardware and software that puts information destined for a printer on the wires physically going to the printer.

Printer sound hood: A printer cabinet made with sound-deadening material.

Programming language: The words, symbols, numbers, and grammar used to give instructions to a computer.

Proportional spacing: Printing in which wider letters (such as M or W) take up more space than narrow ones (i or l).

Pull-down menu: A set of computer command choices that appears only when requested; until then, the menu titles alone appear on the screen.

Random access memory (RAM):   Electronic memory that can be written to and read from.

Read-only memory (ROM):   Electronic memory that can normally be written to only once; a user cannot change its contents.

Relational data base: A data base in which any field or record can be associated with any other other field or record.

RS-422, 423, 232C: Recommended standards (RS) for computer interfaces, from the Electronic Industries Association.

Scrapbook: In the Macintosh, a way to transfer information (text, picture, or other data) between files created with different programs. The Scrapbook operates the same way as the Clipboard except that it is saved on disk. (See *Clipboard.*)

Screen dump: A pixel-for-pixel screen image printed on paper or stored in a disk file.

Scroll arrow, bar, box: On the Macintosh, the symbols along the borders of a window that show the window's position with respect to its contents and allow the user to change the position.

Serial port: An electronic interface for computer devices that sends information in a sequential stream.

Sheet feeder: A mechanical printer accessory that feeds paper, one sheet at a time, into the printing mechanism.

Simplex: A communications channel, such as an ordinary radio or television broadcast, that always works one way only.

Software: The instructions that specify the operation of a central processor and other computer hardware.

Source code, source program: The original instructions (usually in a high-level programming language) that an interpreter or compiler turns into machine code for execution on a computer.

Spreadsheet program: A program that manipulates values laid out in a rectangular grid; the user specifies interrelationships among the values.

Start-up disk, boot disk: A disk with information necessary to start computer operations.

Stop bit: In asynchronous communications, the bit or bits added to mark the end of each character.

Structured data program: Any application program that stores information in a regular, defined way. A spreadsheet is a structured data program; a word processor or free-form graphics program is not.

SYLK file: A data file using the SYmbolic LinK format developed by Microsoft.

Synchronous communications: A method of sending computer data in units of generally fixed size, with a timing (synchronizing) signal at the beginning of each unit. (See *asynchronous communications.*)

System disk: In the Macintosh, a disk containing the start-up and other utility information, including the Finder.

Tab-delimited file: A data file in which tabs separate data elements.

Thermal-transfer printer: A dot-matrix printer design that uses small heated pins to melt small dots of pigment onto paper.

Touch pad: A computer pointing device that the user operates by moving a finger over a flat surface.

Touch screen: A computer screen that allows the user to point at objects by touching the screen itself.

Trackball: A computer pointing device with a large roller that the user turns.

Uninterruptible power supply (UPS): A power system with a battery and a fast switch; if the normal power fails, the UPS quickly switches to the battery before the attached equipment can fail.

Utility program: Software needed to support a computer's operation rather than a user application. (See *application program.*)

Video-controller circuit: An electronic circuit that takes digital information and creates the signals necessary for displaying that information on a CRT.

Video RAM: A portion of random access memory set aside for buffering screen information. In the Macintosh, video RAM stores a bit-map of the screen display.

Visual interface: A modern computer interface using icons and other visually symbolic information instead of pure text.

Warm boot: The process of resetting a computer to its start-up state without shutting off the power.

Windows: In the Macintosh, a technique that partitions the screen display into several independently controlled regions.

Word wrap: Text entry display on a computer in which the software automatically advances to the next line at the end of a word; words are preserved as units.

Write-protect tab: A small part built into a disk jacket that is set to prevent accidentally erasing the disk contents.

Xerography: The most widely used photocopying technology, employing a photoconductive drum and electrostatic image development.

X-axis: The horizontal axis in a two-dimensional graph.

Y-axis: The vertical axis in a two-dimensional graph.

Index

CARY LU

Born in Qingdao, China, Cary grew up in California and received an A.B. in Physics from the University of California at Berkeley and a Ph.D. in Biology from Cal Tech. In addition to making a number of short films for *Sesame Street,* Cary has been an associate producer for *NOVA* and the science and technology advisor for The Children's Television Workshop. He is currently the microcomputer editor for *High Technology* magazine and a nationally recognized authority on office automation.

The manuscript for this book was submitted to Microsoft Press in electronic form; text files were processed and formatted using Microsoft Word.

Cover design and calligraphy by Tim Girvin; drawings by Rick van Genderen.

Text composition in Stempel Garamond, with display in Helvetica Italic, by Microsoft Press, using CCI Book and the Mergenthaler Linotron 202 digital phototypesetter.

Cover art separated by Color Masters, Phoenix, Arizona. Text stock, 60 lb. Glatfelter Offset, supplied by Carpenter/Offutt; cover 12 pt. Carolina. Printed and bound by Halliday Lithograph, West Hanover, Massachusetts.